REAL PEOPLE AND THE RISE OF REALITY TELEVISION

REAL PEOPLE AND THE RISE OF REALITY TELEVISION

Michael McKenna

ROWMAN & LITTLEFIELD
Lanham • Boulder • New York • London

Published by Rowman & Littlefield
A wholly owned subsidiary of The Rowman & Littlefield Publishing Group, Inc.
4501 Forbes Boulevard, Suite 200, Lanham, Maryland 20706
www.rowman.com

Unit A, Whitacre Mews, 26-34 Stannary Street, London SE11 4AB

British Library Cataloguing in Publication Information Available

Library of Congress Cataloging-in-Publication Data

McKenna, Michael, 1969–
Real people and the rise of reality television / Michael McKenna.
pages cm
Includes bibliographical references and index.
ISBN 978-1-4422-5053-6 (cloth : alk. paper) – ISBN 978-1-4422-5054-3 (ebook)
1. Real people (Television program) 2. Reality television programs–United States–History–20th century. I. Title.
PN1992.77.R425M36 2015
791.45'72–dc23
2015002439

∞ ™ The paper used in this publication meets the minimum requirements of American National Standard for Information Sciences Permanence of Paper for Printed Library Materials, ANSI/NISO Z39.48-1992.

Printed in the United States of America

CONTENTS

Preface   vii

Acknowledgments   xix

Introduction: The Cult of TV Personality   xxi

1 The Golden Gut Strikes Again: 1979–1980   1

2 Branding a Genre: Nonfiction, Actuality, Reality!: 1980–1981   33

3 Whackos, Freaks, Eccentrics . . . God Bless America:
   1981–1982   63

4 Sliding down the TV Food Chain: Syndicated Reality:
   1982–1983   91

5 Ebb Tide: 1983–1984   117

Epilogue: From *Real People* to *The Real World*   137

Appendix A: *Real People* Episode Guide   147

Appendix B: Reality-Themed Shows 1976–1992   191

Appendix C: Map of *Real People* Filming Locations, 1979–1984   197

Notes   199

Bibliography   219

Index   223

About the Author   227

PREFACE

Television is a time machine that at any given moment will regurgitate its own past in a quest to fake a "new" trend.—Tom Shales[1]

The above quote by Tom Shales, the renowned television critic from the *Washington Post*, states an immutable truth revealed in the history of American television broadcasting. Originality, seminal achievements, and lasting cultural impact are quite unique. Much more common characteristics in the history of television are replication, repetition, and overexposure of the innovative concepts/themes/genres that emerge periodically. These "hot" trends in programming ebb and flow in popularity and prevalence, but they rarely disappear completely or permanently. Examples in these broad trends/genres in TV history include westerns, variety shows, game shows, sitcoms, character-driven dramas (police, medical, legal, etc.), and, most recently and persistently, the ubiquitous "reality show."[2]

Over the first decade and a half of the twenty-first century, it has become increasingly evident that reality programming has acquired permanence as a standard television genre. The incessant proliferation of reality programming over the last fifteen years has been widely posited by scholars, cultural commentators, and critics as a seminal wave breaking on the shores of American popular culture. Nonetheless, while the intensity and scope of this reality immersion is unprecedented for the genre, it is not the first reality surge to hit the cultural shores; it is just the largest and most recent.

On the whole, scholars, journalists, fans, casual observers of television, and those within the industry have a reasonably accurate knowledge of the shows that established a genre or began a trend in programming. Consequently, members of these informed groups associate the variety show with *Texaco Star Theater* (1948–1956) or *The Ed Sullivan Show* (1948–1971); and the sitcom is eternally linked with *I Love Lucy* (1951–1957), *The Honeymooners* (1955–1956), or, for some, *The Beverly Hillbillies* (1962–1971), which touched off a 1960s inundation of sitcoms, as the 1970s, 1980s, and 1990s each had their own reinvigorating sitcoms. Similar connections are made with the medical show (*Ben Casey* [1961–1966] and *Dr. Kildare* [1961–1966]); the game show (*What's My Line?* [1950–1967] or *The $64,000 Question* [1955–1958]); the police show (*Dragnet* [1951–1959], *Gangbusters* [1952], or *The Naked City* [1958–1963]); and the legal drama (*Perry Mason* [1957–1966] or *The Defenders* [1961–1965]).[3]

As the above brief survey of shows indicates, there are easily identifiable programs that mark the emergence of a new creative form or era in virtually all genres of television. However, there is one genre, the reality show, in which the seminal program is misunderstood, misrepresented, or completely ignored. Consequently, the central goal of this book is to address this deficit by establishing the National Broadcasting Company's (NBC) *Real People* (1979–1984) as the prototypical and most influential program in the first wave of reality programming from the early 1980s into the early 1990s. Illustrative of the impact of *Real People* is the spate of imitators that followed in the subsequent decade. Programs such as *Speak Up America*, *That's Incredible*, *The People's Court*, and a wide array of *PM Magazine*–style offerings rode the wake of *Real People*'s popularity to varying degrees of success. In the process, the economic and artistic viability of reality programming was confirmed.

A more substantive analysis of *Real People* reveals an unrecognized or unacknowledged link with reality-themed programming that has gone unbroken for more than thirty years. In essence, *Real People* is the Rosetta Stone of contemporary reality TV. Within it, one can see the revelation of subgenres of reality programming that are presently indispensable to the format. Whether the unique/intense occupation, the inspirational overachiever, the eccentric collector, the allegedly talented performer, or the just plain weird, *Real People* featured "everyday" characters that would not be celebrated anywhere else on television.[4]

A quick perusal of the fundamental exemplars of modern reality TV programming (*Cops, Deadliest Catch, Ice Road Truckers, Pawn Stars, Duck Dynasty, Ghost Hunters, America's Funniest Home Videos, Extreme Makeover: Home Edition,* etc.) exposes the genetic link between *Real People* and the contemporary crop of reality shows. In point of fact, the wave of reality programming initiated and inspired by *Real People* has never ended. Though *Real People* was canceled in 1984, reality-themed programming did not disappear; the genre flourished in national syndication, and increasingly dotted the landscape of network programming in the late 1980s and early 1990s. However, for a variety of reasons, *Real People* has not received the credit it is due, even though there has been a sizable collection of scholarship produced on reality television.

THE NARROW VIEW OF REALITY

Though there is an increasing volume of analysis of reality TV, a purely historical view of the evolution of the genre has been overshadowed by work in other academic fields. There has been excellent scholarship done in the behavioral sciences focusing on the sociological or psychological aspects of the content in reality shows and the impact on the audience. The liberal arts and humanities have carved out a niche focusing on specific constituencies and their representations in the genre, with extensive work done on issues associated with gender, race, LGBT, and socioeconomic themes. Additionally, in what appears to be an understandable grasp at relevance, many of the studies focus exclusively on contemporary shows—those that were recently or still are on the air—with only a cursory nod to the origins of the genre. Prominent works in the field include Susan Murray and Laurie Ouellette's *Reality TV: Remaking Television Culture*; Misha Kavka's *Reality TV*; Kristie Bunton and Wendy Wyatt's *The Ethics of Reality TV*; and Leigh H. Edwards' *The Triumph of Reality TV*.[5]

The above studies in the behavioral sciences or the humanities do not fundamentally require an in-depth appreciation of the origins of reality TV to be successful. However, in a historical analysis, a more accurate understanding of the roots of the genre will prove both necessary and useful, particularly given the ubiquity of reality TV and the likelihood that the genre is here to stay.

Before credit can be assigned for the creation and popularization of reality-themed programming, several structural issues have to be addressed. To begin with, what is the definition of a reality TV show? By 2014, the genre has been stretched and manipulated so strenuously by American television broadcasters that almost any program with non-performers as featured characters, or even shows with professional performers trying to act like real people, can be classed as reality TV. The result is an epidemic of quasi-reality genres such as the washed-up celebrity show, the semi-scripted reali-dramas, and various talent and game-show-style competitions. All of these categories have clearly reached the tipping point of narrative manipulation. Thus, the artistic result is a manifest by-product of scripting, as opposed to detached observation and documentation. A more purist definition of reality TV is delineated by Richard Crew, in his study of *PM Magazine*: "People portraying themselves, recorded at least in part in their living or working environment, recorded without a script, with events placed in a narrative context and the primary purpose being viewer entertainment."[6] At this point in American culture, the pure form of reality TV has been obfuscated by the quasi-reality, ultrasensationalist fare. However, the primordial core of reality TV can still be traced to the era of *Real People.*

The second question to be addressed is, what constitutes a "wave" or dominant trend in television programming? There is a distinct difference between sporadic or isolated programming in a specific genre and the development of an escalating trend that becomes a standardized genre. A prime exemplar of this can be seen in the development of the made-for-TV film. Made-for-television films had appeared sporadically and successfully as early as 1964. Nonetheless, it was not until 1970, with the popularity of the American Broadcasting Company's (ABC) *Movie of the Week*, that the TV movie began to proliferate, ultimately becoming a standard programming format. Thus, the ABC *Movie of the Week* is credited with creating the wave or trend.[7] A similar chain of events occurred in the reality genre. As the forthcoming introduction will elucidate, there were sporadic examples of highly celebrated reality-themed programs from the 1950s into the 1970s. With the arguable exception of a certain brand of game show in the late 1970s, there was no continuum of reality-themed shows in the subsequent era. In fact, the reality show was virtually nonexistent in the 1970s. The cultural wave or continuing trend of reality TV began with the success of *Real People* in 1979, and the clones that followed in its wake, up to the present day.

THE USUAL SUSPECTS

The reality genre is not without purported candidates for the title of original, seminal, or catalytic reality show. In the last two decades, several programs have emerged, both in academia and the general public, as candidates for the designation. Three shows that are consistently cited are *Candid Camera* (1948–1950, 1960–1967), *An American Family* (1973), and *The Real World* (1992–). While all three of these shows were successful and culturally significant, their links with the origins of the reality genre can be tenuous.

Candid Camera was a hidden-camera program featuring unsuspecting everyday citizens being filmed in often unusual, occasionally exasperating, but almost always funny situations manufactured by the show's production team. At the peak of the subject's frustration and/or incredulity, the show's host, Allen Funt, would appear to relieve the comic tension by telling them they were on *Candid Camera*, and instructing them to "smile" for the hidden cameras. The set-up subjects and circumstances, coupled with the anticipated "reveal," were hugely popular with audiences in the early 1960s, producing a top ten rated program. The popular appeal of *Candid Camera* was built on two principles. The first of these was the "what would you do?" factor. The scenarios made it easy for viewers to imagine how they would act if placed in a similar setup. No matter how outlandish or contrived the scenarios, viewers enjoyed placing themselves in the shoes of the unsuspecting victims. The second founding principle of the show was very basic: make people laugh, though not exclusively at the expense of the subjects. Unlike many modern variants, the purpose of the show was not to expose its participants to physically threatening situations, nor was it to hold people up to scorn or ridicule. To produce these benign laughs, *Candid Camera* relied on skilled writers such as William Saroyan, Woody Allen, Pat McCormick, and Fannie Flagg.[8]

The fact that many of the scenarios required actors delivering scripted or improvised dialogue, in addition to the occasionally elaborate set decorations, works to dilute the purity of *Candid Camera*'s reality status. The show is clearly dependent upon non-performers for its content; nonetheless, the situations in which people were placed were not genuine, but fabricated and manipulated. Thematically, *Candid Camera* lies somewhere between an elaborate sociological experiment and the more modern practical-joke programs, for example, Music Television's (MTV) *Punk'd*. Furthermore, there was uniqueness of form, almost a trademarked quality in *Candid Camera* that made it difficult to re-create artistically, without looking like a blatant counterfeit. Consequently, it did not produce a collection of immediate imitators, and did not give birth to a reality trend or wave.

Another of the purported cornerstones of modern reality programming is the Public Broadcasting Service's (PBS) creation *An American Family*. Originally broadcast from January through March of 1973, the series was a hybrid, a traditional documentary infused with a cinema verité style. The show orbited around the Loud family of Santa Barbara, California, who allowed their personal lives and relationships to be filmed, edited, and presented in twelve episodes. The show struck a chord with its audience, due in large part to the intimate details exposed about the family. The families' revelations, including alcohol abuse, marital infidelity, divorce, and even emerging homosexuality, were not uncommon in 1973. However, using a real family, one with which viewers came to be familiar and likely empathized, added a measure of tension and drama that scripted fiction rarely achieves.

There is no doubt that the Louds and their family travails were real, but was it reality TV? At the time, the show was framed by a variety of labels: documentary, cinema verité, nonfiction entertainment, and actuality. Reality TV did not exist in 1973; and *An American Family* would not create the genre. Though celebrated and widely discussed, the television industry would not act on the popularity of the series by producing similar reality-themed programming in the mid-1970s. *An American Family* stands alone in its time as a cultural phenomenon, but it did not create or promote the reality genre. It is evident that the claims of origination for the show are a result of recategorization, two decades later, after the reality genre had become standard fare.[9]

One of the reasons *An American Family* is often cited as *the* foundational reality show can be found in its similarity to another of the programs regularly credited with starting a wave of reality programming, *The Real World* (1992). A creation of MTV, *The Real World* utilized the intimate surveillance theme; but rather than filming a family, the show would assemble a group of strangers to live together in a well-equipped home. The producers of the show, Mary-Ellis Bunim and Jonathan Murray, cast the program with disparate and often combustible characters chosen selectively, with an eye toward potential drama, tension, and romance. Consequently, supporters of *The Real World* cannot legitimately proclaim it to be pure reality, considering the overt manipulation of cast and setting. In most seasons of the show, the cast were people who would not have been living together were it not for the television production. Nonetheless, the conflicts created within the show are representative of those found in the actual real world, so there are aspects of realism in the show.

At the very least, *The Real World* deserves credit, or blame depending on one's perspective, for popularizing the contrived and manipulated reality show (e.g., *Big Brother* [2000], *Survivor* [2000], *The Apprentice* [2004]). However, even as *The Real World* was being conceived in the early 1990s, reality programs flourished on the major broadcast networks and in national syndication, and had been doing so since the early 1980s. *The Real World* receives and deserves much credit for inspiring the reality programming that followed in the 1990s and beyond, particularly in the arena of cable television. Nonetheless, to suggest that it is the seminal reality show, or mark it as the beginning of the reality trend, ignores more than a decade of reality-themed programming that preceded it. In fact, as *The Real World* was broadening and reimagining the genre, the ripples of the first wave of reality programming initiated by *Real People* were still lapping at the cultural shore.[10]

THE LARGER REAL WORLD

Beyond the effort to establish *Real People* as the genesis of the reality genre, this study also explores the milieu in which the show flourished, an era of dramatic transition for both the television industry and larger American society. When *Real People* premiered in 1979, television was beginning a radical transformation that would not only alter the economics of the industry, but also influence programming and creative decisions. The three major American television networks, the Columbia Broadcasting System (CBS), ABC, and NBC, were facing major challenges from emerging technologies, most notably home video games, home video devices (Betamax, VCR, videodisc, etc.), and cable television. By the time *Real People* ended its run in 1984, 35 percent of the nation's homes had video devices, and the networks had to compete with major cable channels such as Home Box Office, Showtime, Turner Broadcasting System, the Cable News Network, ESPN, Bravo, Nickelodeon, and the Disney Channel. Additionally, federal deregulation of the media produced a surge in the number of independent television stations across the nation, thus increasing the volume of competing local and syndicated programming, and further fragmenting the audience. Consequently, throughout the 1980s, the major networks began to lose an increasing share of the television audience. The smaller network audiences resulted in declining revenue, as advertisers began to spread their commercials around to other broadcast entities, creating competition the big three networks had never before faced. Unfortunately, for the networks, just as their profits began to decline, the cost of producing television shows was increasing dramatically. These economic factors would be compounded by the late 1980s, when NBC, CBS, and ABC were acquired by non-entertainment conglomerates that had a bottom-line management style and massive debt to pay off. [11]

In light of these distressing factors, the ratings success of *Real People* and its reality spawn created an enticing opportunity. Network and independent television producers hoping to cut costs found reality programming less expensive, due to the lack of the high-priced actors and writers with which they normally had to contend. Thus, they had the same ratings potential as scripted programs, with significantly lower production costs and higher profit margins. [12] *Real People* had established the viability of the reality genre, creating the economic and creative model for future reality shows.

The achievements of *Real People* and its reality brethren also began to permeate other aspects of television programming. For many, the most alarming aspect of this development was what many called the "softening" of TV news, or what some came to derisively call "infotainment." Prior to the late 1970s and early 1980s, local and network news would regularly feature what were known as human interest stories, or feel-good news. For example, the CBS network news had veteran TV news journalist Charles Kuralt with his "On the Road" segments, in which Kuralt traveled around the country to meet interesting and heartwarming people, while highlighting the virtues of rural and small-town America. Local news stations would also seek out the heartwarming stories, and feature "how to" or "what to do" segments designed to appeal to local viewers. However, as reality programming grew in popularity, the "soft news" began to crowd out the traditional news coverage. At the same time, news anchors, both male and female, morphed into a more telegenic, charismatic, and engaging breed, while the stoic graying middle-aged male news readers became dinosaurs. News now had to have a personal appeal, be continuously applicable to viewers' lives, and be delivered by likeable TV news personalities.

Another area of the television industry to be influenced by the emergence of reality programming was the syndicated market. "Syndication" is a term used to describe the sale of non-network programming to local stations across the nation. Typically, the programs in syndication were largely reruns of shows and movies that had previously aired on a major network (e.g., *I Love Lucy*, *Gilligan's Island*, *The Brady Bunch*, or made-for-TV movies). There was very little original programming in syndication prior to the 1980s, except for the sporadic talk or game show. Original content created for syndication was likely to produce higher ratings than reruns of an old movie or TV show, but the cost of producing original scripted programs made it an unprofitable enterprise. Accordingly, when the appetite for reality programming was revealed, syndicated producers were willing and able to meet that demand by creating original reality-themed content, because the lower production costs in that genre generated healthy profit margins. As a result, the 1980s featured an array of court shows (*The People's Court*, *Miller's Court*), reality-based dating shows (*Love Connection*, *Singles*), and *Real People*–styled shows (*PM/ Evening Magazine*, *The World of People*, *Look at Us*). The original programming produced for syndication would continue to expand and thrive over the subsequent three decades, becoming one of the most lucrative regions of the television industry.

Beyond the insight into the television industry, *Real People* offers a broad and unique perspective on contemporary American society. Unlike most modern reality shows, which represent or reflect small communities (e.g., the fabricated cast and scenario, or the inaccessible lifestyle or occupation), *Real People* is more representative of its era, displaying the larger fabric of American life. As a result, *Real People* presents a clear window into the evolving American culture of the late 1970s and early

1980s. A close analysis of the segments featured on *Real People* uncovers the emerging "culture wars" that were beginning to roil American society in the 1980s, 1990s, and beyond. Evidence for this assertion can be found in the recurring themes on the show: coastal areas v. mid-America, small town v. big city, traditional values v. modernity in all its forms, and conservatism v. liberalism. Nonetheless, it is important to note that the conflicts among these divergent constituencies were not angry or divisive as they would become later; rather, the differences are portrayed as light-hearted examples of the diversity that makes America great.

Real People could be schizophrenic in its tone and focus, even within a single hour-long episode. The series' run offers a snapshot of opinion on the era's populist totems, including high gas prices, inflation, unemployment, the Iranian hostage crisis, political corruption, government bureaucracy, foreign industry, and a variety of other issues that captured people's attention. The show was also capable of progressivism, focusing on successful and trailblazing women; presenting stories about incredible achievement despite impediment; and advocating for the handicapped, senior citizens, the economically disadvantaged, and even missing children. Notwithstanding these high-minded, even noble efforts, *Real People* was prone to dabbling in the overtly sexual story—what critics at the time referred to as "jiggle TV." Although promoted as family entertainment, and shown in the so-called "family hour" of 8–9 PM, there were enough clothes being shed and sexual innuendo to make most parents squirm while watching with their children. Throughout the six seasons of the show there was a continual stream of segments on cheerleaders, bikini contests, male and female centerfolds, wet T-shirt contests, various scantily clad endeavors, and strippers of all ages, gender, and body type, including a woman who stripped for God.

Nevertheless, the show was not a liberal playground by any means; in fact, *Real People* also effectively mirrored the rising tide of Reagan era neoconservatism. The show regularly satirized big government, big cities, and cultural elitism, while simultaneously celebrating and romanticizing mid-America, small-town life, and traditional values, and promoting an almost reflexive hyper-patriotism. To wit, patriotic iconography such as Mount Rushmore, the waving American flag, the Statue of Liberty, the Washington Monument, and the Lincoln Memorial was frequently displayed. Yet the most consistent and laudable manifestation of this patriotic fervor was the show's efforts to redeem and restore the Vietnam veteran, and to celebrate all of America's veterans. The progressive and patriotic themes provide a useful counterbalance to some of the more ridiculous and salacious segments, as well as acting as a partial shield against the frequent critical accusations of mockery and exploitation of *Real People*'s subjects. Additionally, for students of American popular culture, *Real People* explores most of the major fads and trends of the late 1970s into the mid-1980s, including roller disco, Valley girls, break dancing, preppies, skateboarders, the Rubik's Cube, punk music and fashion, and many others.

At its broadest points, this study examines reality-themed programs from the 1950s to the early 1990s; though in the main, the primary focus is the years 1978–1984. The narrative is largely chronological, punctuated with an examination of the prevailing themes and developments of the era. The book opens with an introduction that explores the sporadic early examples of reality programs from the formative years of television through the mid- to late 1970s, just before the premiere of *Real People*. The core of the book features five chapters, each dedicated to a single television season, over the length of the show's run. The year-by-year analysis includes a review of that season's episodes, as well as the show's evolution and recurring themes. This analysis also traces the emerging wave of reality TV, as well as changes in the television industry and larger American society.

Chapter 1 examines the development of the series, as Fred Silverman empowers George Schlatter to create *Real People*. By the midpoint of its first full season, the show becomes a ratings success and a growing cultural phenomenon. In chapter 2, the reality trend expands across the television landscape, with shows such as *That's Incredible, Speak Up America, Games People Play*, and *That's My Line* dotting network schedules. Chapter 3 details how *Real People* balances its content with a series of offbeat characters, places, and events, while bathing the show in the rising tide of feel-good patriotism engulfing the United States in the early 1980s. In chapter 4, several years into the reality wave, the trend begins to proliferate in national syndication and local programming. In addition to daily syndicated reruns of *Real People*, shows such as *The People's Court, PM Magazine*, a collection of dating shows, and private events made public inundate viewers. Chapter 5 details the final season of the series, during which the show falls victim to plummeting ratings, declining cultural relevance, and a network that is trying to reframe its programming brand.

Finally, there is an epilogue, which briefly reviews *Real People*'s extended legacy, and includes a survey of reality-themed programs from the mid-1980s to the early 1990s, when the reality genre began its transformation. There are also several appendices, including a *Real People* episode guide, a list of reality-themed shows from 1976 to 1992, and a map of *Real People* segment locations.

When *Real People* was canceled in 1984, it was summarily deposited in the bargain bin of American popular culture. This status may be a result of a slightly flawed collective memory of the show as a circus of eccentricity, jiggling bodies, and corny jokes. It is too easily dismissed as kitsch by those with selective memories, or a generation that has never seen the show. It may well be a lack of access that has circumscribed the significance of *Real People*, as the show has rarely been seen in national syndication in the last twenty years, nor has it been released on DVD. Regardless of the cause, the marginalization of *Real People* has clearly obscured its cultural legacy.

A peeling back of the layers of reality programming over the last two decades reveals that *Real People* is the hub from which many of the spokes of the reality genre emerge. Even if one were to argue that it was not the "original" reality show, the ratings success of the show clearly inspired a wave of reality programming that had not been seen previously. *Real People* proved there was an audience for reality programming, and much of that audience would be acculturated to appreciate the entertainment value of reality television in the future.

The transformation of American television that began with the premiere of *Real People* in 1979 would ebb and flow over the next three decades. However, it is important to note that there was no break or cessation between the "old" reality wave and the "new" reality wave of the last decade and a half. Though *Real People* disappeared in the mid-1980s, the subgenres it spawned, and its confirmation of the potential of reality TV, would be the foundation for a genre that would ultimately envelope mainstream media by the early twenty-first century. Ideally, this study will redeem the reputation of *Real People*, and place it in its correct historical context.

ACKNOWLEDGMENTS

Continued thanks are extended to my editor, Stephen Ryan, for supporting my work and having a shared consciousness on the academic and cultural value of television history. I am generally and specifically grateful for the work of archivists, both professional and amateur, who preserve television in all its forms. Special thanks go to the leadership and staff of the Paley Center for Media: Mark Ekman in New York and Martin A. Gostanian in Los Angeles. The same is true of Mark Quigley at UCLA Television and Film Archive, where I benefited from the deep collection and high-quality facilities.

A substantial portion of this project would not have been possible without two travel grants. At Suffolk County Community College I would like to thank Donna Krompinger, the Adjunct Professional Development Fund, and the College Faculty Association. At Farmingdale State College I was the grateful recipient of a New York State/United University Professions IDAP Award for Professional Development.

INTRODUCTION
The Cult of TV Personality

For most scholars and observers, 1948 is considered to be the seminal year in which major network television began to take form. However, television broadcasting in a practicable, though experimental, form emerged in the 1920s. A prominent example of the potential capabilities of television occurred in 1927, when Secretary of Commerce Herbert Hoover agreed to take part in a televised speech for the American Telegraph and Telephone Company. Sitting in front of a transmitter tube in Washington, DC, Hoover delivered an address that would be seen and heard over two hundred miles away in New York City, on a two-inch by three-inch screen. The Hoover experiment produced enthusiastic headlines in major American newspapers, but it did not produce dramatic commercial advancement for television. Over the subsequent decade, television was largely a medium for amateurs and innovators, while also featuring the early stirrings of corporate involvement.[1]

The national coming-out party for television occurred at the 1939 World's Fair in New York City. The Radio Corporation of America (RCA) would operate one of the more popular pavilions at the fair, in an effort to promote sales of its TV sets. Utilizing the corporate-owned National Broadcasting Company (NBC), RCA would broadcast the opening ceremonies from Flushing Meadows. The telecast included an address by Franklin Delano Roosevelt and a speech by RCA president David Sarnoff. At the time, there were only about two hundred television sets within a forty-mile radius, but special receivers had been set up at RCA headquarters and in the windows of several Manhattan department stores. Sarnoff's speech served as a grand, eloquent, if not self-serving, introduction to television. As Sarnoff put it:

> Now we add sight to sound. It is with a feeling of humbleness that I come to this moment of announcing the birth, in this country, of a new art so important in its implementation that it is bound to affect all society. It is an art which shines like a torch in the troubled world. [2]

It was not a coincidence that the following day RCA began selling its first TV sets designed for the general viewing public. For the remainder of the fair, the RCA pavilion would demonstrate television technology for thousands of visitors. In the most popular component of the pavilion, a camera was set up to allow people to appear on a large TV monitor. Visitors were gleeful as they shouted and waved while their friends and family watched them on television. [3] It can be fairly stated that from the very introduction of the medium, people have enjoyed seeing themselves, their family, friends, and other "real people" on television. With that in mind, the emergence of reality TV seems like a natural, even an inevitable development.

The onset of World War II slowed the growth of commercial television in the United States. Not only was there a paucity of programming, some of which was caused by the impositions of war, but television sets were still prohibitively expensive for most consumers. As a result, most of the TV sets were owned by people of means, or by public entities such as bars, where some of the limited programming fare of baseball, boxing, and wrestling would draw big crowds. One of the more unique real-life, real-people applications of television involved wartime air wardens visiting local police stations to view televised lectures on how to properly do their jobs.

In fact, there is an interesting parallel between the early years of motion pictures and those of early 1940s television programming. When motion pictures began to appear around the turn of the twentieth century, audiences were so captivated with the visual wizardry that they were mesmerized watching mundane events like a moving train, birds in flight, urban street scenes, or a man and woman dancing. Many early-adopting television viewers were equally engrossed when images of street scenes, man/woman-on-the-street interviews, and various daily live events such as sporting events or city council meetings were broadcast. For example, the Columbia Broadcasting System (CBS) produced a show entitled *What's It Worth?* where average people would bring in heirlooms or antiques and have them appraised by the erudite Sigmund Rothschild. The viewer's payoff came when the owner was told how much the item was worth.[4]

Another of the unique early uses of non-performers on television occurred in New York City in the late 1940s. Don Weiss, the head of the New York office of the Veterans Administration, was growing increasingly frustrated with his inability to find jobs for disabled war veterans. In a truly prescient acknowledgment of the coming power of the medium, Weiss decided to use television to prove the capabilities of these men. Weiss successfully pitched his idea to station WABD; and a proto-reality show was born. A stage set was created in which the disabled soldiers could prove proficiency in fixing machinery, laying brick, working on automobiles, and varied carpentry tasks. It was essentially a thirty-minute job audition, with a semi-authentic setting, using real disabled men. Over several months, the Veterans Administration received hundreds of offers of employment for the men, while WABD received positive publicity for the nascent medium.[5]

Eventually, television, like motion pictures decades earlier, would move away from mundane reality to more scripted and talent-laden fare. Early budgetary and technical limitations would bind television programming to static stage sets and live performances. Accordingly, there was an early reliance on genres such as variety and talent shows, game shows, sitcoms, and live drama. However, as the 1950s progressed, and the major networks expanded their daily program schedules, there would be opportunities, some orchestrated, some not, for reality-themed programs and for non-performers to capture the attention of the American public.

ACCIDENTAL REALITY STARS

It is difficult to conceive of any broad study of the 1950s, whether academic or popular in nature, that does not include extensive discussion on the activities of United States Senator Joseph McCarthy. In terms of eternal infamy, deserved or not, McCarthy has few equals in American political history. Not only is he the personification of Cold War paranoia and fear-mongering, but his name will forever be linked with political or institutional persecution. Most examinations of McCarthy necessarily explore the role television played in popularizing, legitimizing, and ultimately derailing the senator's campaign to expose Communist elements in American life. The narrative trajectory of McCarthy's television "career" has been widely disseminated—from his initial foray into televised Senate hearings in the early 1950s, which helped make him a national celebrity and respected political champion; to the emerging cracks in his crusading façade, famously exposed on Edward R. Murrow's *See It Now* program; to his ultimate disintegration in front of millions of TV viewers during the Army-McCarthy Hearings in 1954.

A further, though admittedly alternative, analysis of McCarthy's activities reveals him to be one of the earliest reality TV celebrities, while many of his televised appearances epitomize the standard reality drama/ suspense formats. McCarthy transcended politics; he became either the perfect hero or villain to viewers, for whom the drama, suspense, and anger were amplified by the salient reality of the events. The McCarthy-driven Senate hearings of the early 1950s evoked an air of a sixteenth-century church inquisition, with the dogged senator acting as the moralizing grand inquisitor, while the witnesses played the role of obsequious supplicant or degraded heretic. For television viewers, particularly those viewing during the day, when regular programming was sparse in the early 1950s, the real-life drama of these proceedings could be spellbinding. Even when McCarthy's appearances were essentially scripted, as in Murrow's *See It Now* exposés, or his rebuttal of those accusations on a subsequent episode, the senator's personality and performance was the catalytic force.

The real-life drama achieved its zenith as McCarthy plummeted to his nadir in his 1954 investigation of Communist infiltration of the United States Army. With twenty million viewers watching 187 hours of coverage spread over thirty-six days, McCarthy and his equally aggressive and dramatic co-counsel, Roy Cohn, battered and badgered reluctant or suspect witnesses. Given the persistent annual increase in television ownership since he began his crusade in 1950, there were now more viewers able to see McCarthy operate in his natural and unfiltered environment. What they saw was a flood of accusations and implications, but very little solid evidence to justify convening the hearing; nor any exemplars of accomplishment toward the senator's overarching goal of exposing subversive Americans.[6]

The dramatic crescendo of the proceedings occurred when McCarthy tried to impugn the character and loyalty of a young lawyer working in the office of the army's chief counsel, Joseph Welch. In response, Welch delivered a soliloquy that would have been the envy of any television writer: "If it were in my power to forgive you for your reckless cruelty I would do so. I like to think I'm a gentle man, but your forgiveness will have to come from someone other than me." Welch then went in for the rhetorical kill. "Let us not assassinate this lad further, Senator, you have done enough. Have you no sense of decency sir? At long last have you no sense of decency?"[7]

These withering dismissals of McCarthy's tactics are among the most iconic film clips of the entire decade. Even at the time, cultural critics and political pundits recognized how television's reality had colored events. Writing in the May 30, 1954, edition of the *New York Times*, James Reston marked the changing public perception of McCarthy:

> One cannot remain indifferent to Joe McCarthy in one's living room. He is an abrasive man, and he is recklessly transparent. The country did not know him before, despite all the headlines, now it has seen him. It has had a startling but accurate presentation of his ideas, his tactics, his immense physical power, and it is at least basing its judgments now on first hand observations.

Jack Gould, renowned *New York Times* television critic, noted the narrative power of reality television: "The absorbing attraction is to follow the testimony as it goes first one way then another, as first the Army and then Senator McCarthy made their points. On TV it is the drama of unrehearsed actuality unfolding for everyone to see at home."[8]

Though McCarthy and his televised hearings endure as a twentieth-century cultural touchstone, neither the Wisconsin senator nor his hearings were unique in their time, or even the most widely viewed of their kind. This distinction belongs to another proto-reality TV celebrity and US Senator with larger aspirations, Estes Kefauver.

Kefauver, a first-term senator from Tennessee, found his path to national political prominence through an investigation of the criminal underworld in American cities, during early 1951. Over ninety-two days in fourteen cities, he chaired a senate subcommittee as it exposed the dark underbelly of organized crime, often live on local television. The senator's star began to rise in medium-sized cities like Detroit, where his hearings drew stronger ratings than *The Howdy Doody Show*; and in New Orleans, where the hearings were telecast in the evening, reportedly resulting in empty movie theaters and restaurants throughout the city.

With his national celebrity beginning to peak, the Kefauver Committee landed in New York City in March of 1951. The convening of the hearings was heavily covered by the city's newspapers, with the anticipation of a long-awaited Broadway opening or Hollywood film premiere. Not everyone was enthralled with the arrival of the televised spectacle. The Federal Bar Association of New York, New Jersey, and Connecticut publically admonished the senator, stating "that the glaring melodrama created by television lights and cameras does interfere with the quest for truth in a public hearing."[9] Kefauver himself had expressed reservations about having the hearings televised in the various cities, including New York. However, when he arrived in New York, he discovered that a temporary network of twenty-five stations had been set up to broadcast the hearings from the East Coast to the Midwest. With no opportunity to bar the cameras, and newspaper coverage increasing, the hearings morphed into a national phenomenon.

The televised hearings lived up to, if not exceeded, the preliminary hype. Up from the New York underworld gurgled a cast of characters that could have been appropriated from a 1930s Hollywood gangster film. Among those testifying was former New York City mayor William O'Dwyer, who had resigned a year earlier as a result of a corruption scandal that deservedly landed at his feet. There were Joe Adonis, a reputed Brooklyn crime boss, known to be a murderer and an extortionist; Jake "Greasy Thumb" Guzik, former confidant of Al Capone and comic butcher of the English language; and Virginia Hill, former Hollywood actress and girlfriend of mobster Bugsy Siegel, who in her own way was tougher and more acid-tongued that any of the alleged Mafiosi. However, the most compelling and unwittingly dramatic of the criminal witnesses was Frank Costello, reputedly the majordomo of New York's crime syndicate. In spite of his reputation, Costello presented himself as a respected businessman and pillar of his community. Consequently, when called to testify, he was reluctant to appear on television in a sensationalized criminal investigation. As his lawyer stated, "Mr. Costello does not come to submit himself as a spectacle."

In a compromise, the committee agreed to keep the camera from showing Costello's face, instead focusing only on his hands. This was equally if not more dramatic than showing his face; for when the questioning became intense or pointed, his hands were shown in sweaty clenched fists, tearing at papers and tightly gripping a glass. His hands said all that his face could have, and more. As Jack Gould of the *New York Times* remarked, "His was video's first ballet of the hands." The narrative and visual juxtaposition of the down-home, humble, crusading public servant Kefauver and the abrasive, urban, ethnic criminal element was irresistible to viewers. The ratings for the hearings were remarkable, surpassing the 1950 World Series, and on one Tuesday when the hearings ran late, they drew a larger audience than ratings king Milton Berle. [10]

Many of the hundreds of articles appearing in newspapers and periodicals not only described the proceedings, but also analyzed the social impact of the televised hearings. *Life* magazine noted the effect in cities that aired the New York hearings:

> The week of March 12, 1951, will occupy a special place in history. The U.S. and the world had never experienced anything like it. In Detroit the telephone company noticed that for hours at a time normally clogged phone lines went unused . . . thousands of people stayed away from their jobs. . . . Trolley cars in many cities carried half their normal loads. New York cab drivers wasted gas in a vain search for passengers. It became apparent that at least one-fifth of the population had absented itself from normal pursuits.

New York Times television critic Jack Gould offered daily cogent analysis:

> The opening session of the Senate Crime Investigating Committee was nothing less than a Hollywood thriller brought to life. For five and a half hours there were gripping and compelling drama and suspense in watching one of the seamier sides of national life spread out for all to see.

On the public reaction to the hearings, Gould suggested, "Housewives have left the housework undone and husbands have slipped away from their jobs to watch. The city has been under a hypnotic spell, absorbed, fascinated, angered and amused. It has been a rare community experience." [11]

The breakout "star" of the hearings was Estes Kefauver. The senator became a nationwide celebrity, gracing national magazine covers and even appearing on the semi-reality-themed show *What's My Line?* in which blindfolded celebrity panelists attempted to guess the identity/occupation of the guests. In a clear reflection of his television stardom, Kefauver received an Emmy Award for Outstanding Contribution to Television in 1952.[12] Though he experienced a meteoric rise to television stardom and national political prominence, that momentum would not help him achieve his presumptive goal of becoming president of the United States. However, the power of television to create celebrities out of non-performers or real people was now clearly evident. In fact, 1950s television would produce a reality celebrity even more unlikely than two nondescript senators: a Catholic priest.

HIS EXCELLENCY THE MOST REVEREND FULTON J. SHEEN, ARCHBISHOP OF NEW YORK

In February 1952, the DuMont Network began airing a half-hour program entitled *Life Is Worth Living*. The off-camera introduction described it as "a program devoted to the everyday problems of all of us." It was not, however, the "problems" that attracted millions of viewers to the program; it was the single character and star of the show, Bishop Fulton Sheen. A Catholic priest, in a predominantly Protestant nation, would seem an unlikely candidate to become one of the most revered religious figures of the decade, let alone a television star, yet that is exactly what happened. However, Sheen was not a typical parish priest; he was well educated, articulate, and most importantly, a telegenic theologian. After his trademark "Hello friends" welcome, Sheen would spend twenty-seven minutes delivering his sermon, without the aid of a script, cue cards, or teleprompter, often ad-libbing seamlessly. His only props were a blackboard, a stage set made to look like a scholar's study, and his priestly vestments.

Within eighteen months of Sheen's premiere, his show was airing on over 130 stations across the country; drawing an estimated twenty million viewers per episode; and receiving two hundred thousand letters weekly from his audience. Sheen's ratings success is all the more remarkable given that his competition on Tuesday nights was TV superstar Milton

Berle. An oft-repeated quip of the time inquired who are you going to watch, Uncle Miltie or Uncle Fultie? Amazingly, after a later change of network and airdate, Sheen found himself in direct competition with another 1950s powerhouse, *I Love Lucy*. At the peak of his popularity, Sheen was appearing on the covers of national magazines and earning a reported $26,000 per episode, and he won the 1952 Emmy Award for Most Outstanding Television Personality. Given the extent of his fame and acceptance, Sheen's success cannot be solely attributed to the support of fellow Catholics. As a matter of fact, Sheen would often comment upon and utilize the philosophy of other spiritual traditions and institutions; and a steady stream of letters he received was from non-Catholics, as were many of the awards and honors he received over the years. [13]

Undoubtedly, some measure of Sheen's popularity can be explained by a Cold War–inspired revival in American religiosity. Yet more important was the power of television combined with the relatable personality of a non-performer. Sheen was a real person talking about real issues, which struck a chord with viewers. These characteristics would be present in many future reality celebrities, though regrettably, most would not be as high-minded and noble as Bishop Sheen.

During the 1950s, there were also several popular television personalities who, though recognized as professional performers, had built much of their success on the ability to interact with the average person. The two most prominent and prosperous performers in this unique subgroup were Art Linkletter and Groucho Marx. Linkletter built a prestigious five-decade career on his ability to engage in and create entertaining dialogue between himself and members of his studio audience and selected non-celebrity guests. Shows such as *Art Linkletter's House Party* (1952–1969), *Life with Linkletter* (1950–1952), and *People Are Funny* (1954–1961) utilized audience participation, viewer contests, interviews, and, most memorably, a regular segment in which Linkletter asked questions of several young children, often with comedic or poignant responses. Unquestionably, Linkletter had a notable talent for connecting with television viewers; however, were it not for the non-celebrity guests and audience interaction, his career would not have been as legendary. [14]

While no informed observer would ever question the talent and accomplishments of Groucho Marx in film and theater, his comic gift and personality alone would not translate into television success. *You Bet Your Life* (1950–1961) reads on paper as a fairly run-of-the-mill game show, with money awarded to contestants for answering several questions in a category of their choosing. However, the heart of the show was the interview Marx conducted with the contestants. Virtually all of the contestants were non-professional performers, yet many were selected for their unusual skills, occupations, hobbies, or funny stories. Marx's rapier wit would elicit and illuminate the comic aspects of the contestants' lives, often with an off-color double entendre. While *You Bet Your Life* clearly would not have worked without Groucho Marx, neither would it have worked without the real people as a foil. In this case, Marx is a brilliant miner of comedic gold, but the real people are the gold mine. [15]

GAME SHOWS

While proto-reality themes dot the landscape of 1950s programming, in several unique ways the most reality-dependent genre on television was the game/quiz show. The elasticity of the genre produced great diversity of format, from physical challenges and pure luck to specialized knowledge quiz/game shows. Regardless of format, it was the contestants, often described as "the person next door" or "your friends and neighbors," who created the narrative and visual appeal for viewers. The most infamous, though widely popular, of the subcategories in the genre was what came to be known as the "confessional show," often referred to by critics as the "misery shows." The standard-bearer for prime-time misery shows is *Strike It Rich* (1951–1955). The self-proclaimed "quiz show with a heart" was hosted by Warren Hull, and typically featured contestants purposely selected for personal stories that were designed to resonate with an audience. In essence, the more woeful and desperate the story, the more likely it was the contestant would make it on the air. The standard format began with the contestants being introduced and interviewed by Warren Hull. Slowly, the tales of misfortune would unfold as the camera panned in on the guests. A sampling of the more emotional stories includes a childless couple who wanted to adopt but could not afford the adoption; parents who needed money to pay for an operation for their blind, hearing-impaired, and physically disabled child; and families that had grown too large at ten, twelve, even seventeen children, and needed help with the basic necessities. There was a constant stream of widows, single mothers, sickly children, war veterans, and homeless or hungry families. The common thread among contestants was a desperate economic need, a willingness to reveal intimate, even embarrassing details of their lives, and the hope of winning money to offset some of their problems.

The quiz segment of the show followed the interviews, featuring reasonably easy general-knowledge questions or "name that tune" challenges. Of course, after their tales of misery, home viewers were eager for the contestants to win as much money as possible. The final segment of the show utilized what was called the "Heartline," which allowed the TV viewers to call in offering their own assistance to the woebegone. Home audience members called in to pledge additional money or other aid, such as a place to live, free clothing, and occasionally medical care. Some years after the show was canceled, a producer acknowledged that many of the Heartline calls had been prearranged to ensure legitimacy. The most heartwarming of the contestants would often return to the show to provide an update of their circumstances, while also validating the help they had received in earlier appearances.[16]

Not surprisingly, *Strike It Rich* was consistently accused of exploiting its downtrodden guests. Critics pointed to the unseemly nature of the intimate personal details being exposed, as well as the camera techniques used, such as tight close-ups on weeping parents or sick children, including one episode with a tight camera shot of a disabled boy's legs as he struggled to walk with heavy leg braces. The most prominent TV critic in the nation, Jack Gould, of the *New York Times*, led the cultural assault, calling the show "an instance of commercial TV gone berserk," and suggesting it was "a show that callously exploits human anxiety to sell the products of a soap manufacturer and does it with a saccharine solicitude that hits the jackpot in bad taste."

Strike It Rich even ran afoul of city and state officials in New York. In 1954, it was revealed that dozens of people had come to the show's New York City studio hoping to appear on the show. When these unfortunate souls could not get on the show, many were stranded in the city, including a destitute family of eleven from Maryland. The New York City welfare department was compelled to extend financial assistance to get the family home. In response, the welfare commissioner called the show "a national disgrace." In another embarrassing episode, an escaped fugitive appeared on the show, winning $165 and a place to live. In the aftermath of these incidents and mounting criticism, politicians became involved, initiating a criminal investigation and proposing bills in the state legislature to protect viewers from shows like *Strike It Rich*. CBS buckled under the public scrutiny and canceled the prime-time version of the show in early 1955, though a daytime version would continue until 1958. The controversy and condemnation surrounding *Strike It Rich* foreshadowed a frequently critical response to reality-dependent programming in the future.[17]

Though *Strike It Rich* did have a daytime programming presence, unquestionably the most prominent and successful of the daytime misery shows was *Queen for a Day* (1956–1964). This confessional show was targeted toward the female viewer at home during the day. On a daily basis, four or five women would be called from the studio audience to be interviewed by host Jack Bailey. In truth, the contestants for each show were preselected and placed in the audience. The women were chosen for the depth of sadness in their personal lives and their level of neediness, but also for their ability to look forlorn, frumpy, and unattractive on camera. The physical appearance of the women was heightened by the contrasting use of glamorous fashion models to display the daily gifts awarded to the winner. Upon being called on camera, the women would be prompted by Jack Bailey to detail their depressing circumstances and explain why they deserved to be Queen for a Day.

Much like *Strike It Rich*, there was a litany of sick children, dying relatives, starving or homeless families, and various other depressing stories. At the end of the program, after each woman told her story, the contestants would be assembled together on the stage. At that point each woman would have her misery summarized, after which the studio audience would be encouraged to applaud for their favored Queen, with an on-screen applause meter determining the winner. Bailey would then shout to the winner, "I now pronounce you . . . Queen for a Day," and she would be cloaked in a red sable robe, with a crown placed on her head, often with tears flowing from the winner and many in the audience. Though the show was a ratings powerhouse, drawing 50 percent of the audience in many television markets, it never drew the same volume of criticism hurled at *Strike It Rich*. This is likely due to its primary existence as a daytime show, which placed it in a category of programming that could easily be dismissed or ignored, as opposed to prime-time programming, which was taken more seriously and subject to more comment and critique.[18] Several other confessional shows aired in the 1950s, including *Glamour Girl* (1953–1954), in which the "needy" or "deserving" women were awarded with gifts for their troubles, most notably a twenty-four-hour beauty makeover; and *On Your Account* (1953–1956), in which contestants had their misery assessed by a panel of judges, while earning money by answering questions.[19]

At the opposite end of the reality-dependent game show spectrum was the quiz show, particularly the specialized-knowledge format. In the summer of 1955, CBS premiered *The $64,000 Question*, airing at 10 PM on Tuesday nights. Initially, the appeal of the show was the unprecedented amount of money available to contestants. The money itself was enough to create some measure of tension; however, the producers of the show amped up the drama by carefully selecting the contestants. Not only were many of the participants emblematic of the guy/gal next door, but their fields of expertise often seemed incongruous with their perceived station in life. For example, there was Gino Prato, a shoemaker from the Bronx, who was an expert on opera; Redmond O'Hanlon, a New York City police officer, whose category was Shakespeare; Marine Captain Richard McCutcheon, whose topic was cooking; and arguably the most famous contestant from the show, Dr. Joyce Brothers, a twenty-eight-year-old psychologist, who was an expert on boxing and ultimately won the $64,000 grand prize. Many of the breakout "stars" of the show were not only relatable to viewers, but also remarkable in their knowledge. The format of the show was also brilliantly crafted to stretch and build the tension over several weeks of a contestant's run. Within several weeks of its premiere, *The $64,000 Question* was the number one rated show on television, reaching a peak audience of fifty-five million in September of 1955, when Marine Captain McCutcheon became the first contestant to win the $64,000 prize.[20]

As is often the case in television programming, success breeds replication. After the meteoric rise of *The $64,000 Question* came other big money quiz shows, such as a spin-off from the original, *The $64,000 Challenge*, which had popular alumni from the parent show competing. Other popular quiz shows included *Tic Tac Dough* (1956–1959), *Name That Tune* (1953–1959), and *Dotto* (1958). Most noteworthy of the big money imitators was a show entitled *Twenty-One*, which premiered in March 1956. From the beginning, the show's producers, Jack Barry and Dan Enright, faced intense pressure from their commercial sponsors and heavy competition from other quiz programs. Like their successful competitors, *Twenty-One*'s producers created a show built on nail-biting dra-

ma and excruciating tension, coupled with the carefully screened personalities of the meticulously selected contestants. Within the televised
game, two competitors answered questions from a diverse group of categories, with higher points awarded for more difficult queries; the ultimate
goal was to be the first to attain twenty-one points. To amplify the drama
contestants were sequestered in a glass-walled "isolation booth," which
prevented them from seeing each other's point total until the game was
over. For even more dramatic effect, ties up to and including twenty-one
points were possible, thus ensuring two strong competitors could appear
together for several weeks.

Because these programs were so reality dependent, the merits or competition of the game itself were not enough to ensure ratings success.
Consequently, the *Twenty-One* producers chose their contestants as if it
were a Broadway production. Their greatest success was in casting a
villain, in the form of thirty-one-year-old Herbert Stempel, a struggling
graduate student from Queens, New York. Known to his friends and
family as "the walking encyclopedia," Stempel had impressed the producers with his amazing knowledge in a broad array of topics. Nonetheless, he was deemed completely un-telegenic in both his appearance and
personality, bordering on extremely unlikeable. Barry and Enright decided to accentuate these characteristics with the hope that viewers would
tune in to see Stempel lose. The producers crafted him into an unpleasant
know-it-all by dictating how he dressed, his haircut, and his on-air man-
nerisms and speech. The artifice worked to a point, particularly in the
show's ratings, but Barry and Enright realized that the American public
would rather root for someone to win, as opposed to hoping for someone
to lose. They needed a fair-haired hero, and they found one in Charles
Van Doren.

A scion of a renowned and award-winning literary and academic family, Charles Van Doren, thirty, was an English instructor at Columbia
University. He was also the antithesis of the unappealing Stempel; Van
Doren was handsome, pithy, modest, and self-deprecating, in spite of his
obvious erudition and intelligence. As Dan Enright said of Van Doren,
"he was the kind of young man you'd love to have your daughter mar-
ry."[21] In December of 1956, after having won over $50,000, Herb Stem-
pel was defeated by Charles Van Doren. Thus began the short career of
the era's greatest reality celebrity. During an unprecedented fifteen consecutive appearances, Van Doren became a national hero and icon, grac-

ing the covers of national magazines and guesting on TV talk shows. America's "favorite egghead" was even promoted as bulwark against the looming threat inherent in the emergence of Elvis Presley. As Karal Ann Marling has noted in her book on 1950s culture,

> Charlie Van Doren had provided an almost irresistible contrast to Elvis; he was articulate, conservative, neatly barbered—all the things Elvis appeared not to be. Unlike the sensual, some would say downright dirty Elvis, he was cool, restrained and cerebral, the perfect hero, it would seem, for American teens in the age of Sputnik.[22]

The newly minted celebrity had won $129,000 on the show when he finally lost in the spring of 1957. Van Doren transitioned into a regular position as a "cultural correspondent" on NBC's *Today Show*, at a salary of $50,000 a year. Van Doren seemed the perfect man, who now had the perfect life.

Unfortunately for everyone involved, the off-camera manipulation of contestants was not limited to coaching how they looked and acted on the set of the show. In the late summer of 1958, a contestant on the quiz show *Dotto* exposed a scheme in which contestants on that show had been given the questions and answers in advance of their appearance. In short order, the other quiz show dominoes began to topple, ultimately reaching *Twenty-One* and Charles Van Doren himself. Though the youthful professor denied any wrongdoing, Herbert Stempel, after attempting extortion from Dan Enright, vindictively confessed the show's guilt, including Van Doren's, to reporters and law enforcement. The fabricated reality villain now seemed to be living up to that caricature. Eventually, in a stunning fall from grace, in front of a congressional committee, Van Doren admitted his culpability in fixing his appearances on *Twenty-One*. It was a sad public end to a brief but remarkable personality-driven phenomenon.

Undoubtedly, the ethics of Barry, Enright, and the other producers and participants in the quiz show scandal can be easily assailed. Yet in a substantive way they were captives of their own genre and the medium in which they worked. The saturation of the game show format in the late 1950s created intense ratings competition. Furthermore, in the reality-dependent quiz show genre, producers quickly learned that it was the contestant's personalities, quirks, and narrative appeal that produced ratings success. In fact, the ratings for a specific game show could fluctuate wildly, even though the prize money and question format stayed the same. Viewers tuned in for the personalities; when a show had an engaging contestant the ratings would spike upward, while the reverse would occur with less engaging contestants. Given the confluence of these factors with ratings expectations and the ability to manipulate reality, it is not at all surprising that the outcomes were predetermined. However, that reasonable understanding did not protect the television networks or their sponsors from the taint of scandal. To cleanse themselves they purged all the major quiz shows (*The $64,000 Question, The $64,000 Challenge, Dotto, Twenty-One*) from the lineups almost immediately when the scandal hit the media. [23]

The smaller prize money game shows were still a viable genre, though largely during the daytime schedule; but the big money quiz show would not prosper again in prime time for almost forty years. Collaterally, the disappearance of big money quiz shows eliminated one of the platforms for reality-themed programming. In fact, reality-dependent programming acquired a stain that caused it to appear only sporadically over the next twenty years. The big three networks felt more secure manipulating fictional characters in sitcoms, westerns, and dramas than risking the inevitable criticism that would come from stage-managing real people in a reality-themed program.

BRANCHES OF THE REALITY TREE

The 1950s also featured a collection of miscellaneous reality-themed pieces. One with a similar motif to shows like *Strike It Rich* and *Queen for a Day*, but with a comedic tinge, was *It Could Be You* (1956–1961). On a typical show, host Bill Leyden would walk into the studio audience and call out the name of an audience member. It was not a random act; with the help of family members and "spies," the show's producers had assembled a biographical narrative of the targeted contestant. The subject would then listen as funny or mildly embarrassing stories, or occasionally tales of woe, were revealed to viewers. To take the edge off of being set upon, the contestants were awarded gifts or given the opportunity to win prizes. Periodically, the show would surprise people at their home or job. However, *It Could Be You* was not as maudlin or cruelly exploitative as its confessional show cousins. There was a warmhearted nature to most of the daily episodes, which included family reunions, long-lost friends reunited, and the solving of small-scale problems. But as with most reality-dependent series, it was the people and their stories that created the viewer interest.[24]

One of the more unique reality-themed shows of the decade, *You Asked for It* (1950–1959), featured what were called at the time "human interest" segments. The central plot device of this weekly program was the ability for viewers to write letters requesting what they wanted to see in future shows. Culled from several thousand letters each week, the viewer requests fulfilled leaned toward the odd and sensational. Features included a one-armed wallpaper hanger on the job; men fighting wild animals such as bears, anacondas, and alligators; a six-hundred-pound cowboy riding a horse; swallowers of goldfish and swords; a Hopi rain dance using a rattlesnake; and a reenactment of William Tell's shooting of an apple off someone's head. Even more revealing of the audience may have been the requests that were not granted. According to the show's host, Art Baker, the producers received requests to see a man executed in the electric chair, a reenactment of the burning of Joan of Arc at the stake, and, from multiple viewers, high-speed car crashes. This sensationalist format would be mirrored more than two decades later by reality shows such as *That's Incredible* and *Games People Play*.[25]

Another stalwart reality TV subgenre, the courtroom show, was also in an embryonic stage in the 1950s. Examples in this field include *Divorce Court* (1957–1969) and *The Verdict Is Yours* (1958), both of which dabbled in reality by using "real people stars" or "real legal professionals" in their presentations. Also noteworthy was the show *Divorce Hearing* (1958–1959), a pseudo-documentary featuring real-life marriage counselor Dr. Paul Popenoe talking to authentic couples in troubled marriages. Foreshadowing modern reality shows, the couples often found themselves in heated confrontations and shouting matches. These court shows were deemed by some as the "trash TV" of their day. United Press International television critic John Crosby minced no words when he said, "*Divorce Hearing* is the most disgusting program on television." He further opined, "It occurred to me watching this [*Divorce Hearing* and other court shows] that real people are entirely too real for television. The actors impersonating real people on these shows, God knows, is bad enough. But at least they can keep their passions sufficiently under control to talk coherently." With the benefit of hindsight this critique seems a remarkably prescient analysis of the early twenty-first-century reality program.[26]

THE 1960S

The quiz show scandals of the late 1950s made the three networks and many TV producers wary of the pitfalls in using real people to create entertainment, especially in the prime-time hours. There were still game shows, talk shows, and human interest programs on during the daytime; and there were sporadic news programs, non-news documentaries, and public opinion/man-on-the-street segments. However, the reality-dependent shows and the reality TV celebrity would recede in an avalanche of scripted fare, in the form of sitcoms, westerns, drama series, and variety shows. In fact, the one reality show to create a cultural legacy in the 1960s, *Candid Camera* (1960–1967), was actually a reboot of a program with origins in the formative years of television in the late 1940s. The forebearer of *Candid Camera* was a radio program transformed into a TV show called *Candid Microphone*. Eventually renamed *Candid Camera*, the program aired sporadically in the 1950s—until 1960, when *Candid Camera* began a very successful seven-season run on CBS, including four consecutive years in which it was one of the top ten rated shows on television.[27]

The show was created and hosted by Allen Funt. A characteristic episode featured several manufactured scenarios that placed unsuspecting non-performers in a position that would possibly test their honesty, credulity, altruism, and ultimately their sense of humor. This hidden-camera formula was described in the show's opening narration as "people caught in the act of being themselves." Funt was aided in his comic efforts by a cadre of actors who facilitated the scenarios, some of which were crafted by well-known writers such as Woody Allen, William Saroyan, Pat McCormick, and Fannie Flagg. At the heart of most of the comic setups were everyday occurrences that went awry. For example:

> Driving a car with no engine into a service station and having a mechanic examine it.
> Placing a guard on the Pennsylvania/Delaware border to inform drivers that Delaware was closed for the day.

Setting up a trampoline store in which recently hired secretaries
   watched clients bounce through the ceiling and disappear.
Setting up an office in which new employees had to contend with an
   out-of-control mimeograph machine.

Occasionally, the show would border on the truly voyeuristic: secretly
filming people at work, or people combing their hair or grooming in a
mirror. The comic payoff for the audience was what Funt called the
"reveal"—the moment he would enter the camera shot and inform the
unsuspecting subjects they were on TV. It should be noted that everyone
who appeared on the show had to sign a release form to have their
likeness used in the show. According to Funt, very few people refused to
sign the form, perhaps reflecting a universal desire to be on TV.

Candid Camera was broadly popular within several constituencies.
The viewing public responded by making the program one of the highest
rated on television, including second-place finish among all shows in the
1962–1963 season. The network and the show's producers appreciated
not just the success of the show, but also the smaller budgets, with low
production costs being one of the eternal appeals of reality television.
Candid Camera even found vocal pockets of interest and support in academia, particularly in the social sciences. Various sociologists and social
psychologists like Philip Zimbardo noted the value of Americans being
able to see themselves as they really are, as well as the potential clinical
applications of *Candid Camera*'s techniques. In fact, when the show was
only sporadically aired in the 1950s, Funt did consulting work for
psychologists to make ends meet. The show was not universally praised;
it was susceptible to the critiques that most reality-dependent shows seem
to attract. *Candid Camera* was called invasive, misrepresentative, exploitative, and cruel. Funt alluded to the occasional need for cruelty in humor,
saying, "If you want to know what holds the man together . . . you apply a
real jolt and see where the cracks appear." A particularly harsh critique in
The New Yorker called Funt and his show "sadistic, poisonous, anti-
human and sneaky."[28]

Though the show was canceled by CBS in 1967, the *Candid Camera*
formula, and Funt's propensity for using real people, continued for two
more decades. After 1967, Funt produced periodic TV specials, but made
his biggest splash in 1970, when he released an X-rated feature film
called *What Do You Say to a Naked Lady?* It was essentially the *Candid
Camera* hidden-camera approach, but with full frontal nudity creating the

humorous situations and subject reactions. Funt would return to the risqué fare at the height of the reality wave in 1982, by producing a new version of his classic show for the adult-entertainment-themed Playboy Channel on cable television.

Despite the tremendous ratings success of *Candid Camera*, the show stands alone as the only prominent prime-time reality-dependent show of the 1960s. This fact runs counter to the course of television history, in which success with a genre produces a mass replication, if not a saturation of similar programming. That did not happen with *Candid Camera*, for three reasons. First, in the wake of the quiz show scandal of the previous decade, there was still some residual trepidation about any programming that relied on "non-performers" for entertainment. Second, the *Candid Camera* formula of hidden surveillance was difficult to re-create without looking like an unvarnished, explicit appropriation, possibly producing legal action. Third, there was just not the demand for reality-themed shows within the industry or among viewers. Scripted programs were drawing large and loyal audiences with a seemingly endless appreciation for sitcoms, westerns, and variety shows. Though reality-themed programming was definitively cheaper to produce, the costs of financing television production were not as exorbitant as they would be in subsequent decades. Consequently, there was neither the creative nor financial impetus to produce a wave of reality programming in this decade. [29]

THE 1970S

Reality-themed programming would begin a slow and sporadic emergence in the 1970s. While sitcoms, variety shows, character-driven dramas, and made-for-TV movies were still predominant, by the end of the decade the creative stagnancy and growing production costs of these genres created a small opening for reality-dependent programming to establish itself, and thus begin the transformation of the television industry. For many scholars and observers of television, the Public Broadcasting Service's (PBS) *An American Family* (1973) stands as not only a pinnacle achievement in the reality genre, but as the genesis of the genre. Of course, the central thesis of the present study would dispute the latter contention; however, the cultural impact of the series cannot be reasonably disputed. The narrative core of *An American Family* was the Loud family of Santa Barbara, California: parents Bill and Pat, and their five children, Lance, Delilah, Michele, Kevin, and Grant. The family agreed to let cameras into their home in May 1971, to film their day-to-day activities. The show was conceived and spearheaded by producer/director/documentarian Craig Gilbert, who was also a fixture in the family home during the filming. The result, after eight months of intrusive chronicling, is a hybrid of the traditional documentary and an exercise in cinema verité. Given the unique nature of the circumstances, the family appears remarkably unselfconscious with the cameras around. The Louds seem so much more "real" than the subjects on modern-day reality shows that portray people's personal lives and relationships.[30]

In a flash of post-broadcast recognition, the Louds would regret their naiveté and openness; for during the twelve episodes of the series the family had some highly intimate moments revealed, including probable alcoholism, the public emergence of a homosexual son, alleged marital infidelity, and eventually the onset of divorce proceedings. The public response to the series was diverse and often passionate. To begin with, the show drew approximately ten million viewers per episode, which was a remarkably high rating for non-network television, particularly given that it was a PBS offering, and thus slightly less accessible than major network programming, which may well have discouraged viewers who reflexively dismissed such fare. Whatever the reason, much of the debate generated by the show took on a distinctly academic and intellectual bent.

Newspapers and periodicals across the nation featured analysis and critiques from sociologists, anthropologists, and even mental health professionals. Included in these responses were the predictable jeremiads on the collective American family and society in general. Quite unfairly, the Louds became a symbol and central example of America's moral and cultural decline. A *New York Times Magazine* article on the series is emblematic of the overwrought condemnation of the Louds:

> When sorting through the experience of viewing the Louds, my first realization was that all of the avenues of culture as I have understood them were missing from the Loud family life. If there is such a thing as negative culture or culture minus, the Louds have it.

The same article also revealed the reflexive conservative response to the stereotypically California clan, and liberalism in general:

> I think the Louds have escaped the small town mores of an earlier
> America. They have been educated and led into a large vacuum, and
> like the rest of us are cast out without the structure of work and relig-
> ion that used to shape the days. We have so much freedom we are now
> cultural Neanderthal.[31]

These critiques are similar to those voiced in recent years as the reality
genre has continually slid down the slippery slope of morality and social
responsibility.

In most assessments of *An American Family*, the central question
posed was, how authentic and representative was the Loud family? Acclaimed anthropologist Margaret Mead was a vocal supporter of the series, declaring the show to be "as new and significant as the invention of
drama or the novel—a new way in which people can learn to look at life,
by seeing the real life of others interpreted by the camera." On the other
end of the spectrum was the renowned Sociologist Herbert Gans, who
diminished the impact of the Loud family by calling them "a sample of
one" and doubting the deeper implications of the series, saying that "all
the talk about the show's meaning is ill founded. It is a single family
portrait and nothing more."

Much like participants in modern reality shows, the Loud family
found themselves greatly disappointed with how they were represented.
The mother of the family, Pat, was surprised by the end product—"I think
they have dealt badly with our honor and trust"—pointing out that the
producers "left out all the joyous, happy hours of communication and
fun." Bill Loud, the father of the family, was equally dismayed. "If they
filmed 25 normal scenes and five bizarre scenes a day, they picked the
five bizarre scenes and only one of the normal ones for the finished
piece." This selective if not manipulative style of editing became the
lifeblood of the "fly on the wall" style of reality shows that proliferated
beginning in the 1990s.[32]

Despite their initial disappointment, the Loud family did not shun the
public spotlight. Months after the show aired, members of the family
were still granting interviews and appearing on various TV talk shows,
most notably *The Dick Cavett Show*. In the aftermath of the series, perhaps the most prescient and revealing quote came from the oldest son,
Lance, who had emerged as openly gay during the filming. Lance celebrated and concurrently mocked the family exposé and collateral fame:
"The series was the fulfillment of the middle class dream that you can

become famous for being just what you are. This is actually the greatest thing I've done to date."[33] If the truth could somehow be extracted, this would have to be the credo for most of the modern participants in reality programming.

It is easy to see why some people might point to *An American Family* as the genesis of the modern genre and a subsequent wave of reality programming. Clearly, similarities exist in how the PBS show and modern reality shows are shot and edited. The social commentary and criticism produced by the show are reminiscent of contemporary reactions. Just as the Loud family was upset with their representation on their show, many modern participants bemoan their allegedly unfair characterization on a given show. And while it was not the reason they did the show, the Loud family, particularly Lance, seemed drawn to the flame of cheap celebrity, as are virtually all modern-day reality subjects.

All that being said, *An American Family* can just as easily be called a traditional documentary, or an experiment in cinema verité in the mode of *Woodstock* (1970), *Hospital* (1970), and *Grey Gardens* (1975). That *An American Family* has been labeled a seminal reality program is a consequence of the search for a reasonable and culturally comfortable explanation for the origins of a now dominant genre. It is a recategorization of the show, decades after it aired. However, in point of fact, *An American Family* exists in splendid isolation. There was no easily definable collection of imitators that followed in its successful footsteps; nor were there subgenres of reality programming produced by those attempting to capitalize on an emerging trend.

The most successful and closest thematic descendant to *An American Family* is *The Real World* (Music Television [MTV], 1992); but there was an almost two-decade gap between the two shows. The break between the shows is too wide to make a strong case that the PBS show gave birth to the commercial success of the MTV offering, or the other reality-themed shows that proliferated in the 1990s; though there are some observers who point to *The Real World* as the seminal reality program that touched off a wave of reality media. Undoubtedly, *An American Family* created a cultural mark in its time, but it did not produce a "wave" that led to the growth of reality media; that distinction belongs to *Real People*.

The mid- to late 1970s would produce one of the enduring syndicated TV stalwarts of 1980s reality programming, *PM Magazine*, also known as *Evening Magazine* in some local markets. The show began to air on KPIX in San Francisco, on August 2, 1976. The show was essentially a local thirty-minute newsmagazine, with self-help, how-to, and entertainment options geared toward the Bay Area market. KPIX was one of a string of five local stations across the nation owned by a broadcasting entity known as Group W. When *Evening Magazine* became successful in San Francisco, Group W decided to replicate the format on its other stations. By 1978, the format was being sold and syndicated to non–Group W stations, as *PM Magazine*.

Over several years in the late 1970s, a rigid format for the show emerged. Each local *PM Magazine* had its own set of telegenic male and female hosts who would introduce each of the stories and features. The show's appearance was also standardized by using uniform animated graphics and theme music for each local variant. The unique component of *PM Magazine* was the dual foci of the show, which allowed it to present segments that were of both local and national origin. By the early 1980s, Group W had created a cooperative production structure that allowed local stations to craft their own *PM Magazine* geared to their market. Each local station in the syndicated chain agreed to create segments of local origin; these local segments were then placed into a pool of stories from which any other local station in the co-op could select. In other words, a station in Austin, Texas, in addition to its own locally produced stories, had access to segments filmed all over the nation. This was quite a web of national coverage when you consider that by the mid-1980s there were almost one hundred stations in the *PM/Evening Magazine* network.[34]

Former *PM Magazine* executive and later professor of communications Richard Crew offers an encapsulation of the finished nightly product:

> Each *PM Magazine* contained two, six-minute people-oriented stories, the mandatory locally-hosted wraps, and a set of three short lifestyle "tips" covering areas like health, how-to advice, and restaurant reviews. The resulting blend gave each market's PM show national scope, a quality look, and an important local identity.[35]

There is a reasonable debate to be had over whether *PM Magazine* influenced the creation of *Real People*, or whether *Real People* fueled the popularity of the *PM Magazine* format. The original *PM Magazine* predated *Real People* by over two years, and additional local versions aired in a handful of markets by the time *Real People* premiered. However, it was not until after *Real People* (as well as its imitators) became a massive ratings success that the *PM Magazine* brand began its own tremendous growth. Clearly, the national success of reality programming made the local variety more appealing and viable to programmers around the nation. The nascent cable network Showtime also delved into the hybrid newsmagazine/reality realm with an occasional show entitled *What's Up America?* (1978–1981). Given the more liberal content restrictions on cable, the show often delved into more intense, even adult subject matter than would be found on broadcast television.

If one is willing to look well down the limited food chain of 1970s reality-themed programming, they will find shows such as *The Gong Show* (1976–1980) and *The $1.98 Beauty Contest* (1978). Both of these shows were born out of the unique creative talents of Chuck Barris. The game show impresario Barris was also the brain behind reality-tinged shows such as *The Dating Game* (1965–1973) and *The Newlywed Game* (1966–1980), both of which drew their entertainment from real people contestants. *The Gong Show* became a hugely popular daytime talent show by employing some of the least and oddly talented performers one could imagine. The highlight of every episode was usually the dismissal of the worst contestants with the flamboyant sounding of a gong, delivered by a panel of lesser celebrities. *The $1.98 Beauty Contest* was an updated *Queen for a Day*, but with an alleged wink to satire, as the contestants engaged in talent and swimsuit competitions. Both of these shows were undeniably crass and exploitative, yet entertaining to their own constituencies; though television critics and social commentators were not among them. [36]

The Barris stable of shows could not have been done without real people or amateur performers, thus again affirming the entertainment value of real people. However, these shows exist on the shadowy periphery of 1970s reality-themed programs, more evocative of television's past, rather than presaging its immediate future. Shows such as *PM Magazine*, *What's Up America?*, and Charles Kuralt's "On the Road," and to a lesser degree programs like *The Gong Show*, reveal the potential opportunities for reality-themed programs. The missing element was a catalytic agent to expand and accelerate the presence of reality programming in the national consciousness. *Real People* was the missing ingredient and transformative force that would cement reality programming as a fixture in the television industry, beginning in 1979.

I

THE GOLDEN GUT STRIKES AGAIN

1979–1980

On June 8, 1978, Fred Silverman began his reign as the president of the National Broadcasting Company (NBC). Six months earlier, Silverman had been lured away from the American Broadcasting Company (ABC) with promises of more money, executive perks, and extensive power to shape NBC into a network that reflected his philosophy of television programming. To many observers, both inside and outside the television industry, the money and power awarded to Silverman appeared well deserved. At forty-one years old, Silverman had dedicated all of his adult life to television. In 1960, while at the Ohio State University, he had written a master's thesis assessing ABC's prime-time schedule from 1953 to 1959. He then thrived as a programmer at independent stations WGN in Chicago and WPIX in New York, until landing an executive position at the Columbia Broadcasting System (CBS) in 1963. While at CBS he rose to the position of programming chief, in which he was responsible for the production and scheduling of classic hit shows such as *The Mary Tyler Moore Show* (1970–1977), *All in the Family* (1971–1983), *M*A*S*H* (1972–1983), and *The Waltons* (1971–1981). Frustrated by a staid, cautious, and stagnant executive culture at CBS, Silverman jumped at an opportunity to become the president of ABC Entertainment in 1975.

While it was certainly a professional milestone for Silverman, and he was widely respected among his peers, few in the television industry expected his ascendency to alter the status quo of the major networks.

Nonetheless, in three years at ABC he was able to achieve what many in television had thought unimaginable. In 1976, after more than two decades as the perennially lowest-rated network, ABC finished first in the Nielsen ratings, dethroning CBS, the twenty-year reigning champion. Silverman had engineered this reversal of fortune with a deft programming touch and with a little help left over from his ABC predecessors. The result was a lineup of ratings powerhouses, including *Happy Days*, *Starsky and Hutch*, *Charlie's Angels*, *Three's Company*, *Laverne and Shirley*, and the groundbreaking mini-series *Roots*.[1]

However, Silverman was not without his vocal critics. For more than a decade there had been an almost continuous critical drumbeat assailing the excessive sex and violence on television; by the late 1970s it had become a deafening torrent for the executives at the three major networks. Though he was not alone in his programming tastes, Silverman was regularly singled out for the violence in such shows as *Starsky and Hutch* and *Baretta* and various made-for-TV films. He was also alternately credited and blamed for the use of over-the-top sexuality and objectification of the female form in his shows—what the critics derisively called "jiggle TV." Whether it was the bikini-clad female detectives on *Charlie's Angels*, the equally underdressed beauties on *Three's Company*, or just the continual stretching of the boundaries of sexual content and imagery, Silverman appeared to many as the standard-bearer of moral decay in the nation's most powerful medium. Equally irritating for the social critics was that in the ultracompetitive and ultimately unoriginal arena of television, it was not long before the other networks were trying to match the sexually charged Silverman formula. The success of ABC guaranteed there would be even more bounce in jiggle TV.[2]

In early 1978, Silverman's contract with ABC was up for renewal; most industry insiders assumed he would stay with a number one network that was essentially his creation. However, NBC offered Silverman opportunities that ABC could or would not match. Not only did NBC offer a huge salary increase and executive incentives, but he was also presented with a more prestigious title, president of NBC broadcasting, which included control over the company's entire entertainment division, in both television and radio. There was also an additional enticement designed to appeal to Silverman's purportedly massive ego. As the distant third-place network, NBC presented a clean slate upon which Silverman could craft another remarkable "worst to first" transformation. Transforming NBC into the number one network was a daunting challenge. In the 1977–1978 season, NBC had only two original programs finish in the top twenty rated shows, and just a small collection of programs considered success-ful, notably *Little House on the Prairie*, *The Big Event*, *The Rockford Files*, *CHiPs*, and *Quincy*. As a mark of the weakness of NBC program-ming, its most reliable program, both in ratings and revenue, was the long-running *Tonight Show Starring Johnny Carson*. Some observers of television mockingly said that NBC stood for "Nothing But Carson."

In hiring Silverman, NBC had added a man who even at a young age was one of the legendary programmers in the history of the medium; someone so well known and respected that in the fall of 1977 he was deemed worthy of a *Time* magazine cover story, in which his program-ming instincts earned him the sobriquet "the Man with the Golden Gut." In addition to the programming brilliance, NBC was also purchasing some cultural cache. Silverman brought with him name recognition and badly needed positive publicity, if not credibility, for a struggling net-work. As a measure of Silverman's status and influence, on the day in January of 1978 when his defection was announced, the Wall Street stock price of ABC dropped $1.75 a share, while stock in the parent company of NBC, the Radio Corporation of America (RCA), jumped $1.25.[3]

Though Silverman's defection to NBC leaked into the media in Janu-ary 1978, his contract with ABC was not officially over until June of that year. Being extremely disgruntled, ABC decided to hold Silverman to his contract even though he would have no role or presence at the network offices. Consequently, Silverman spent four months in limbo, where he was no longer at ABC, but could not yet begin his duties at NBC. That interregnum allowed time for a great deal of speculation and rumination as to what Silverman would do when taking the reins at his new network. Much of this media speculation was negative, based largely on Silver-man's reputation as the mastermind of jiggle TV and the dumbing down of network TV. Illustrative of this analysis was an *Esquire* magazine article entitled "The Dangers of Television in the Silverman Era." In his piece, Richard Reeves suggested that "something is forcing the quality of television down—and Fred Silverman is that instrument." He further jabbed, "All that he has proved is that he is the best of desperate men . . . the overriding, invariably successful value in Silverman's world seems to be: do it if you can get away with it." On a lighter note, Silverman became a semi-regular target in Johnny Carson's late-night monologues, and political comedian and future *Real People* contributor Mark Russell quipped that the Golden Gut would change the name of the *NBC Evening News with David Brinkley* to "Laverne and Brinkley."[4]

To the surprise of many industry observers, when Silverman emerged from his four-month hiatus he appeared to have experienced a philosophical renaissance. In his first address to NBC affiliate station managers, Silverman pledged that NBC would make a commitment to "quality" programming, both in the entertainment and news division. In essence, he promised that under his leadership NBC would not only be the ratings leader, but also the most respected network. So passionate was his emphasis on the high-minded and quality programming angle that he soon felt obliged to stress, "I don't want anybody to get the impression NBC is going to be the second public television network." In subsequent press interviews, Silverman acknowledged spending his four months off "rethinking his career choices and having a crisis of conscience." Whether due to the wave of criticism and jokes he endured, or the recognition of NBC and this legacy-defining job, Silverman seemed genuinely committed to destroying his reputation as "an impresario of trivial light entertainment, and a champion of the new wave of sexually titillating series."[5] Even more confounding to TV critics and observers alike was the fact that Fred Silverman actually followed through on his high-minded promises, at least initially. Silverman would be even more committed to another of his stated goals, the production of innovative, trend-setting programs that would reimagine the medium.

Because of his delayed start on the job, Silverman had little opportunity to apply his principles to NBC's already constructed and announced 1978–1979 television schedule. The best he could reasonably be expected to do was tinker with time slots and plan for the inevitable cancelations of underperforming shows. Yet Silverman would not or could not wait to begin crafting his ideal network. Almost immediately, he found an opening to merge his primary goal of quality and innovation. While perusing shows that had been produced as series pilots (first episode) but not placed on the fall schedule, Silverman discovered a show entitled *Lifeline*. The program was an intimate documentary-style film with voice-over narration. What set the show apart were the remarkably intimate real-life portrayals of real doctors and patients. All the more unique was that the cameras followed the doctors to their homes, providing candid images of their personal lives. Silverman found the show to be extraordinary, and quickly determined to make space for it by removing an already slated new series from the schedule. The now canceled series, entitled *Coast to Coast*, was described by industry insiders as an "airborne combination of ABC's *Three's Company* and *Love Boat*," both of which had been part of Silverman's "light and jiggly" stable just several months earlier. But that was the past; Silverman now saw *Lifeline* as the future of television, stating that "it could be the single show on any network this fall that could change the face of prime-time." The narrative content of *Lifeline* was a progenitor of the medical reality show. Cameras were indeed in the operating rooms and living rooms of the doctors. It was serious drama and tension, occasionally enhanced through the acknowledged use of re-creations.[6]

Lifeline premiered on September 7, 1978, at 10 PM, with mixed results. The ratings for the show were unfailingly miserable; on several occasions it finished as the lowest-rated show on television for the entire week. However, the television critics were generally much more receptive to the show than was the audience. The widespread critical acclaim combined with Silverman's faith in his own intuition led him to stay committed to the show well after most executives at NBC wanted to concede defeat. In fact, Silverman pushed his figurative chips to the middle of the table by engaging in what NBC publicity claimed was "the most dramatic programming decision in the history of television." Silverman would air an episode of *Lifeline* on three different nights in one week in November, during the all-important sweeps period. The ad campaign promoted the dramatic, nonfiction nature of the show as "a new dimension in television drama . . . the epitome of classic drama—only this time the life and death are for real." This desperate gamble in scheduling and the larger experiment with innovative programming failed, as *Lifeline* would be canceled by late 1978.[7]

Although disappointed by the failure of *Lifeline*, Silverman was not ready to discard the reality concept, particularly since *Lifeline* had earned him what he seemed to crave at that point in his career: critical acclaim and respect. What he further needed was for the critical cache that reality programming was creating to be matched by ratings success. Silverman's first genuine opportunity to create that type of show came in the fall of 1978, as he was able to cancel shows that were performing poorly. The replacement of these canceled shows with new programs to be aired in the new year was known as the "second season." On a single day in

December, Silverman canceled nine of the nineteen shows NBC had on the air. He now had a new chance to try out a reality concept that would register with audiences.[8]

After watching a local show in New York City featuring segments on local points of interest, and inspirational or unique local citizens, Silverman decided to try and create a broader, high-concept show with a national scope. To bring his concept to life, Silverman contacted veteran TV producer George Schlatter, who had a list of quality credits, most notable being the creator-producer of the groundbreaking NBC variety show *Laugh-In* (1967–1973). In short order, Schlatter created an outline for a show focusing on real people, their lives and communities, and pitched it to Fred Silverman, who quickly agreed to the format and the title, *Real People*. Though originally conceived as one or two hour-long specials, the mandate was expanded to encompass six hour-long episodes to air as part of the second season in the spring of 1979.[9] Given the green light, several formative decisions were made by Schlatter and approved by Silverman. The show would comprise a mixture of taped segments punctuated by introductions and witty banter by the hosts, broadcast in front of a live studio audience in Burbank, California.

Schlatter and his production team then began to look for topics, events, and subjects to feature on the show. Staffers combed through newspapers and magazines and contacted local NBC affiliates to find viable stories. Following that selection process, field producers and film crews were quickly dispatched across the nation. This left Schlatter with the task of assembling the hosts of the show. It was decided upon early in the creation of the show that the hosts should not overshadow the real stories and subjects being featured. Consequently, the hosts/correspondents of the show would essentially be a cast with no nationwide name recognition or network prime-time television experience. Included in the cast were Sarah Purcell, an actress who had worked in local television in San Diego and Los Angeles as a morning talk show host; Skip Stephenson, a stand-up comedian with a PG-13-rated routine and a midwestern persona; John Barbour, a stand-up comedian and television character actor, who was also credited as producer on the show; Bill Rafferty, a comedic actor, who operated as a "roving reporter"; and Fred Willard, the only host with something of a national track record, as a costar of two quirky television comedies, *Fernwood Tonight* (1977) and *America 2-Night* (1978). There would also be two special commentators, Mark Russell, a political comedian with a penchant for satirical songs, and Jimmy Breslin, a curmudgeonly acid-tongued writer for the *New York Daily News*, who had developed a national reputation for his writing.[10]

Real People was given an 8 PM Wednesday time slot, and an April 18, 1979, premiere date. It was a challenging time slot for several reasons. To begin with, in the previous three months that slot had been something of a ratings wasteland for NBC, first with a program called *Supertrain*, one of the biggest critical and financial flops of the decade, then with several weeks of repeated variety specials. Second and more intimidating, *Real People* would be opposite a top fifteen rated program, *Eight Is Enough* on ABC, and a reliable ratings earner, *The Jeffersons* on CBS. Although Wednesday at 8 PM was a dead spot in the NBC lineup, it would prove to be an advantage for *Real People*, as the expectations for any show in that spot would be very low. In fact, the ratings for *Real People* in the spring of 1979 would not be a determinative factor in the show's future. NBC was winding down a disastrous ratings season that left it as the distant third-place network. There was no way to even salvage ratings respectability, thus *Real People* was not under as much pressure as other shows may have been.

The pre-premiere publicity was built largely on the reputation of producer George Schlatter and the unique reality concept. In a number of national newspaper interviews, Schlatter became alternately the promoter and defender of the reality premise in general, and his show specifically. In his comments, Schlatter tried to conceptualize the show: "What we're doing is the theater of reality . . . real people and what they're saying and doing. We don't tell them what to say." As he further explained, the show was also trying to "raise the American eccentric to his proper place in the public esteem." The highlighting of eccentricity produced mocking dismissal from some in the TV industry, even though they had not seen an episode. When one interviewer noted that some observers had called the project a "traveling freak show" and a "*Gong Show* on wheels," the creator counterattacked. In an impassioned rebuttal, Schlatter proclaimed, "*The Gong Show* and *The $1.98 Beauty Show*, that is the theatre of humiliation . . . those shows say, 'How humiliating can we be? How degrading and distasteful can we be with the use of people?'" Schlatter then explained the difference with his show: "We're not dealing with freaks, we're dealing with individuals. Some of the people are a little unusual, some of them are eccentric, but all of them have their dignity."[11]

Real People cast photo, back row left to right: Fred Willard, Skip Stephenson, Bill Rafferty; front row left to right: John Barbour, Sarah Purcell. *NBC / Photofest* © *NBC*

NBC's larger publicity campaign played heavily upon two main themes: the reality format, and the uniqueness and eccentricity of the people featured on the show. NBC promotional material described the show as "a madcap collage of people, places and events celebrating the unusual lives of ordinary Americans." Subsequent promotional ads during the short season reinforced the "everyman" quality of the series by citing positive reviews from real viewers, such as a schoolteacher, a nurse, a telephone operator, a sound engineer, and a secretary, each of whom was quoted in effusive praise of the show: "Halleujah! The inside story of what life is really like," and "the kind of show that is about plain folks just like me."[12]

The six episodes of the abbreviated mini-season undoubtedly paid off on the premise of uniqueness and eccentricity. It became clear very quickly that the unique subjects featured were diverse enough that they would begin to fall into subcategories of eccentricity; for example, the uncommon occupation or pastime; those who live unusual day-to-day lives; those with a non-mainstream world view; and those so unique they defy categorization. Viewers were introduced to John "Sherlock Bones" Keane, a private investigator from San Francisco who specialized in finding missing pets for his clients; a professional panhandler named Omar the Beggar; a New York doctor who operated the Vampire Research Center; a husband and wife in Miles City, Montana, who operated the smallest television station in the United States; and local car dealers who starred in their own whacky commercials.

Some of the more unusual pastimes featured included health food advocates who ate dirt for its nutritional qualities; a club for self-professed ugly people; a basketball game played by people on donkeys; extreme male and female weightlifters at Gold's Gym in Santa Monica, California; a Neurotics Anonymous meeting; a man who lived a hermetic life in a desert shack; and a man who drove and lived in a passenger airliner he had converted into a mobile home. *Real People* also engaged with the late 1970s cultural fascination with science fiction and UFOs created by movies and TV shows like *Star Wars*, *Close Encounters of the Third Kind*, and *Battlestar Galactica*, among others; the result being a string of segments on visitors from, and visits to, outer space. There were several people who had made or were planning to make "contact," including "Space Ship Ruthie"; Ed Vanelsen, who claimed to regularly engage with aliens who lived in his home; and several people who were building their own spacecraft, one of whom was a former NASA scientist.

   Despite Fred Silverman's protestation to the contrary, there were aspects of jiggle TV evident in the first six episodes, as there would be
throughout the run of the series. Salacious segments included a feature on
Kelly Everett, a New York City woman who stripped for God; a visit to
the male strip club Chippendales; and a tour of erotic lingerie store Frederick's of Hollywood in Los Angeles, California. Unfortunately, the odd-
ball characters and bouncing bodies tended to inaccurately shape the
reputation of *Real People*, both when it originally aired and subsequently.
Yet as George Schlatter promised, there were always people and events
that had a deeper, more inspirational tone. The initial offerings in this
field featured stories on Carl Brashear, the first black American man to
become a US Navy deepwater diver ("frogman"), despite the loss of one
of his legs; Lesa "yo-yo" Worly, a female trucker from Tennessee; a man
who invited destitute families to live with him and his wife; a grateful
eight-year-old boy taken in by his grandmother in New York City; and a
collection of active and accomplished senior citizens who were learning
the newest disco dances, competing on rowing teams, and editing newspapers.
   Another recurring and often unacknowledged layer of a still develop-
ing *Real People* reflected a deepening vein of populism and patriotism
that was beginning to bubble up in American life. Mark Russell and
Jimmy Breslin were overt conduits of the populist fare, with Breslin
ranting about the excessive price of sneakers ($40), and Russell spoofing
government bureaucracy, waste, and hypocrisy. Yet ordinary subjects
also longed to have their voices heard; they were complaining about and
refusing to pay taxes—one called the Internal Revenue Service "a com-
munistic mafia organization"; they were fighting corruption, living off
the grid, and in subtle ways resisting the cultural, political, social, and
economic axis of New York, Washington, DC, and Los Angeles. [13]
   Not surprisingly, given the competition and unique concept of the
show, the ratings for *Real People* in its mini-season run were not strong.
In fact, they were awful; the program regularly finished at the bottom of
the Nielsen ratings, one week finishing fifty-second of sixty-one shows.
Nonetheless, Fred Silverman was undeterred; when talking about the
show he confidently spoke of the strong and broadening demographics of
its audience, its "breakout potential," its "word of mouth," and the encouraging innovation of the program. Silverman was not discouraged by
lukewarm reviews from national TV critics. The show was termed "un-

even" by *Daily Variety*, while John J. O'Conner in the *New York Times* said of the show, "We are thus quickly thrust back into the familiar television territory of non-substance, into the kind of product unlikely to grab the fancy of editors and reporters anywhere." O'Conner's haughty comments are exactly the type of coastal elitism that *Real People* would periodically mock and skewer in its features. More than most critics, Tom Shales of the *Washington Post* understood the content and potential of *Real People*:

> Is *Real People* really a new idea? Sort of; it's half an idea, at any rate, and that's more than usual for television. As half an idea, it deserves far more than half a chance. It deserves a chance and a half. Besides, *Real People* moves prime-time television another step in what many believe to be its inevitable direction; informational variety rather than the standard old Chug-Chug entertainment forms.

In addition to giving *Real People* the artistic benefit of the doubt, Shales was moderately prophetic in his view of the future of television; and he saw that future in *Real People*.[14]

Of all the segments presented in the first season, there was one that fully revealed the seemingly insatiable desire of Americans to achieve some measure of fame. The "taste test" was a constructed scenario in which Skip Stephenson posed as a TV pitchman who was presiding over a commercial taste test for a new soda called Sweet Thing. In front of a TV camera, subjects were given the soda to drink and asked to offer a critique. Almost to a person, they all sipped the drink and offered very positive comments on the product directly into the camera. In fact, *Real People* had created a concoction that was designed to taste terrible. After they thought the camera was off, everyone who had praised Sweet Thing admitted to not truly liking the soda. So anxious were these subjects to be in a TV commercial, they lied without being prompted by producers. In many people's minds, that type of self-directed deception has become the foundation of the modern reality genre in the twenty-first century.

In the end, ratings and reviews mattered little in determining the future of *Real People*; rather, it was Silverman's faith in his own skill and intuition that would prevail. On the sixth and final episode of the abbreviated season, the hosts announced to the live studio audience in a dramatic and celebratory fashion that *Real People* would return to NBC in the fall. After a hiatus of two months, NBC began repeating the first six episodes on July 25.[15] The summer reruns produced another round of magazine and newspaper articles on the show, and revealed an early subaltern promotional strategy. There was a concerted effort to create an equivalency between *Real People* and a cultural phenomenon of a decade earlier, *Laugh-In*. Beginning in 1968, *Laugh-In* not only produced stellar ratings, but also carved into American culture like a knife. The show helped promote into the mainstream consciousness the 1960s counterculture; a wave it then rode to great success and relevance. *Laugh-In* influenced the stretching of the bounds of acceptable content on television, both socially and politically; it contributed multiple catchphrases into the national lexicon and drew an eclectic mix of cameo appearances, from John Wayne to Richard Nixon. To further reinforce the desired equivalency, NBC ran several weeks of *Laugh-In* reruns during the summer of 1979. In addition to having the same producer, George Schlatter, the shows did have some familiar attributes, particularly in reflecting the emerging zeitgeist of their eras. The prime difference was that *Laugh-In* measured the politically liberal and socially freewheeling elements of American culture, while *Real People* would tap into the growing neoconservatism welling up in the early 1980s.

The opening of the 1979–1980 television season was a cautiously hopeful time for NBC and Fred Silverman. One of the shows with the most "buzz" coming into the season was *Real People*, which had momentum built up from the first season having been repeated for six weeks leading into the opening of the fall schedule. On Wednesday, September 5, 1979, *Real People*'s second season opened with new graphics and theme music, but with a continued emphasis on the everyday citizen. The show's initial filmed opening featured several real people (construction workers, police officers, flight attendants, nurses, students, families) offering an excited "Welcome to *Real People*," upon which the theme music would strike up and announcer Jack Harrold would say, "Tonight, live from NBC in Burbank, with videotape and filmed inserts from practically every place else . . . this is *Real People*."

For the second season there was one significant cast change that would essentially establish the core of the cast for the remaining seasons. Fred Willard, disappointed with his role and the content of the show, left the series to dedicate himself to his acting career. Replacing Willard was Byron Allen, an eighteen-year-old wunderkind comedian who had been seen on *The Tonight Show* by George Schlatter and hired immediately, even though he was enrolled in the University of Southern California at the time. Allen added some needed diversity to the cast as a young black man, at least fifteen years younger than any of the other hosts. Mark Russell continued to be a frequent contributor, but Jimmy Breslin would become less of a presence as the season proceeded.

By the end of season two, each of the hosts had crafted their own on-air persona and pattern of interaction with the others. The two most effective comic foils were Skip Stephenson and Sarah Purcell. Skip had a milquetoast midwestern persona sprinkled with an ability to deliver mild sexual quips and double entendre. Sarah was a more polished TV performer, an attractive accomplished "modern" woman. Their largely scripted dialogue often had Skip making a slightly risqué remark that would leave the demure Sarah blushing and flustered. Skip also regularly took on the role of smug male chauvinist, whom Sarah repeatedly dismantled with a mild 1970s feminist-inspired retort. There was an effort to create a similar lighthearted back-and-forth between Byron Allen and John Barbour, the comedy emerging from the alleged cultural chasm between the young black man and the middle-aged white man. This relationship never consistently clicked, but each man individually was very effective in representing his demographic cohort in larger society.

Another significant element of the *Real People* formula, audience and viewer participation, began to crystallize in season two. By the middle of the season, the *Real People* production offices in Burbank were receiving approximately five thousand letters a week from viewers. Production assistants would sort the mail into representative categories, such as cast mail, straight mail, miscellaneous, photo requests, funny want ads, story ideas, special requests, bloopers, negative mail, consumer ideas, X-rated signs, posters, names, pet peeves, children's jokes, and newspaper and billboard typos.[16] This volume of mail was whittled down to extract items and issues that might be viable as future stories or for use in the viewer participation segments of the show. There were several categories of viewer participation: the funny or unbelievable photo; humorous or mistaken advertisements or classifieds; viewers' comments on previous stories or opinions on issues of the day; funny stories read by the hosts or audience members; jokes; and even poems. Each submission was accompanied by the viewer's name and hometown, and the promise of a *Real People* T-shirt.

Each episode also incorporated active participation by members of the studio audience. This included introducing the cast and making comments or jokes on the salient issues of the moment. Here, again, the populist edge of the show cut through the more frivolous elements. The late 1970s were a dark and depressing time in American life. In an era recently emerged from various rights movements, the antiwar movement, the cultural hangover from Vietnam itself, and Watergate, the American people were more comfortable speaking their minds than they had ever been. In the summer of 1979, President Jimmy Carter suggested the United States was suffering a "crisis of confidence" in daily life. The *Real People* studio audience's comments were a manifestation of that crisis, with satirical and biting comments on issues like the energy crisis, high gas prices, interest rates, unemployment, taxes, inflation, corrupt politicians, the Cold War, and the taking of American hostages in Iran. It was mostly humorous, but also tinged with anger and frustration. As it moved forward, *Real People* would evolve as that angry populism transformed into the hyperpatriotism of the Reagan era.

This series' dipping of the toe into the previously sacrosanct waters of news, and even reportage by non-news entities, would be increasingly bemoaned by newspaper columnists and members of network news divisions throughout the 1980s. *Real People*, specifically George Schlatter, was not subtle or apologetic about the incursion into news. During a typical episode, at least once or twice a show the hosts would be featured sitting at a desk, with a projected image at their side to help them deliver their introductions, looking very much like news anchors. George Schlatter believed that news was entertainment and he consciously tried to meld the two; as he said before the show even aired, "This is the first show to get into that gray area between news and entertainment; so therefore it feels a little different." When confronted with accusations of blurring the line, Schlatter loudly countered by saying, "We're not doing it right then, I want to *erase* the line." With a retrospective view, it is obvious that *Real People* was not alone in this process; it was the beginning of the end for pure television news.[17]

Creating a full season's worth of material would be a true test of the capacity of reality TV to renew itself over the long run of a series. Were there even enough intriguing or inspiring people, places, and events to fill up an entire season? As it turned out there were more than enough, an almost never-ending supply. Season two featured over two hundred segments filmed all over the country. Since the broadcast of the first season the producers had received thousands of story suggestions, most of the whacky, eccentric type. The result was a collection of human and animal oddities in the theater of the absurd. The animal segments fell into the category of cute or amazing; for instance, "Buddy the Wonder Dog," who drove a car with his human companion; a water-skiing squirrel and dog; a monkey that worked around a farm riding a tractor; a toilet-trained cat; trained turkeys; Andre the performing seal; racing goats; and an ugly dog contest. The unique panoply of human absurdity and communal endeavor was also on full display. Some of the uniquely "talented" included "Mr. Backward," Pleni Wingo, who walked backward everywhere he went; a man who pulled an oversized top hat on to his upper body, painted lips on his stomach, and made his belly button whistle; a man who hypnotized lobsters; and a colorful array of knife throwers, mind readers, psychics, and collectors of pets, memorabilia, and assorted junk.

Unusual jobs were also a strong audience draw and good time filler for *Real People*. This category included some well-known minor celebrities, such as Ted Giannoulas, the San Diego Chicken, the most famous sports mascot of the late 1970s and early 1980s; the Unknown Comic, Murray Langston, who gained fame on *The Gong Show* for doing his act with a paper bag on his head; and Famous Amos, who went from homeless to being a chocolate chip cookie magnate. More anonymous people were examined as well: Captain Sticky, a three-hundred-pound man from San Diego, California, who wore a homemade superhero costume while campaigning for consumer protection; Laurie Cabot, known as the "official witch" of Salem, Massachusetts, though she was a decidedly nonthreatening witch; and a real-life Cupid, who for a fee would show up and shoot his arrows into "love targets." Extremes of age were also prominent; there was a ten-year-old disc jockey; a twelve-year-old evangelist; a ninety-three-year-old lifeguard; and a coterie of senior citizen cheerleaders and Olympians.

Real People also proved itself capable of examining uncommon, though not unusual, occupations. To wit, season two featured an effective piece on a group of loggers in Oregon. During the segment, viewers are exposed to the dangerous work of clearing forests, but also the personalities—how they interact, how they spend their free time; the phrase "work hard, play hard" is apt. Later in the season there was a similar exploration of the lives of seasonal lifeguards at busy Jones Beach, Long Island. The

Promotional ad for *Real People*, **November 14, 1979,** *New York Times*, **C33.**

lifeguards are a diverse group in age (from nineteen to ninety-three), in race, and finally in gender, as women had only recently started to be accepted into the corps. Between jokes about girls in bikinis and being beach bums, the guards are shown saving lives and keeping the peace. There is no sensationalism, no absurdity; it is a straightforward depiction of genuinely interesting people who have an uncommon lifestyle. It is difficult to watch segments such as these and not see the prototype for a much later staple of reality TV, with shows like *Deadliest Catch* (2005), *Dirty Jobs* (2005), *Duck Dynasty* (2012), etc.

During an era in which commentators lamented the loss of community life in American society, *Real People* countered that representation with an exploration of subcommunities that found enjoyment in their shard connections. There were conventions spread across the nation for people who did not seem likely conventioneers: bald people, roller coaster enthusiasts, ventriloquists, ghost town inhabitants, Edsel owners, low riders, jugglers, and hoboes. The American people have a deep competitive drive that emerges in a variety of forms both pro and con, but *Real People* would expose competitions and contests that revealed the offbeat and quickly disappearing localized community event. These events were staged anywhere, from small towns to big cities, and required not just physical skills, but other innate abilities. Included in this lineup were a hollering contest; belly bumping fights; the search for America's ugliest person; bathtub races; downhill racing with outhouses; camel racing; hot-air balloon racing; a boat race with homemade boats made from milk cartons; a prison rodeo; "Bogginhole" four-wheel-drive mud races; a jump rope contest; and various barroom "tough man" competitions. *Real People* was further active in plotting the fads that were sweeping the nation. Season two had several segments exploring the roller disco phenomenon drawing in people of all ages; the steadily rising number of joggers; the birth of "Ultimate Frisbee"; and numerous UFO stories, which were increasingly more widely accepted among the general population.

Most of the truly outlandish *Real People* segments would be classified by many as harmless, even wholesome escapism. However, *Real People* was casting a wide net when it came to viewers; to draw adults, sex was the default device. Given the prohibitions of broadcast TV, there was no nudity, but there were a good number of bouncing body parts in close-up, accompanied by freely flowing double entendre and sexual innuendo. Although it was promoted as family entertainment, and aired in the so-called "family hour" of 8–9 PM, there were enough clothes being shed and off-color jokes being made to make most parents squirm uncomfortably while viewing with their children. Even in its sexual themes *Real People* found a way to appeal to diverse interests, as the segments included a visit with the Dallas Cowboys cheerleaders; a party for former male centerfolds from *Playgirl* magazine; a nudist restaurant; the twenty-fifth-anniversary party for *Playboy* magazine, held at the Playboy Mansion; the Miss Physique contest; a best legs contest for men; female mud wrestling; and a segment on a widely reported national story about a young woman who was fired from her job for sitting on top of a copy machine and making photocopies of her buttocks.

While most of the segments in season two could be deemed harmless exhibitionism, in which the subjects and audience were laughing with each other, there were several features during the second season that teetered on the line between thoughtful tolerance and winking mockery. Of course, George Schlatter had consistently stated in media interviews that *Real People* would not exploit or embarrass its subjects. Periodically, over six seasons, *Real People* did present segments that appeared to have been inspired by a desire to promote genuine diversity and understanding by focusing on people who had alternative lifestyles, or views outside of the perceived social ideal. On occasion, however, the style of presentation and the unpredictable response of the audience actually produced the opposite result. There were several exemplars of this consequence in the 1979–1980 season. One segment early in the season featured a husband and wife who were saving money for sex reassignment surgery for both of them. In the filmed piece, the couple's daily activities were captured by cameras as they cross-dressed: the husband walking around town in short skirts and heels, while the wife walked around in men's work clothes and boots. The segment used the Ethel Merman song "Together (Where Ever We Go)" for a soundtrack. The punch line of the piece was the reaction of others as they recognized what was happening before them. The quick double takes, craning of necks, and overall incredulity of the local citizenry produced riotous laughter in the studio audience, and presumably with many home viewers as well.

The unfortunately obvious question to be asked was, who was being laughed at? Was it the gawking locals, or the husband and wife stretching the bounds of accepted mainstream American life? A similarly uncomfortable tone permeates a segment on John and Greg Rice, twin dwarves labeled the world's smallest real estate agents. While the piece was clearly designed to have some inspirational message, it is difficult not to hear the studio audience chuckle as the twins face height-challenging obstacles such as trying to get into and drive a massive automobile, eating with a booster seat, and being unable to reach a public bathroom urinal. The integrity and inspirational qualities of the Rice brothers emerge largely intact, but it is a comedic, some might say mocking presentation. A feature on "full-figured" swimsuit models also produced seemingly unintended snickers and laughs among audience members. Here again, the intentions of the producers are unclear; the audience laughter on the finished episode could be manipulated, the volume of the laughter could be modulated, enhanced, or reduced for desired effect in postproduction. A number of cultural and TV critics honed in on these examples, or some of the more eccentric characters, and marked the show as unworthy of serious consideration. H. F. Waters in *Newsweek* was particularly reproachful when he said, "An undertow of almost casual cruelty eddies beneath most episodes . . . at its most grotesque, *Real People* implies that America is a freak show staged for the detached amusement of us, the 'norms.'"[18]

Contrary to the above critique, *Real People* was able to present pieces that were sincerely inspirational, heartwarming, or reflective of those giving back to their communities. One of the popular and widely celebrated stories from season two focused on Carol Johnston, a competitive college gymnast who was aiming for the 1980 Summer Olympics. What made Johnston remarkable was that she had accomplished these achievements despite missing the lower half of her right arm. In the segment she is shown performing rigorous gymnastic disciplines with one arm, but also performing the tasks of daily life that could be difficult with one arm. In another sports-related feature, Fred Thompson, a successful black professional, is celebrated for his efforts in helping inner-city black and Latino children escape poverty by coaching a track-and-field team, with the ultimate goal of having the students earn college scholarships. In yet another example, there was a piece on a group of Chicago police officers who sacrificed their off-duty hours to dress up as clowns and entertain ill children at local hospitals.

Though not necessarily inspirational, there was another subcategory of *Real People* designed to stir emotion: those segments steeped in populism and/or patriotism. As noted earlier, 1979 was another year in a decade-long slog through one of the most difficult and divisive eras in American history. Compounding the actual problems was the depressed state of mind of many Americans. What President Carter called a crisis of confidence was further inflamed when in November 1979 a mob of radical Islamist students entered the American embassy in Tehran, Iran, and took

The Show That Started A "Real" Trend
Real People

8:00PM

★ The silver dollar
 handout! Millionaire
 gives it away!
★ A true Nielson family!
 All 500 get together!
★ Black track coach trains
 girls to win!
★ A dog that drives a car!
★ Plus a ventriloquist's
 convention — and
 more!

Sarah Purcell
John Barbour
Skip Stephenson
Byron Allen
Bill Rafferty

Promotional ad for *Real People*, April 30, 1980, *Newsday*, B53.

the staff hostage. The fact that the United States could not get its citizens released immediately seemed to many people another sign of increasing American impotence.

The American public responded to their newly degraded status in a variety of complex ways. Some reflexively looked back nostalgically to a time when America was the dominant force in the world, and domestic life was simpler, safer, and more stable. As with most nostalgia, the memories were idealized, if not manufactured, and certainly not uniformly shared by all; but they resonated nonetheless. Other Americans responded by constantly complaining, though offering no workable solutions, while many others reacted by looking for somebody to blame. They pointed at various targets, including the government, liberal ideology, the rich, Wall Street, corporations, and even the big cities along both coasts (New York, Washington, DC, Los Angeles, San Francisco), which monopolized the media, the national economy, and political power; all while allegedly ignoring the middle of the country. *Real People* had its eye on this pulsating anger and frustration early in its run. In season two these forces manifest themselves in a number of segments bathed in populist sentiment and patriotic imagery.

In a bit of self-serving populism, *Real People* had a season-long recurring theme attempting to undermine the credibility of national Nielsen TV ratings, in essence questioning what seemed like corporatized control of television. The premise was to talk with families named Nielsen across the country, none of whom actually had their viewing habits officially monitored. Typically, the people interviewed had opinions that differed from the published ratings, with many watching little or no TV at all. Host John Barbour framed it in late 1970s populist rhetoric: "It's all tied up in New York and Hollywood by men who are out of touch with the rest of the country. They accept almost no input from anyone else."[19]

A "fighting city hall" theme was found in the unusual story of Dennis Holland, a Costa Mesa, California, man who had spent over a decade building a massive wooden ship in his backyard. Holland, his wife, Betty, and their children eventually moved into the ship when they had trouble maintaining their house as well. After receiving numerous complaints, the local city government ordered the ship removed. Holland refused, and became something of a David fighting the Goliath of repressive government. The super-rich were skewered in a piece that explored Fiorucci, a very upscale store in New York City. During the segment there was a mocking slant toward the elitism of snobby shoppers who watched as a model paraded through the store in ridiculously overpriced and sometimes outlandish ensembles.

A curious fusion of nostalgia and anti-corporate populism pitted actor Clayton Moore, who played the Lone Ranger on television in the 1950s, versus Jack Wrather and his production company, which owned the rights to the Lone Ranger character. Though the show had ended years earlier, the sixty-five-year-old Moore still did public appearances wearing the iconic black mask of the Lone Ranger. To protect his interests, particularly with a new Lone Ranger film in the works, Wrather won a court order preventing Moore from wearing the mask in public or calling himself the Lone Ranger. *Real People* presented Moore as a sympathetic character who just wanted to make adults and children happy, while the businessman is viewed as greedy and conniving. After the filmed segment was shown, Moore was introduced to the studio audience, which responded with a rousing ovation. The Clayton Moore story would become a national cause célèbre that *Real People* would continue to follow until Moore won the right to wear the mask once again.[20]

In 1979, as it had been for the previous thirty years, the global Cold War with the Soviet Union was the prevailing threat to the American way of life. Any issue, no matter how trivial, that engaged the Soviet Union in any way was likely to inspire swift and impassioned patriotism. In the summer of 1980, the Soviet Union was going to host the Olympics in Moscow. However, in late 1979, the Soviets invaded Afghanistan. The world community, led by the United States, responded in vehement protest, with the US threatening and ultimately following through on a boycott of the Moscow Olympics. Coincidently, *Real People* had taped a segment on the town of Moscow, Ohio, which had already planned an alternative Olympics for those who did not want to support the Communist regime. The segment itself was fairly predictable, with local citizens alternately taking shots at Communism and celebrating American life. In a fortuitous stroke of timing, the segment aired just three days after President Carter had proposed the American boycott. Consequently, the segment struck an unanticipated patriotic chord with the audience. A few weeks later, the greatest moment in American sports history occurred when the United States Olympic hockey team defeated the Soviet team on the way to winning the Olympic gold medal at Lake Placid, New York. Not long after the inspiring upset victory, *Real People* presented a short feature on the team and introduced the team's head coach, Herb Brooks. The coach received a thunderous ovation from the audience, and the episode was the highest rated of the season.

One of the frequent patriotic themes *Real People* would employ over the length of the series was the elevation and celebration of American war veterans. This was not a common motif in American popular culture in the late 1970s. In the post-Vietnam era there was great disillusionment with the military and a desire to forget the turbulence and suffering of the lost war. Unfortunately, in the effort to forget the war, many veterans were also forgotten, if not forsaken. Season two featured a pair of segments celebrating military service. One segment focused on the town of Chickamauga, Oklahoma, the home of a former US Cavalry fort where residents re-created and reenacted the cavalry life with exciting riding displays. The other poignant military-themed segment was a piece on the Tuskegee Airmen. During World War II the Tuskegee Airmen was a segregated unit of black fighter pilots serving in the European theater.

Though their service was recognized at the time, after the war the Airmen were largely forgotten. *Real People* filmed one of their reunions and interviewed them about their service. Though forced to serve in segregated units, denied promotions, and not decorated like their white counterparts, the men were neither bitter nor angry; rather, they were proud of their service, their fellow Airmen, and their country. It was an emotional segment that reached a climax when the Airmen were introduced to the studio audience in Burbank. There was thunderous applause and a number of teary-eyed hosts and audience members. It was the kind of heartwarming patriotic story at which *Real People* excelled, and that the public seemed to desire. Clearly, the American public was desperate to feel pride in their country and themselves, a hunger *Real People* would actively feed for the next four seasons.[21]

RATINGS AND RECEPTION

Real People's ratings had not been strong during its abbreviated inaugural season in the spring of 1979. However, in the fall, *Real People* slowly began to build ratings momentum week after week. In the first week of October it cracked the Nielsen ratings top twenty, at number twenty. By late November, *Real People* was consistently beating its primary time slot competition, *Eight Is Enough*, and beginning to break into the top ten rated programs. By mid-February of 1980, *Real People* was the fourth-rated show on television, drawing twenty million viewers and trailing only *60 Minutes*, *Three's Company*, and *Dallas*. In the final tally of the season, *Real People* finished as the fifteenth-ranked show, NBC's highest-rated program. The performance of the show was a bright spot in an otherwise disappointing season, as NBC would finish a distant third to CBS and ABC, respectively.[22]

The critics' reviews of *Real People* were not as unequivocally positive as the ratings outcome. The disparaging reviews of the show typically pivoted around two common refrains. First, how real was *Real People*? The second recurring critique focused on the alleged cruelty or mocking tone in many *Real People* segments. The claims of fakery or contrivance led to snide revised names for the show: "Fake People," "Real Fakes," "Real Fake People." These accusations were vehemently denied by the producers and cast; as Sarah Purcell protested, "There is no dressing up of the interviews on our show. No more than on an interview on a newscast. We report what we see and the camera is rolling. There is no stretching of the truth, even though people have accused us of that."[23] Protestations aside, the camerawork on the show often dictated the action; for instance, with a camera placed in a room to film as a subject enters. The show also had two flat-out hoaxes during the season, most notoriously during a segment on professional panhandler "Omar the Beggar," who turned out to be noted prankster Alan Abel. However, despite these cited examples, *Real People* was more real than not, and the subjects were much more genuine than they would be twenty years into the growth of the genre.

The other frequent criticism was the accusation of cruel mockery and exploitation. As Associated Press television writer Peter Boyer suggested, "*Real People* has established itself by working a mixture of one-liners and filmed shorts on human folly—dancing on a thin line between humiliation and comedy . . . *Real People* walks that line with heavy boots." H. F. Waters in *Newsweek* was more literary and melodramatic in his condemnation: "Amid the weekly parade of weirdos, loonies, cranks and screwballs and the hoots and cackles from the live studio audience, stumbles the ghost of Quasimodo in flight from the Paris mob." The Catholic Church even weighed in on the impact of *Real People*. The New York Archdiocese labeled the show one of the ten worst programs for children, in terms of content and visual imagery.[24] Some of these allegations were valid, but it is hard to define the extent to which people outside of media centers would have shared these views, particularly during an era in which tolerance, sensitivity, and political correctness were not aggressively enforced in the American social consciousness.

The positive reviewers were able or willing to evaluate the show based on the totality of its offerings, the whacky and eccentric but also the inspirational and heartwarming. Gary Deeb of the *Chicago Tribune*, one of the more acerbic TV critics of the era, saw the deeper appeal of the show when he said, "*Real People*, the Wednesday night potpourri of eccentric America, is one of the silliest, zaniest programs on television. It also happens to be one of the cleverest and most courageous when it comes to exposing those government and big-business bogeymen who frequently make life miserable for the average citizen." Other reviewers noted the pieces on the Tuskegee Airmen and Carol Johnston as exemplars of the potential quality in the show, despite the more frivolous fare.[25]

One other repeated theme in most reviews or assessments of *Real People* was recognition of the innovative nature of the show, and the potential for the birth of a new genre. Even reviews that doubted the quality of the show noted its innovation: "The things that make *Real People* noteworthy have less to do with its content, which ranges from dull to delightful, or its pace, which is pell-mell, than with its potential influence on the rest of television, which is considerable." Though the show was less than a year old, the *Chicago Tribune*, in a retrospective on the end of the 1970s, named *Real People* one of the most important shows of the decade, calling it "the originator of the newest trend toward 'reality programming' and a populistic gem."[26] As the above quote illustrates, it is noteworthy the alacrity with which the phrase "reality programming" or "reality television" was beginning to make its way into the lexicon of the television industry. George Schlatter echoed the voices that proclaimed the innovation of *Real People* when he opined, after the second season, "I think *Real People* has had a profound effect upon television. It is reflecting the mood of the country and is putting more emphasis on the individual. It is very patriotic. It shows that the little guy is important. It is a positive statement about America and the youth of America."[27]

Perhaps the most important consequence of *Real People*'s second season, particularly for the future of the genre, was its financial statements. Industry periodicals determined that *Real People* cost approximately $450,000 to produce per episode, with the profit per episode at $150,000. This made *Real People* the fourth most profitable program on NBC's schedule. Yet TV executives looked at those numbers more analytically. The most profitable show on NBC was *Little House on the Prairie*, but that show cost $650,000 to produce per episode, and finished sixteenth in the Nielsen ratings, while Real People cost $200,000 less, and finished fifteenth. Additionally, *Real People* had no major stars and required no high-priced writers, neither of which was true of *Little House*. In its second season *Real People* had proven the ratings potential of reality, but just as significant, it became an increasingly preferable economic option for NBC and the other networks. Leonard Goldenson, chairman of ABC, noted the economic value of what he was still calling "actuality shows," when he said, "We will never select an inferior program because it is cheaper. But when we can choose between programs of comparable audience appeal, our confidence in their future cost levels will be a determining factor." In other words, if the less expensive reality shows can draw ratings similar or superior to scripted programs, studios will lean toward reality programs. Thus emerges the calculus increasingly used by television executives over the subsequent thirty years.[28]

INCREDIBLE REALITY

On March 3, 1980, ABC premiered its own reality-themed show, entitled *That's Incredible*. The show had been announced in November of 1979, just as *Real People* ascended the Nielsen ratings. After airing as a one-time special entitled *Incredible Sunday*, the show moved to its permanent spot on Monday night at 8 PM. The similarities between *Real People* and *That's Incredible* were evident very quickly; as one reviewer said, "Now, nobody could possibly miss the connection between *That's Incredible* and *Real People*; the former is as close to a clone as one can risk. It may not be long before these shows are fighting over the same freaks and kooks for their sideshow."[29] In form and structure the shows were remarkably similar. *That's Incredible* featured filmed segments introduced by hosts (John Davidson, Cathy Lee Crosby, and football star Fran Tarkenton) in front of a studio audience. *That's Incredible* tried to differentiate itself from *Real People* by focusing on extraordinary events or people, not everyday events or average people. As an early ad for the show exclaimed, "It's all about things that just can't happen . . . and the people they happen to." That translated into people displaying "unique talents," people surviving harrowing, life-threatening moments, and people performing daredevil stunts. In an effort to carve out some original ground, host Cathy Lee Crosby tried to describe the show in its broadest terms: "Our show is about people demonstrating what they do, how they survive, or why they are involved in a variety of situations. But we won't degrade them or what they do. The material is real human interest which can't be described as news and certainly not comedy."[30]

The first season of *That's Incredible* offered an array of unusual spectacles and curious human activity. The more attention-grabbing segments included a sky diver who escaped from a straitjacket before pulling the rip cord on his parachute; a ski jumper performing a stunt while set on fire; a blind track star; a house with an "unexplainable" black ooze bubbling through the floor; carnivorous plants; a man who catches bullets in

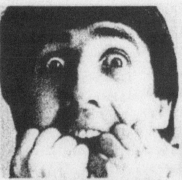

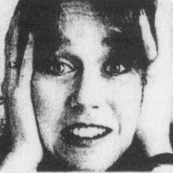
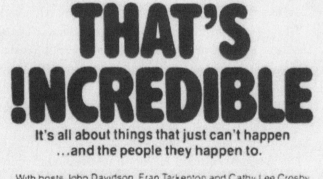

Promotional ad for *That's Incredible*, March 3, 1980, *New York Times*, C18.

his teeth; a dog who found its way home from 1,500 miles away; a rooster who plays tic-tac-toe; an early form of bungee jumping; and a litany of ghost stories, psychic practitioners, paranormal activities, and various medical and physical curiosities.

The public reception for this reality clone was extraordinary, leaving many invoking the show's title in response. The premiere episode ranked as the fifth-rated show of that week, besting *Real People*. From that moment to the end of the season in May, *That's Incredible* rarely finished out of the top ten in the Nielsen ratings, ultimately finishing the season ranked as the number nine show, again ahead of *Real People*. The remarkable ratings for *That's Incredible* can be explained by several factors. First, there clearly was an unsated appetite among the viewing public for reality programming. Even with *Real People* already a growing ratings success, *That's Incredible* was able to garner outstanding audience shares, with both shows drawing over twenty million viewers per episode. Second, there is the content of the show, particularly the spectacular stunts and daredevil antics, which were not available on any other shows on television, creating a quality unique to *That's Incredible*. Finally, there was a massive promotional campaign for the show during ABC's broadcast of February's Winter Olympics. Those Olympics were a ratings powerhouse for ABC, and the network promoted *That's Incredible* incessantly to a large and receptive audience.

The critical and industry reception for *That's Incredible* was not as favorable. It appears that for critics and industry insiders, their revulsion toward *Real People* was compounded by the success of *That's Incredible*, and thus, they looked to halt reality television before it grew any more prominent. The Associated Press TV writer was blunt: "I looked very carefully and saw nothing at all incredible, or even interesting in the entire hour (or was it 90 minutes?). What was interesting, perhaps even incredible, was that ABC so clearly imitated an NBC show, *Real People*. I mean *That's Incredible* barely even bothered to use a different set." Bill Carter of the *Baltimore Sun* condescendingly sniffed, "It's startling; it's improbable, it's staggering; it's stupefying; it's uncanny. (It's just a mite sickening.) It's incredible alright, but it's true. *That's Incredible*, a new ABC show, is emerging this spring as a certifiable hit on TV (Yes, it's certifiable)." Tom Shales of the *Washington Post* had been a supporter of the original *Real People* format, but by the summer of 1980 he had grown weary of the expanding genre. "The trend is already way out of hand and perhaps a glut will help end it. In the meantime, we must suffer unwarranted exposure to the antics of wackies and the insufferable and obnoxious ravings of televised neighbors one would never tolerate in person."[31]

Although those involved in the production and presentation of *That's Incredible* defensively proclaimed their show's originality, George Schlatter dismissed those claims, suggesting, "*That's Incredible* would not be on the air if *Real People* hadn't proven there was an audience." The aphorism "A rising tide lifts all boats" was wholly applicable to the influence of *Real People* on the reality genre. Not only did the show inspire a raft of clones and derivatives, but it also inflated a predecessor in reality, *PM Magazine*. The half-hour syndicated program predated *Real People* by more than two years, and produced content with similar themes to that of the NBC offering. The cooperative structure of the Group W franchise's story pool ensured that each local *PM Magazine* would be different from the others in some way, but they would also share a good number of similar segments. The typical *PM Magazine* featured unique personalities, occupations, hobbies, and destinations, as well as style and cooking segments with TV celebrity Chef Tell. Examples of widely aired segments include shark attacks, female private detectives, a New York City modeling agency, Nazi hunters, UFO encounters, conspiracy theorists, a rodeo school, various tourist stories, medical mysteries and marvels, and a swath of ghost stories and paranormal exploits.[32]

When *Real People* premiered in April 1979, *PM Magazine* aired on just over thirty stations across the nation. By the summer of 1980, *PM Magazine* was approaching ninety stations in small, medium, and large cities. Of particular note was the addition of New York and Los Angeles to the Group W fold, not coincidentally after the very successful second season of *Real People*. A number of local stations around the nation that did not want to join the Group W consortium created their own "people" shows, such as New York's WCBS series *To Life* and Los Angeles' KNXT's *Two on the Town*. So broad was the footprint of reality TV by the summer of 1980 that a number of shows and documentary styles were lumped in with the emerging genre. Programs like the Public Broadcasting Service series *Non-fiction Television* were deemed reality TV, albeit for the intellectual and socially conscious set. Even the venerable *60 Minutes* was coupled with the reality trend, though again of a higher-brow news-based variety. The producers of *60 Minutes* and network news divisions in general did not appreciate being classified thusly, as they saw shows like *Real People* and *That's Incredible*, and others soon to follow, as encroaching upon and thereby tainting TV news. It would become an ongoing battle that TV news would ultimately lose. As CBS News president William Leonard bitterly forecast in early 1980, "There isn't enough mediocrity to go around in fiction. In five years, I think more than 50 percent of programming will be informational." Leonard's prediction was off by about fifteen years, but it is reflective of the attention paid to, and fear created by, reality TV, even in its embryonic stage. [33]

As it turned out, the greatest threat to the network status quo would not be an emerging and expanding genre; rather, it was the dark, looming cloud of cable/pay TV. Even in the nascent medium of cable television reality programming was budding. Home Box Office (HBO), which was spreading across the country, accumulating four million subscribers, though it had not yet telecast a 24-hour-a-day schedule. In 1980, the network created a "reality magazine" show entitled *Crazy and Wonderful*, which featured unique and eccentric people, as well as a collection of animal and lifestyle features such as "a woman who thinks she can fly, and a man who trained his pet cockatoo to answer his phone." HBO's pay TV competitor Showtime (SHO) also had its own version of a reality series, called *What's Up America?* This semi-regular special actually premiered in October of 1978, airing just twice, only to be revived and more regularly scheduled after *Real People* gained popularity. *What's Up America* trod familiar ground, featuring segments on topics such as BB guns; female boxers; urban cowboys; Elvis Presley impersonators; chariot racers in Pocatello, Idaho; and a couple who lived year-round on Liberty Island in New York Harbor. However, pay TV did not have the same content restrictions as "free" network television did; as a result, *What's Up America?* could include sexually explicit segments on pornographic film actors, strippers, prostitutes, and a nude beauty pageant. Cable television would be a haven for adult-themed reality programming from that moment forward, with notable examples being *Real Sex* (1989–2009), *Cathouse* (2005–), and *Taxicab Confessions* (1995–). [34]

Even in the late 1970s and early 1980s cable television would prove to be the Wild Wild West of reality television. When cable television franchises were being granted to cable entities in American cities throughout the 1970s, there were certain conditions imposed. Standard among them was the promise that cable companies would provide free airtime to the general public, in what came to be known as cable access programming. Cable access revealed an even more pure vision of reality, not filtered by producers or network executives. The consequence was a broad assortment of self-produced programs in which people espoused political views, showcased their varied artistic talents, and hosted their own talk shows, some of which were pornographic in nature. Across the nation, largely anonymous people were on display, creating and presenting their own narratives. It was reality TV at its most raw, and it would grow as cable television grew in size and scope.[35]

As the 1980s began, the big three networks were just beginning to recognize and, equally important, acknowledge the various threats to their previously unchallenged audience share. The most immediate threat was cable television, which was no longer just movie channels like HBO or SHO, but broadcast cable entities such as ESPN, CNN, and Superstation WTBS, which began to draw viewers throughout the broadcast day. At the beginning of 1980, industry analysts estimated that just fewer than 20 percent of America's seventy-six million homes had some form of cable television. For the remainder of the decade, as more homes were signed up for cable and the number of channels began to grow, the audience share for networks continually eroded. As if that were not enough, viewers' eyes were diverted by the growing number of home video game consoles that were filling up hour upon hour for many young Americans. At the same time the availability of home video recording devices was slowly increasing, essentially allowing viewers to take control of their daily viewing habits, particularly the ability to avoid commercials and watch one show while recording another. Whatever the proximate cause, the result was a loss in viewership, and corresponding ad revenue, which changed both the economic and creative environment of television.[36]

Nonetheless, in the upcoming 1980–1981 television season, the three broadcast networks were still the center of the TV universe. In that narrow core of creativity and economic power, reality television was beginning to reach its first zenith, in which *Real People* was still the brightest light in the sky.

2

BRANDING A GENRE: NONFICTION, ACTUALITY, REALITY!

1980–1981

The 1980–1981 television season had one of the most tumultuous beginnings in the history of the medium. On July 21, 1980, the Screen Actors Guild (SAG) and the American Federation of Television and Radio Artists (AFTRA) carried out their threat to have all working actors go on strike. At the heart of this work stoppage was the actors' demand for an increase in their share of the film and television producers' revenue from the growing pay TV and home videocassette and disc market. The strike shut down production on virtually all scripted television and film sets across the nation. Rather than plying their craft, film and television actors, famous and anonymous, were instead walking picket lines. The longest strike in television history ended in late October with the actors winning a small measure of their original demands.

One consequence of the strike for the big three television networks was a stalled rollout of their fall schedules. With the strike coming in July, most series had only completed a fraction of their episodes. This left the networks scrambling for programming to fill in at least the first two months of the fall season. The result was a mélange of old and a few new episodes, repeated and new made-for-TV movies, specials, miniseries, and live sporting events.[1] Fortuitously for the National Broadcasting Company (NBC), *Real People* and other reality programs were not directly impacted by the strike. Not only did the shows not require unionized actors for most of their content, but performers in special categories, such as documentary or news, which *Real People* may or may not have actually been, were not prevented from working by the strike. Consequently, *Real People* never stopped production, and was able to open the season on September 17 with an original episode and never suffer a lull in scheduling.

Following a remarkably successful season in 1979–1980, George Schlatter and his production staff changed little. The hosts remained Sarah Purcell, Skip Stephenson, John Barbour, Bill Rafferty, and Byron Allen, with special commentary by Mark Russell. One of the unexpected developments from the first full season was the ongoing celebrity status of the hosts. The initial host selection process had been one in which nationally known performers were avoided so that the real people would not be overshadowed. However, having been seen by twenty million people per week, the hosts were now prominent cultural figures. Sarah Purcell was featured on the cover of *TV Guide* and several lifestyle magazines, and also fielded acting offers. Skip Stephenson and Byron Allen were now headliners on the national comedy circuit; and Bill Rafferty and John Barbour were hosting and appearing in various other TV vehicles. In fact, all of the hosts could be seen individually on programs such as *The Tonight Show* with Johnny Carson, or collectively on the *Family Feud* game show, where they competed for charity and gave host Richard Dawson a *Real People* T-shirt.

As celebrated as the hosts had become, by necessity the viewers and the people of America had to be the stars of the show. Schlatter understood this and included as much viewer participation as possible. Studio audience members were increasingly used in the second season to poke good-natured fun at the cast, or to make flirty comments to their favorite host. More illustrative of American life in 1980–1981 were the topical comments of the studio audience and the contributions of the larger home audience. It has been said by political scientists, historians, and political pundits that it is the economy, specifically an individual's pocketbook/ wallet, that determines the level of national happiness and view of the future. With the American economy still struggling mightily in 1980–1981, the populace was in a general state of unease. The hosts and viewers reflected and fueled these feelings with comments, jokes, and jabs at topics such as high unemployment, inflation, gas prices, and rising interest rates. Other enduring complaints infused with contemporary populist fervor included women's liberation, political corruption, the Cold War, and various quality-of-life issues. There were also fleeting hot-button issues considered: the hostages in Iran, the Equal Rights Amendment, the 1980 presidential election, and the "Mariel Boatlift" from Cuba.[2]

Here is a sampling of the commentary on the various topics noted above:

Politics

Audience member: I think we would get more people to come out and vote if we had a category, *none of the above.*

The cast: Whenever election time rolls around, the voice of the politician is heard around the land . . . one symbol is the Republicans, their symbol is an animal known for its memory, the elephant; the other group is the Democrats, with another well-known animal, the donkey . . . and this year the symbolism is especially clear . . . if the Democrats make an ass of themselves the Republicans will never let them forget.

Audience member: The Supreme Court won't allow prayer in school, and that's too bad, because with the Supreme Court we've got, we need all the prayer we can get.

Women's Liberation/Equal Rights Amendment

A letter from Allan and Mary Warren, Toledo, Ohio: When the white man discovered this country, Indians were running it, there were no taxes, no debts, and women did all the work . . . tell me why the white man thinks he could improve on a system like that?

Sarah Purcell: Sexual equality is hard to attain . . . you can't follow it to the letter . . . all women are not equal to men; in many cases they are better.

Cold War

> Audience member: The Russians invaded Afghanistan in the interest of peace, a piece of Afghanistan, a piece of Poland, a piece of Denver, and so on and so on . . .

Mariel Boatlift

> The cast: This week we traveled the land and saw much concern for the people in other countries . . . we'd like to shake the hands of the people of Afghanistan, but we can't because they are across the sea; we'd like to shake the hands of the people of Poland, but we can't because they're across the sea; and we would like to shake the hands of the people of Cuba, but that we can do because they're all over here with us.

Though there was gloominess, frustration, even anger over the state of American affairs, *Real People* regularly tried to temper this negativity with some hopefulness, as the cast suggested on the season premiere: "We have seen a nation facing clouds of controversy . . . we found a lot of folks who think the sun is long overdue. So it helps to remember what Mark Twain said when he was walking with a friend in the rain, and the friend said, 'Do you think it'll stop?' and Twain looked up and said, 'It always has'; and that is the spirit that makes America great."[3] With thirty-five episodes already produced, and mountains of viewer mail/comments/reactions, *Real People* producers had a strong conception of the stories and people that would resonate with their audience. Nonetheless, with twenty-five episodes scheduled for the new season, *Real People* did have a looming problem. With the number of reality-themed programs increasing across the various levels of television, there was a greater demand and competition for stories and themes, particularly original content. Consequently, in season three *Real People* continued to focus on the core themes and stories that had driven it to the top of the Nielsen TV ratings. As was the case at the inception of the show, and would be throughout, the eccentric lifestyles, hobbies, or habits were the foundation of the program. Despite occasional criticism of such programming, *Real People* would not try to hide its affinity for the unique and unusual. In fact, in most episodes the opening titles and narration made light of this propensity: "Once again NBC presents *Real People* . . . a probing introspection of unique personalities in the prime of their creative years; some are about thirty, some are about forty, but one or two have no idea what they're about."[4]

One of the more frequent criticisms leveled at *Real People* during its first two seasons was the charge that the show exploited or humiliated some of its subjects. George Schlatter and the cast fought off these charges, often by suggesting they were celebrating independent spirits. However, in season three, there were several segments in which the audience was laughing at, not with, the eccentric. A prime example of this contradiction was a visit to Memphis, Tennessee, to meet Prince Mongo. A man in his mid-thirties, Prince Mongo claimed to be a visitor from the planet of Zambodia. When host John Barbour arrived at his house, in an upscale, well-groomed neighborhood, he found a front yard filled with junk and rusted-out cars. Inside he found the home of a hoarder, with all manner of debris, including the skeletons of his in-laws from their home planet of Zambodia. In the interview, Mongo rambled incoherently about his travels through space and his special powers. It is not immediately clear to viewers whether he was a brilliant actor, a burnout from the 1960s counterculture, or seriously mentally ill. What is clear is that the video narrative is mocking in tone, though given Mongo's antics, it would have been difficult to have it be anything else; and the studio audience was rolling in laughter. The hilarity does not dissipate, even though Barbour talks to a doctor who claims Mongo suffers from manic-depressive psychosis. Whatever his status, it feels inappropriate and unkind to be laughing at him.

Another interesting figure was Rollerena, a New York City man in his mid-twenties, who would change out of his business suit and into the outfit of a good fairy, with tutu, magic wand, and roller skates. Rollerena is shown skating through Central Park while tossing pixie dust and touching people with his wand. In the segment there are the requisite incredulous locals and park dwellers, but also subtle hints, and likely audience assumptions, about Rollerena's sexual preference. It is difficult to know exactly what the viewers and audience members were laughing at, but it does not seem like supportive encouraging laughter. The season also featured two different stories about men who preferred to wear dresses/skirts in their daily lives. The filmed segments featured the men walking around town, going to work, seemingly oblivious to people's reaction to them. Again, there are equal parts exposition and explanation, but the subtle tinge of mockery is evident in the final segment.[5]

There were also the oddly talented: a man who played the ironing board as an instrument, a college student savant on all things related to TV game shows; a man who claimed he could control the weather; a therapist who helped people sing their stress and troubles away, and a seventy-year-old "disco queen" who danced the night away at Studio 54 in New York City. People and their pets were a continuing staple, with Arnold the pig, who was treated like a family member by his owners; a man who trained house cats to be guard animals; a chimpanzee who rode a tractor and oversaw farm animals; and a woman who dressed cockatiels in fancy costumes and taught them to sing and dance to pop songs.

With twenty hours to fill over the course of the season, the most reliable and repeated category of story was the whacky event/convention/ contest. Not only was it a good time filler, but it was relatable for many viewers, and it had a small-town community aura that appealed to many people around the nation. There were competitions of all kinds: barstool races; a kissing contest; a whistling contest; staring contests; a mud bowl football game; a senior citizen beauty contest; female arm wrestling; an underwater pumpkin carving contest; a contest to determine the world's fastest oyster shucker; and several types of rodeo, notably an all-black rodeo, a gay rodeo, and a children's rodeo.

In the twenty-first century, unusual jobs or working environments acquired an ubiquity that engulfed the reality genre. It was already familiar territory for *Real People* by season three, which featured a man who played the violin in a men's room; a man who raised snails for use in restaurants; a professional dog walker; a New York City cat doctor who made house calls; champion female wrestler the Fabulous Moolah; and a professional "garbologist" who sifted through celebrity trash. In fact, during the segment, the garbologist (Alan J. Weberman) is arrested by the Secret Service for rummaging through former president Richard Nixon's trash. Of all the interesting workplaces featured, the one that garnered the most attention was the one created by weight loss expert Richard Simmons. In his Beverly Hills gym, Simmons is shown working out with primarily obese women, while in drill sergeant fashion he cajoles, yells, insults, and pushes the women to work out more intensely. Yet the women featured in the piece loved Richard Simmons, many of them crediting him with saving their lives. From this initial appearance, Simmons would branch out into other television appearances, including his own show, and later a hugely successful series of home video workout tapes. Simmons was a rarity in the reality world of the 1980s, in that he was one of the few people to parlay an appearance into a much greater level of fame and fortune. This of course is common in modern reality television, but in that first wave of reality the subjects were marginalized, not celebrated.

Though it promoted itself as a family show, and aired in the 8 PM family hour time slot, *Real People* regularly featured segments seemingly designed to appeal to the more adult members of the family. Consequently, there were voluptuous women skiing in bikinis; a charity athletic competition between cheerleaders and airline stewardesses; a fashion show with custom-made bikinis for men and women; a male exotic dancing contest; female body builders; a bathing-suit tan lines competition; a

Promotional ad for *Real People*, September 24, 1980, *New York Times*, 72.

gigolo convention; and an erotic bakery in New York City, where baked goods were shaped like body parts and sexual positions, though none were shown in the segment. One of the keys to the success of *Real People* was the ability to balance the content of the show. To wit, as a counter to the absurdity, superficiality, or sexual content, there were always more substantive stories and people presented. This approach produced segments on jobs and workers that were unique but not unusual, such as the best waitress in America; a park ranger in Yosemite National Park; the first professional female rodeo clown; Oklahoma monks who were also volunteer firemen; female longshoremen; and a woman who cleaned windows on the Empire State Building.

During its run, *Real People* had great facility with inspirational stories. It was one, if not the only, redeeming quality of the show for many viewers. Season three was crowded with inspirational, heartwarming, and arguably a bit cloying stories. There were several segments on disabled subjects, including fourteen-year-old Suzy Gilstrap, a paraplegic girl who was pursuing a career in acting; the shortest man in America and the trials and triumphs of his daily life; a competition for skiers with various disabilities; and ballet classes for wheelchair-bound senior citizens. Age was not an obstacle for several of these featured subjects; for instance, the members of a senior baseball team, some over eighty years old; a fifty-year-old boxer who was fighting age discrimination to earn a license to fight professionally; and another fifty-year-old man, who returned to college to play football on the college team while living in his car to afford tuition. Socially inspirational stories examined the Arthur Mitchell Dance Troupe in Harlem, New York; "Shabba Doo" Quinones, who taught dance in inner cities; Utah police officers who drag-raced teens to keep them off the streets; a Harlem, New York, artist who painted murals on iron store gates to beautify the neighborhood; a school for American Indians; and a family with nineteen children, fifteen of whom were adopted.

However, the most well-known of these inspirational stories was that of twenty-two-year-old Terry Fox, who was running across Canada to raise money for cancer research, after having lost his right leg to the disease. Sarah Purcell visited and ran together with Terry Fox as he traveled along highways and through small Canadian towns. Viewers could see the difficulty with which Fox ran, yet his determination was what shone through. Terry Fox became a national story, not just in Cana-

da, but in the United States as well. *Real People* would follow the story
with updates throughout the season, which sadly included Terry Fox
having to cut short his crusade due to a recurrence of his cancer, which
was tearfully announced by Sarah Purcell.

Ronald Reagan's campaign and eventual election in the fall of 1980
unleashed a wave of born-again patriotism in American culture. From its
genesis, *Real People* had bathed itself in patriotic iconography, highlighting a waving American flag, Mount Rushmore, and the Statue of Liberty
in the opening of every episode. Season three had more of that feel-good
Americana, with a train trip through the majesty of the Alaskan wilderness; a woman who painted everything she owned red, white, and blue;
and a Hungarian-American immigrant, Peter Toth, who created wooden
sculptures to honor his adopted land of the United States. The 1980–1981
season also contained a recurring theme that would grow in prominence
over the remaining years of the show, the celebration of the US military
veteran. This season had two emotional reunions. First was a gathering of
Japanese Americans from the 442nd Infantry Combat Team, who fought
in World War II, and many of whom had friends and relatives held in
internment camps. The men recounted their exploits in the war, and
shared a reunion with other, non-Japanese soldiers, who greeted them
warmly. The emotional crescendo came when the men were brought on
stage and introduced in front of the studio audience, many of whom wept
openly, as did several cast members. It is noteworthy that this event was
held well before the federal government issued a report condemning the
internment; and you can almost see in the eyes of the *Real People* audience the sorrow and guilt for an embarrassing episode in American history.[6]

The second gathering was not nearly as feel-good; rather, it was tinged
with an anger that rarely showed itself in the older generation of war
veterans. The core of the segment was a reunion of prisoners of war from
World War II and the Korean War. The segment begins simply as an
introduction to the men and their stories, with a very collegial air. They
reminisce about missing the American flag and creating their own out of
sheets and old clothes while in the prison camp. They also recount in a
matter-of-fact way their experiences with post-traumatic stress disorder
and other lingering maladies. At that point, the segment takes a turn, as
some bitterness begins to emerge in the interviews, particularly for the
lack of compensation for their lingering issues. One veteran suggests,

"We haven't been forgotten, we have been ignored." Another says, "All they want is a little piece of America for what they did, that's all," as he breaks down in tears, to be consoled by a fellow POW. Despite the anger, all the men agree they would go back and do it again.

As the piece ends, the strains of "America the Beautiful" begin to play, and a John Barbour voice-over intones, "These men gambled everything on America, they put their lives on the line for her, and even though the government may not have fully paid its debt, the men still consider themselves winners because they live in such a land." The men are then introduced to the studio audience as "unsung real American heroes." *Real People*'s advocacy for veterans of all wars was sincere and enduring, as will be shown repeatedly over the coming seasons.[7]

Running parallel with the patriotic theme was a populist bent, which focused on fighting big government, or taking control of one's life. Included in this collection was a woman in Atlantic City, New Jersey, who refused to sell her home to make way for a casino, which was ultimately built around her house; a Klamath Indian and World War II veteran who was fighting the US government for ownership of tribal lands; and a Minnesota man who had been building his own highway for twenty-five years because the government would not. Finally, there was a story that would have resonated with almost every family in America. The father of the Holmes family of Santa Cruz, California, had become disgusted with his family's "addiction" to television. To cure this malady, Jim Holmes created a system wherein his children would have to pedal an exercise bike to produce power in order to watch television. It had the desired effect; the children watched less television, and their performance in school improved, as did the family relationships. The Holmes family became minor celebrities, with stories in newspapers and TV shows across the nation and in Europe. People from all across the nation contacted Jim Holmes and asked him for instructions on how to build his "Pedal Power Cycle." *Real People* was reaching into people's homes, often twenty million a week, and striking a chord that resonated in a tangible way, as evidenced by thousands of letters pouring in weekly to the *Real People* production offices in Burbank, California.[8]

Though there was a more crowded field of reality offerings on television, *Real People* separated itself from the pack in the Nielsen ratings, finishing as the twelfth-rated show for the entire season. Despite the dazzling ratings, *Real People* found itself enmeshed in the often angry pushback from critics who had already had their fill of reality TV. As many critics found themselves compelled to rail against the "glut" of reality television, *Real People* was lumped in with lesser-quality, derivative programming. It was guilt by association, though the show was not beyond reproach. A *TV Guide* cover story on the show offered a pointed question: "*Real People*: Entertainment or Exploitation?" In the article when accusations of exploitation were raised, George Schlatter sharply rejected the premise: "You want freak shows? I'll tell you what . . . Go talk to those bandits up at ABC . . . *That's Incredible* are the freak hunters. They're the exploiters." Though they may have hurt the creative sensibilities of Schlatter and the hosts, negative reviews were not going to alter the standing of the show with its viewers. [9]

For many people, both inside television and in other areas of public life, mainstream parody is a sign of arrival or cultural resonance. If that is true, *Real People* had arrived by 1980–1981. *Real People* and reality TV in general were targeted by *Saturday Night Live* in May 1980. In a skit entitled "Real Incredible People," Steve Martin, Bill Murray, Gilda Radner, Jane Curtin, Laraine Newman, and Harry Shearer hosted a reality show highlighting incredible people who turned out to be less than such. As the faux skit said:

> And now, it's time for *Real Incredible People*! The show that believes that real people are incredible . . . we'll visit a man who has never opened his mail . . . we'll look at a woman who had the shape of her nose *surgically altered* . . . and we'll show you a man who gets around in what he calls an electric wheelchair.

It was not one of SNL's best, but many would say it was an honor to be lampooned by the original cast in its last year. [10]

Another TV icon, Bob Hope, took his shot at reality TV in one of his annual specials, *Bob Hope's All Star Comedy Look at TV's Prime Time Wars: Will the People Strike Back?* In the celebrity-filled program there was another skit poking fun at the mélange of *Real People*, *Speak Up America*, and *That's Incredible*. A little further down the comedy food chain was *Mad Magazine*, which spoofed reality TV in a comic satire entitled "That's Real Incredible People." These spoofs were mocking and satirical in tone, but they shine a light on the public's growing familiarity with and acceptance of the reality genre. The 1980–1981 season would further reveal the expansive and elastic nature of reality programming.

REALITY GROWS

The established economic viability, combined with the ratings success of *Real People*, and later, *That's Incredible*, ensured that in the largely unoriginal medium of television, there would be other productions attempting to capitalize on an emerging trend. What surprised many television insiders and industry observers was the volume of new reality-themed shows, and the pliability of the genre, which allowed this type of programming to function effectively at all levels of the medium, from the networks to national syndication, at almost any hour of the day.

Just as at the start of the wave, NBC would lead the way in scheduling new reality shows. At both the Columbia Broadcasting System (CBS) and the American Broadcasting Company (ABC) Fred Silverman had developed a reputation, not one universally celebrated, for taking popular characters off of a successful series and creating a new show featuring said character(s), known in the TV industry as a spin-off. For example, at CBS, the ratings powerhouse *All in the Family* spun off *Maude* and *The Jeffersons*, while on ABC *Happy Days* spun off *Laverne and Shirley* and *Mork and Mindy*. Silverman would use that same programming tactic with the reality genre, with one necessary adjustment. Unlike today's television landscape, which can and does create entire series around one or a collection of reality subjects, in 1980, there were not enough hours of airtime on network and cable television for niche reality programs to prosper. Consequently, instead of taking individual subjects from *Real People*, Silverman would take some of the most popular themes (viewer opinion, crazy events/contests, and kid stories) and dedicate entire series to those formats.[11]

Primary among these spin-offs was a series entitled *Speak Up America*. This hour-long reality series was born out of two developments recognized by George Schlatter, and acknowledged by Fred Silverman. First, having spent a year and a half sifting through volumes of viewer mail laced with opinion, anger, and frustration about the state of American life, Schlatter came to believe that the American people were desperate for a forum or format that would allow them to have their voices heard without filtering by journalists, politicians, or self-proclaimed leaders. In an era before Internet message boards, social media, websites, and blogs, when talk radio had not yet grown into a balkanized world of anger and finger pointing, there were few forums for the mass public to be heard. The second development was the early bubbling up of the culture wars that would emerge in the 1980s and turn into a boiling cauldron in the 1990s and beyond. The lines grew more indelible each year; neoliberalism v. neoconservatism, big government v. small, internationalism v. isolationism, traditional values v. modern morality, religious revivalism v. secular impositions. It was at the confluence of these two developments that *Speak Up America* was founded. As George Schlatter stated while promoting the show,

> The time is right . . . the country is facing very serious issues including an inflationary economy, merchandise that quickly becomes obsolete, drugs, alcohol, a political system that is out of sync with the average American . . . and on and on. We would like the people of this country to get involved with serious issues, to speak out. [12]

As much as they could, Silverman and Schlatter wanted to re-create the formula that had worked for *Real People*, in essence creating an extension, though not an imitation of, the original. As a result, the creative similarities between the two shows are manifold. *Speak Up America*, just like *Real People*, was given an abbreviated trial season in April 1980, to both gauge its potential and establish some name recognition for a full-season run beginning in the fall. The spin-off would also have film/video features introduced in front of a live studio audience by a cast of moderately obscure hosts. There would also be significant viewer participation through incoming mail, studio audience interaction, and even live opinion polling from some cable viewers.

From its formative stages it was understood and expected that *Speak Up America* would create and attract controversy and heated commentary. Less anticipated were the depth and sources of the subsequent criticism and commentary. The two-week preview in April featured filmed segments on provocative subjects such as the pending 1980 Summer Olympics boycott; the use of artificial insemination for selective breeding; the drafting of women into the military; the threat of nuclear war; the killing of baby seals; and alternative sexual lifestyles, with open marriage, group marriage, and homosexuality explored. These hot-button issues produced the expected critical response, but the primary target of most TV critics and industry observers was the tone and presentation of the show, particularly the persona of one of the cohosts, Marjoe Gortner. A child evangelist turned actor, Gortner used both of those talents in delivering fiery, impassioned monologues. Most reviews of the show cited Gortner's personality as the most disconcerting aspect of the show. Many compared the host to Howard Beale, a character in the 1976 feature film *Network*. In the film, Beale is an aging network TV news anchor who slowly loses touch with his sanity after having been informed of his impending dismissal. The artistic hallmark of the film is the angry populist ranting of Beale on live television. Most notably, Beale enflames his audience and instructs them to open their windows and yell, "I'm mad as hell and I'm not going to take it anymore." Marjoe Gortner had no interest in a balanced discussion of the issues; it was literally an "us versus them" battle cry. "Us" was the average working or middle-class Americans; "them" was the super-rich, the corporations, the government, the establishment. As he said in the opening episode, "They can't solve our problems; half the time they are our problems. For the next hour it's going to be us giving it to them."[13] John J. O'Conner described the preview episodes as a "disturbing exercise in populist demagoguery." The other source of criticism caught Silverman and Schlatter somewhat off guard: NBC local affiliates and the NBC news division. So one-sided and derogatory were some of the early episode segments that many local affiliates balked at airing the show in the fall because they thought it violated television's fairness doctrine. NBC news executives were angry with the show because it was tackling hard news issues but doing so in a sensationalistic way, with a frivolous entertainment approach they felt denigrated everyone in the news division.

Despite the criticism and complaints, Silverman committed to *Speak Up America* for the fall schedule. With promises to level the unbalanced presentation and rein in Marjoe Gortner, the show premiered on Friday, August 1, 1980. The series was clearly less overtly inflammatory and politically biased, more like its parent show, *Real People*. There were segments on Hollywood gigolos; a Mr. Tush contest; police prostitution stings; the slaughter of whales; the upcoming presidential election; homosexuality in the military; the failing auto industry; and some assorted whacky characters. The new season also featured a T.G.I.F. (Thank God It's Friday) segment from a different city each week, in addition to a semi-regular feature with basketball star Earvin "Magic" Johnson, typically related to young people. Even with the philosophical changes, cast additions, and stronger adherence to the *Real People* formula, *Speak Up America* was not successful in any measurable way. Critics eviscerated the show, several opening their reviews with gag lines like "Shut Up America," "Speak Up America Speaks Down," "Keep Quiet America," and one claiming the show should be called "Throw Up America." An interpretive reading of the array of reviews for the series makes it clear that many critics genuinely detested *Speak Up America*, arguably with justification. However, there is already, just eighteen months in, a visible reality fatigue, almost an aversion to any unscripted fare on the part of television critics and commentators. Many of the reviews of *Speak Up America* reference all the other major reality shows, as if to tar them all with one literary brush. Associated Press television writer Peter Boyer could not hide his disgust: "If television's 'reality' plague has proven anything, it is that the premise of using real Americans for entertainment was better as an idea than as a fact. The creatures go by many names, *Real People*, the prototype, *That's Incredible*, *That's My Line*, *Games People Play*. The most odious of them is called *Speak Up America* on NBC." It is almost as though these critics were reacting in fear, afraid that if reality took hold the way many had predicted, their utility as critics would expire; would the public need or want a review of a reality show?

As bad as the reviews were, they would not have mattered if the show's ratings had been strong. However, despite a strong promotional campaign linking *Speak Up America* to *Real People* and *Laugh-In*, coupled with a six-week head start on the fall schedule and little competition from opposing original programming due to the actors' strike, the show never established an audience. After several weeks of finishing as one of the lowest-rated shows on television, in early October, *Speak Up America* was the first new show canceled in the season. Though the number of fans for the series appeared limited, they were dedicated to the show. George Schlatter claimed that more than two hundred thousand letters had arrived at his offices protesting the cancelation. Schlatter placed some of the blame for the failure of the show on one of its most pointed critics: "I think it created enormous resentment in the news departments, because we were doing things that they should have been doing but weren't." He was also still clearly committed to the populist forum, looking for new ways to pursue themes raised on *Speak Up America*: "Someone has to deal with these issues in more than the minute or so they get on the evening news."[14]

GAMES PEOPLE PLAY

Some of the more popular recurring segments on *Real People* were those featuring unusual skills, pastimes, and competitions of all kinds. In the 1980–1981 season, NBC took that theme and hoped to have it grow into a full-fledged series of its own. Like NBC's other reality-themed programs, this competition-based reality show was given an April preview run, with designs on a full season in the fall. Originally entitled *The Sunday Games*, the show had a superficially global scope, as it was intended to be a tie-in with the 1980 Moscow Olympics, which NBC was supposed to air, before the United States boycott made that impossible. As NBC promotional material suggested, "The purpose of the Sunday Games is to pay tribute to the average man who takes part in sports activities for the sheer enjoyment derived from a competitive situation." In the preview, these competitive situations included a Venice, California, roller-skating skills competition (barrel jumping, roller dancing, hotdogging, wind skating); in Tuscaloosa, Alabama, the Collegiate International Chug Off, a chugalug drinking contest; in Chicago, Illinois, America's toughest bouncer contest; from New York City, a double Dutch jump-rope competition; and from London, a military skills competition called the Field Gunnery Meet.[15]

With NBC betting heavily on reality in the fall of 1980, the competition-themed show was guaranteed a spot on the schedule, with some minor alterations and a new title. On Thursday, August 21, *Games People Play* premiered in the 8–9 PM time slot. The primary host of the show was television sports personality Bryant Gumbel, with his athlete cohosts, Mike Adamle, Johnny Bench, Donna de Verona, and Los Angeles TV personality Cyndy Garvey. *Games People Play* took a different tack from that of *Real People* or *Speak Up America* when it came to hosts. Unlike its NBC reality brethren, *Games People Play* used well-known sports personalities who not only would draw some of their fans, but might also provide some measure of sporting credibility for the odd array of competitions featured on the show.

As the show began its full season it resembled *Real People* in presentation, but there were aspects of *That's Incredible* evident as well. There were inescapably whacky events such as a belly-flop contest; fast-talking disc jockeys; greased pole climbing; the Janitor Olympics; a bathtub regatta; and a shark rodeo. There were also some personality-driven segments on the Special Olympics; a seven-year-old billiard prodigy; an elderly softball player; an eighty-four-year-old mountain climber; and an eighty-two-year-old racetrack stable boy. Additionally, there were several segments that veered toward contrived sensationalism, with "death-defying" escape artists; high-speed car racing; and made-for-TV stunts like a car jumping over twenty-four Mack trucks.

The critical reception for *Games People Play* ranged from dismissive to disdainful. Some who deigned to offer a critique typically placed the show in a recently named subcategory called "trashsports." The term was used to describe programs that featured nontraditional or made-for-TV sports competitions. Shows placed in this class included *The Superstars* (1973), *Battle of the Network Stars* (1976), *The World's Strongest Man* (1977), *Celebrity Challenge of the Sexes* (1977), and now *Games People Play*.[16] Once again reviewers were not content to allow a new reality show to stand on its own; it had to be lumped in with and often stained by the work of other reality shows. The few reviews that judged *Games People Play* singularly often grudgingly acknowledged the appeal of reality TV, while condemning the content of the show: "'Games People Play' is a new NBC series showing totally insignificant athletic events such as belly-bumping, and hot-dog eating. It is staged, manipulative and artificial. But judging by last night's debut, it could become a surprise success, simply because it is beautifully and slickly produced. Many will ignore the dross and enjoy the show."[17] The above critique proved accurate, at least temporarily. In the first month and a half of the series' run, *Games People Play* was able to post very respectable Nielsen ratings numbers, including finishing among the top ten programs for the week. However, the actors' strike had delayed the start of most scripted series; meaning in the relatively successful first six weeks, the show was airing against repeats of series, specials, and made-for-TV movies. When the strike ended, and original programming appeared, *Games People Play* began a precipitous drop in the ratings. By early December, NBC had given up and canceled the series. For all intents and purposes, NBC's experiment with expanded prime-time reality programming had failed less than halfway through the season.[18]

Though *Games People Play* was not a highly influential program, it did presage one of the major themes in later reality programming, the involvement of celebrities. In the first decade of the twenty-first century, celebrities, many of them on the downside of their careers, or limited in talent, found themselves featured in reality shows that were hugely popular (e.g., *The Apprentice, The Surreal Life*). *Games People Play* was one of the few 1980s reality shows to feature prominent celebrities from sports, TV, and films. Those who took part included Erik Estrada, Larry Wilcox, Gary Coleman, Jack Klugman, James Coburn, Gil Gerard, Scott Baio, Reggie Jackson, Charley Pride, Greg Evigan, Joan Van Ark, Arte Johnson, Tanya Tucker, Bruce Jenner, Mike Connors, and F. Lee Bailey. *Games People Play* also had the unusual distinction of producing an international celebrity. During the brief run of the series, the Toughest Bouncer contest was featured; a contestant in that event was Mr. T. The mohawked, gold-encrusted intimidator would rise to global stardom in *Rocky III*, and later on his own hit TV series, *The A-Team*. Though it is common for modern reality shows to produce national celebrities, that process rarely occurred with 1980s reality programs.

NBC's third effort to spin off *Real People* was *Real Kids*, a reality show geared for the junior set. This show made no effort to conceal the relationship to the parent series. To begin with, Sarah Purcell was utilized to introduce the first of two preview episodes, one in March, one in May. The *Real People* set was featured, and a collection of hosts from age seven to eleven were used to introduce filmed segments and live presentations. It was essentially a *Real People* episode but with child hosts, and all kid-friendly segments. The segments were such that they could have appeared on the parent show; they featured, for instance, a twelve-year-old stunt girl; an eleven-year-old girl learning to ride racehorses with famous jockey Willie Shoemaker; an eleven-year-old boy who twirled unusual items like typewriters and kitchen sinks; a visit to a bubble gum factory; a peanut-butter-eating contest; and a search for the new star of the Broadway show *Annie*. The spring previews of *Real Kids* did not transition into a regular series during the subsequent fall for two reasons. First, the ratings were not strong, certainly not on par with *Real People*. Second, NBC had tried and failed to expand its reality presence with *Speak Up America* and *Games People Play*; and thus, without an evident sure thing, they did not take a chance on what was likely a niche program. The singular legacy of *Real Kids* was found in one of the hosts of the show, Peter Billingsley, who would become a contributor to and then host of *Real People* beginning in the fall of 1981.

NBC's chief competitor in the reality realm, ABC, also tried to capitalize on the wave by expanding its offerings. In a titular respect the network spun off from "incredible" to "amazing," creating *Those Amazing Animals*. The show was a clone of *That's Incredible* in format, with studio hosts Burgess Meredith, Priscilla Presley, and Jim Stafford, as well as Joan Embery and Jacques-Yves Cousteau as contributors, and filmed segments from all over the world and occasional in-studio presentations. The typical segments focused on animals and their interactions with humans, and the inner workings of the animal kingdom. Stories included a drug-detecting police dog; a grizzly bear who attacked his trainer; queen bees fighting to the death; wild mustangs in the American West; various stories on the American bald eagle; the amorous exploits of Frazier the Lion; baby elephants; a singing dog; a truck-riding raccoon; and a flock of geese who mistook an airplane for their mother. [19]

Critics paid little attention to *Those Amazing Animals*; it was overshadowed by the actors' strike, the controversy surrounding *Speak Up America*, and the scramble to fill empty schedules. Additionally, the wildlife theme of the show left little to criticize or find objectionable; there were no larger implications or statements about American society. The ratings outcome for *Those Amazing Animals* was somewhat predictable. As a reality show, its production had not been inhibited by the actors' strike. Thus it was original programming when there was very little of it on the air. However, the show was up against ratings powerhouse *60 Minutes* in the Sunday 7 PM time slot. The series would hold its own in the Nielsen ratings from August through late September, but when *60 Minutes* began airing new episodes, and the strike ended, *Those Amazing Animals* began to plummet in the ratings. The show would finish out the year, but it was not renewed for a second season. [20]

ABC also produced a reality pilot in 1980, entitled *All-American Pie*. The show was hosted by former pro football great turned actor Joe Namath. The hour-long show originated on location in Youngstown, Ohio, and featured segments from all over the United States. The finished product leads one to believe that the producers watched *Real People* and *That's Incredible* and decided to take a little of the formula for each and create a show. The features included a visit with a driving instructor in San Francisco, who had to deal with his students as well as the twisting hilly terrain of the city; passersby in New York City's Foley Square being questioned on their opinion on a piece of modern art composed of two large garbage cans; a two-minute compression of what a married couple looked like as they slept for eight hours, including tossing, turning, and pillow stealing; a Hollywood makeup artist playing pranks on his subjects; Sunday dinner with a South Philadelphia, Pennsylvania, family; a look at a Chicago, Illinois, phone answering machine; café patrons discussing the "perfect ten"; and women in a beauty salon revealing what they liked about men. As was the case with many TV pilots, ABC had conceived of the program as a test to see if the finished product would be viable as a regular series. In this case, the show had been financed and produced in early 1980 in the wake of the remarkable ratings success of *Real People* and *That's Incredible*, but the end result either was viewed as subpar and not worthy of filling a valuable time slot, or just did not fit into ABC's plans for the fall. Consequently, *All-America Pie* was aired in the ratings dead time of August, where it attracted little attention.[21]

Despite the failure of ABC's expanded reality offerings, the network still had a major reality success in *That's Incredible*. During its abbreviated first season in the spring of 1980, *That's Incredible* had drawn large audiences by presenting uniquely talented individuals, spectacular events, some inspirational stories, and sensational made-for-TV death-defying stunts. In the 1980–1981 season, the show increased the number and amplified the danger of these stunts, with tragic results. In season one, a subject tried and failed to catch a .22-caliber bullet with his teeth, producing minor injuries, but also suggesting that a few inches in another direction could have been fatal. In season two, several *That's Incredible* stunts produced serious injury. In one stunt, novice stuntman Stan Kruml planned to walk through a 150-foot-long flaming tunnel. During the filmed effort, Kruml fell down, suffering serious burns that destroyed his fingers down to the third knuckle. In another bizarre stunt, a twenty-five-year-old, Steven Lewis, had two cars racing toward him at speeds over 100 MPH. Lewis planned to jump over the cars as they passed under him; but he did not reach the correct height, and had both his lower legs mangled. And in the most sensational of all, daredevil Gary Wells reenacted a motorcycle jump, at Caesars Palace casino in Las Vegas, that had seriously injured Evel Knievel in 1967. Wells crashed during the jump, suffering a ruptured aorta and severe fractures of the pelvis, skull, and legs.

For those critics, TV insiders, and observers who were disturbed by the reality trend, these events created a feeding frenzy of opprobrium. *Newsweek* published an article entitled "Is It Incredible or Inexcusable?" In the piece, several interviewees pointed the finger at *That's Incredible* producer Alan Landsburg, who deflected blame for the events by suggesting the men who performed the stunts were responsible professionals, and that thirty other equally hazardous stunts had been completed with no injuries. The scandal landed on the cover of *People* magazine, with an article entitled "That's Incredible—or Is It Reprehensible? TV Mayhem Stirs Protest over a Top-Rated Show." In the *People* article, George Schlatter attacked *That's Incredible*, possibly in an effort to separate and immunize his show: "We are directly opposed to the kind of stunts they use, and were offered all of them . . . *Real People* is classic character portrayal, *That's Incredible* is a carnival." Of course, the botched stunts were a small part of the series, but they stained the perception of the show, and tainted the reality genre further. This scandal did not immediately impact the series' ratings, especially in the early weeks of the TV season. However, by the end of the season, the show's Nielsen numbers began to slip against strong competition from *Little House on the Prairie*; by season's end *That's Incredible* fell out of the top twenty rated programs, never to return.[22]

Of the three networks, CBS was the least active, and seemingly the least interested in the reality wave. This reticence to follow a trend was not unusual for what many called the "Tiffany Network." CBS had been so successful, and consequently arrogant, in the previous two decades that it rarely followed any trends that it had not set in motion itself. For instance, CBS stayed committed to western and rural-themed programming into the early 1970s, well after most shows of that genre had faded away. And when the made-for-TV movie began to transform television in the early 1970s, the number one rated network thought it was a fad, and was slow to produce what became a staple of television schedules. Therefore, it is not a surprise that CBS was relatively slow to develop reality-themed shows.

The Tiffany Network's initial effort was a show entitled *That's My Line*. The hour-long show was built around unique, unusual, outlandish, and even normal jobs and vocations, as well as the personalities of the people engaged in these endeavors. The finished product had the air of a game show; the title was a take-off on the long-running game show *What's My Line* (1950–1975); it was created by veteran game show producer Mark Goodson; the host was Bob Barker, widely known for his work on *The Price Is Right*; it even broadcast from the *Price Is Right* studio, with that show's distinctive-voiced announcer, Johnny Olsen.

However, aside from the game show trappings, *That's My Line* was really a clone and expansion of the occupational segments on *Real People* and *That's Incredible*. The show featured subjects such as the world's most expensive clothing store; window washers working on skyscrapers; various strippers and risqué occupations; several ingenious inventors; a man who made airplanes out of spare parts; a professional gambler; a Hollywood stunt school instructor; and most notably, a studio segment in which James Randi ("the Amazing Randi") discredited a well-known practitioner of psychic power. *That's My Line* aired as three specials in the summer of 1980, and was later placed in the Tuesday night 8 PM time slot in February 1981. Notwithstanding a reasonably good showing in the summer ratings, when relaunched in February the show failed abjectly, finishing at the very bottom of the weekly ratings. As for the critics, they showed their fangs: "It is nominally about people with weird professions, but its purpose is not to give facts but to entertain in the most vapid way. The events shown are contrived, uninteresting or insignificant; and insultingly coated in rehearsed 'ad-libs.' The program is thus an insult to anyone that views it." Once again, they often attacked not just one reality show, but all of them: "Like grass fires, or acne, as quickly as viewers wipe away one of TV's reality shows, another pops up . . . the latest is CBS' *That's My Line*." Not surprisingly, the show was canceled in April 1981, with reruns airing through much of the summer. [23]

CBS experimented further in the genre with a hybrid variety/reality show special entitled *Kenny Rogers' America*. In November of 1980, when the special aired, Kenny Rogers was one of the more successful musical pop stars in the country. At that time, the variety show was a tired, out-of-style genre, but reality was deemed fresh and innovative, thus the old was infused with the new to create this special. In the program, Rogers sings some of his well-known songs, as do the Commodores and Kim Carnes. But Rogers also plays the reality host role, as he plays touch football with the Pittsburgh Steelers; learns how to farm in Iowa; rides a giant slide in Wisconsin; drives a truck through New York City traffic; judges a Kenny Rogers look-alike contest; and visits the Tuskegee Institute in Alabama. The show performed well in the ratings, finishing in the top twenty; but it was not a realistic option for a series, given the cost of a nationwide production, coupled with the expense of paying a huge star like Kenny Rogers, assuming he would even make that type of commitment. Nonetheless, the show is illustrative of television's experimentation with reality themes, and the seeming industry assumption that the genre had acquired some measure of permanence, as well as further confirmation of the elasticity of reality themes that would allow it to be used in a diverse array of formats. [24]

Even the Public Broadcasting Service (PBS) found itself being associated, willingly or not, with the reality TV wave. During the 1980–1981 season, PBS stations across the country aired a series entitled *U.S. Chronicle*. The show was hosted by newsman Jim Lehrer, and featured segments of local origin on topics such as tugboat workers in New York City; the lives of young black youths in Seattle, Washington; and the prescription drug industry, to name a few. It was not unlike other PBS documentaries, but in the fall of 1980, with TV awash in reality, *U.S. Chronicle* was viewed differently. Some reviewers even cited its similarity with shows such as *Real People* and *Speak Up America*. This was an early indicator of how reality TV would begin to dilute and erode the credibility of television documentary over the next twenty years. [25]

Such was the fascination, if not inundation, of reality TV, that critics took note of the leakage of real people and realistic themes into many scripted programs in prime time. For instance, there was a rash of television films classed as docudramas, which featured true stories of triumph, despair, illness, and perseverance. Even more emblematic was the utilization of non-actors, or real people, to portray specialized roles or even themselves. Of course, this was not a new trend in television; it just became more evident when grouped with the rising tide of reality programming. In the most obvious cross-pollination, Carol Johnston, a one-armed gymnast featured on *Real People*, was starring as herself in a TV movie about her life. [26]

In an ironic development, just as the wave of reality TV was rising, an early practitioner in the form was stepping aside. Charles Kuralt had been traveling the highways and back roads of the nation looking for unique people, places, and events for thirteen years. His five-minute "On the Road" segments had appeared on the *CBS Evening News* since 1967, where they often sampled and surveyed the quickly fading small-town values and people. These were the type of stories that might appear on *Real People*. However, in October 1980, CBS News ended the segments, bringing Kuralt off the road. An adequate explanation for ending the segment was never offered in the press, but it is quite probable that the news division's antipathy toward the incursion of reality entertainment into the news realm caused concern about how "On the Road" would reflect on CBS News' reputation.[27]

The networks also tried a variety of reality-themed programs outside of prime time. In April 1981, CBS broadcast a week-long trial of a show entitled *Real Life Stories*. The show was produced by Alan Landsburg, who was also responsible for *That's Incredible* and *Those Amazing Animals*. At the heart of each episode were families who volunteered to have their daily lives recorded by a film crew. The filmed segments were then introduced by the show's hosts, actress Barbara Feldon and psychologist Tom Cottle, in front of a studio audience. After viewing the segments the hosts and the studio audience would offer opinions and advice related to the families' circumstances. Each family had some unresolved drama to be explored; to wit, a couple's bankruptcy caused by a heart attack suffered by the husband, who still could not return to work; a family in which both the husband and wife believed the woman's place is in the home; and a conflict between a woman's teenage children and her live-in boyfriend. The segments were designed to inspire sympathy/empathy, as well as debate, as there surely would be when discussing a "woman's place" or the morality of a live-in boyfriend. Mix in some pop psychology from host Tom Cottle and some audience comment, and you have a neatly wrapped hour of drama, without the need for a script, actors, or a director. It was what a number of reviewers called "a real life soap opera."[28]

In the fall of 1980, New York's CBS affiliate began airing a daily half-hour reality-based show geared toward women, *The Lives We Live*. At the core of this program were three women, none of whom were professional performers; rather, they were "real" women chosen through an open casting call. The women were all in their thirties and at divergent stages in their professional and private lives. The program had no moderator or script; the women would just have a spontaneous discussion on the topic of the day, often related to family, health, career, and various issues important to women. There were also occasional guests, frequently drawn from the hosts' personal lives, including their children, friends, and co-workers. *The Lives We Live* would run for a year and a half, and be copied in format by several shows throughout the country. Though neither *Real Life Stories* nor *The Lives We Live* were long running or memorable, you can see in them formulaic television DNA of later daytime talk shows

(*Sally Jessy Raphael, Jenny Jones, Dr. Phil*, etc.), which would come to saturate TV schedules from the late 1980s forward. [29]

Late-night network television was not immune to an experiment in reality. In the fall of 1980, *Saturday Night Live* was in a state of flux; the original cast and producer of the hit late-night show had departed, to be replaced by an entirely new cast who were not faring well. One of the shows considered as an occasional fill-in, if not a permanent replacement, for *Saturday Night Live* was a program called *Roadshow*. Chuck Braverman, the producer-director, described the show as "a mix of non-fiction and fiction combining serious subjects and mere titillations. It looks at lifestyle, cultural milestones, and flights of fantasy." The narrative hub of the show was a bus trip in which the cast, headed by John Candy, drove across the country. The bus stopped long enough to visit the "real Animal House," a fraternity at Louisiana State University; a wild Halloween parade in Carbondale, Illinois; and a graphic women's sexuality seminar in New York City. Braverman had produced the reality-themed show *What's Up America?* for Showtime, and it was clear that he was trying to push the boundaries of network censorship by airing sexually explicit material that was acceptable on cable TV, some of which did not get past NBC's standards and practices. Despite positive reviews, notably from Tom Shales of the *Washington Post*, *Roadshow* did not develop beyond the initial airing. [30]

CBS tested its own late-night reality hybrid, called *No Holds Barred*, on Fridays in the fall of 1980. The setting of the show was a cabaret-style club, with Canadian Kelly Monteith acting as studio host. True to reality form, there were taped segments from locations around the country. That meant a mud-slinging contest in Arcadia, Florida; a ride on a New York City subway; a television dating service; tryouts for a women's basketball team; a brothel in Deadwood, South Dakota; and various other views of what producer Alan Landsburg called "the crackpot side of life." The show ran for several episodes into the late fall, but it would not make a substantive mark on television or American culture. [31]

Though the results of the network's new prime-time reality programming were a major ratings disappointment, the genre was still viewed as having great potential, particularly in areas of TV where inexpensive and easy-to-produce content was needed. Syndication of shows to local stations across the country was a perfect match for reality programming. There were several new reality franchises syndicated for the 1980–1981 season. *The World of People* was a daily half-hour program, generally shown in the late afternoon, with a presence in forty-four markets across the country, including Boston, Los Angeles, and San Francisco. The show is an inescapable clone of *Real People*, but presented in the *PM Magazine* format, with no studio audience, just a collection of filmed hosts who introduce segments. The program's specialty was the event/contest/convention subgenre of reality TV; as the show's introductory narrative suggested, "It is an exciting celebration of people and the fascinating things they do; for fun, for free, for love or for challenge." The segments on *World of People* are already standard reality form: camel races; technology conventions; a visit to Gilley's honky-tonk, where the urban cowboy fad was born; a canine Frisbee-catching contest; female mud wrestling; zany inventions; Greek week on a college campus; eating contests; skateboarding; and countless other conventions and contests across the nation. *The World of People* was the embodiment of reality TV's potential; it was slickly produced and broadly appealing, cost only $15,000 per episode, and filled up two and a half hours of airtime per week for a local station.[32]

A further indication of reality's prospects is found in the efforts of independent producers to sell reality pilots to local stations. Trade shows and broadcasting conventions were the middle ground where ideas were conceived and deals struck. For the 1980–1981 season, a number of syndicated reality pilots were up for sale; for example, *Fantasies Fulfilled*, a show in which celebrities and average people had their fantasies realized. In the first episode, actor Walter Matthau fulfills a dream to announce a horse race at Santa Anita racetrack in California; and a woman gets to dance a tango with actor Cesar Romero. There was also a game show element, used to determine who would have their fantasies fulfilled. The producers called the show "a cross between *Real People* and *Fantasy Island*." *The Amazing World* was a one-hour magazine show that focused on travel adventures all over the globe, with segments on white-water rafting, exploring lost cities, discovering magical islands, and visits to "hometowns." Advertisements for the show called it "a show for today, with real people, living real life international travel adventures, in an age when adventures seem out of reach." In addition to shows like these, which emerged as finished pilots, there were untold reality proposals that never reached the production stage.[33]

The year 1980 featured the arrival of another program that infused an old format, the daytime talk show, with reality components. *Hour Magazine* was a daily syndicated program hosted by Gary Collins and Pat Mitchell, broadcast in over one hundred markets across the nation. The show was produced by Group W, the same company that produced *PM Magazine*. *Hour Magazine* had elements of *PM Magazine*, *Real People*, and *The Phil Donahue Show*. This included filmed features on topics such as food cooperatives, the women's rodeo championships, female construction workers, a gym for handicapped children, a hospital ward for premature babies, and regular visits with celebrities and numerous public events. There were also studio interviews with celebrities, newsmakers, and average people with interesting stories to tell on issues like male menopause, families surviving illness, weight loss, and other compelling topics. There were also medical segments with a rotating cast of doctors, and lifestyle tips from various contributors. Some aspects of the show were quite serious, while others were the standard lighthearted reality fare. A *Boston Globe* article likely summed up many people's view of the show, when it entitled its review "It's Just a Poor Man's Donahue: *Hour Magazine* Tries to Be Serious but Ends Up Innocuous." Though it might not have been high-quality programming, *Hour Magazine* would become a staple of daytime television for eight years. [34]

The powerhouse of syndicated reality remained *PM Magazine*; by the summer of 1981 it would be shown in over 120 markets across the nation. Given the cooperative nature of the *PM Magazine* format, the more stations broadcasting the show, the larger the pool of stories from which they all could choose. Here is a random sampling of episodes on channel 5 in Schenectady, New York, for the week of March 9–13, 1981:

Monday: An unusual hockey game where kids are pitted against their mothers; a nineteen-year-old escape artist; Chef Tell makes Polish Meatballs; Dr. Wasco on sugar products and dental health; a visit to Zurich, Switzerland.

Tuesday: A visit to *TV Guide* headquarters; a 450-lb skiing champion; Mary Gregori builds storage shelves; Capt. Carrot on indoor pollution; Sharon Wolin visits an area bookstore that works on the barter system.

Wednesday: A new operation that partially restored a deaf woman's hearing; the world's first car orchestra; Chef Tell makes Veal Gou-

lash; Dr. Wasco on a breakthrough for cataract sufferers; Cathie
Mann meets Hollywood stand-ins.
Thursday: Snow skiing on barrel staves; a man who uses applejack for
fuel; Chef Tell makes Rice Salad; Jazzercizes for the knees.
Friday: World championship power boat racing; a woman who has
collected 130 stray cats; ice fishing in the Adirondacks; Capt. Carrot has exercises to help relaxation.

The unique aspect of *PM Magazine* was that a station just fifty miles from
Schenectady could broadcast a very different program on the same evening.[35]

By the summer of 1981, there were cities and towns across the nation
that had as much as twelve hours of some variant of reality television
available to them on a weekly basis.

Though it was not immediately evident, there were several developments
in the TV industry in 1980–1981 that would ripple through the remainder
of the decade and beyond. The actors' strike in the summer of 1980 had
given TV actors a larger slice of the profits of the productions in which
they worked. Television production companies, not wanting their profit
margins limited, began to look for ways to cut production costs. For most
series, professional writers and actors were still a necessary component;
therefore, cuts were made in other places. Single episodes or entire series
set in exotic locales like Hawaii would either have to shoot on a Hollywood soundstage or not be produced at all. Series with high special
effects costs, such as *The Incredible Hulk* (1978–1981) and *Buck Rogers
in the 25th Century* (1979–1981), would also have to be scaled back,
canceled, or never even produced. The same was true of shows that
utilized extensive action segments, such as *B.J. and the Bear*
(1979–1981) and *The Dukes of Hazzard* (1979–1985), particularly car
chases or elaborate stunts. The determinative mitigating factor for a show
could be its rating; a top twenty show would likely be immune to these
financial strictures; but just as likely, a proposed show that had any of
these profit-draining qualities might not even be attempted. It did not go
unnoticed in the TV industry that during the actors' strike, reality programs did not have their productions shut down the way scripted programming had. For many producers and TV studios, what reality may
have lacked in quality and artistic respect was balanced by the lower
budgets, the greater control of production, and of course, the potential

profit. Therefore, while much of the networks' 1980–1981 reality-themed programming was a failure, the economic value of reality TV was becoming increasingly accepted by the industry. [36]

One of the most notorious reality failures of the season was *Speak Up America*. Though the ratings were terrible and the critics' reviews eviscerating, *Speak Up America* had an element that was a dramatic innovation presaging the future of media. A hallmark of the show was the debating of contentious political or social issues. To expand its viewer participation, and hopefully raise interest, *Speak Up America* developed a relationship with a cable entity in Columbus, Ohio, known as QUBE. In 1977, the Warner-Amex cable company created a "talk back TV" service for the community of 580,000 people. QUBE allowed home viewers to press a button on a remote control and have it register at a central database. This capability allowed for an experimental exercise in gauging immediate public opinion. For example, early in live episodes of *Speak Up America*, a series of questions was posed, and QUBE viewers were able to enter a vote, the results of which would be announced by the end of the show. The populist questions posed included: Should both men and women be drafted into the military? (49 percent yes); will you vote for Jimmy Carter or Ronald Reagan in the 1980 presidential election? (51 percent Carter); do you support the Equal Rights Amendment? (55 percent yes); who Shot J.R. [on *Dallas*]? (none of the above); should military spending be increased? (yes). [37]

QUBE was utilized by PBS for similar purposes, to gauge public opinion on several public affairs programs, usually on controversial issues. Locally, QUBE technology was used to create "interactive" educational programming and monitor home security systems; and by the winter of 1980, viewers could order items from American Express' Christmas catalog with their remote control and have the item delivered to their front door. QUBE had interactivity between broadcaster and viewer, something that is vital in the modern TV industry; it was shopping from home before the Internet, and entire channels dedicated to that purpose; it was centralized home security, with twenty-four-hour monitoring of fire and theft, as well as panic buttons for medical or police emergencies. In short, QUBE was the future; it was interactive, innovative, and expansive; it offered every available cable channel, including adult networks; and it had a pay-per-view component that broadcast sporting events and first-run Hollywood films. By 1983, Warner-Amex cable would expand

QUBE to Cincinnati, Pittsburgh, Dallas, Houston, and Saint Louis; but the operational and expansion costs coupled with less-than-expected subscriber interest caused QUBE to cease operations in 1984. Though it ultimately failed, QUBE and its proto-technology are the embodiment of a threat that would slice off large chunks of the network audience over the subsequent twenty years.[38]

For NBC, the 1980–1981 season was another disappointing outcome. Despite an early-season ratings advantage, due in large part to reality programs and the special-event miniseries *Shogun* and *Centennial*, NBC still finished as the third rated network. Even more alarming, NBC's profits had plummeted, from 122.1 million in 1978 to 75.3 million in 1980. Though not completely fair, much of the blame for these failures was leveled at Fred Silverman. For many in the industry, Silverman had made bad decisions on programs such as *Supertrain*, *Speak Up America*, *Number 96*, and others, combined with some bad luck in the US boycott of the 1980 Moscow Olympic Games, which were intended to provide strong ratings and massive promotional opportunities. There were also failures and declines in daytime and late-night programming, including with the venerable *Tonight Show Starring Johnny Carson*.

On July 1, 1981, Fred Silverman resigned his post as president of NBC, after failing to secure the vote of confidence he sought from NBC's parent company, the Radio Corporation of America. Though Silverman had failed to elevate NBC to number one in the ratings, he would leave an indelible mark on the history of the reality genre. From his support of *Lifeline* to his creative impetus in *Real People*, and even his commitment to ratings flops such as *Speak Up America* and *Games People Play*, Silverman had established the viability of the genre and set in motion the inexorable growth of reality programming. Succeeding Silverman as the chairman of the board and chief executive officer was veteran producer Grant Tinker. Though he was not a fan of reality TV, Tinker was compelled to leave *Real People* alone, largely because it was one of only three NBC shows in the top twenty of the Nielsen ratings.[39]

3

WHACKOS, FREAKS, ECCENTRICS...
GOD BLESS AMERICA

1981–1982

The early 1980s were a difficult time of transition and retrenchment for the television industry. The greatest contaminant to the stasis of the medium was the growth of pay/cable television. That cable TV would become a drain on network TV's audience share was becoming a widely accepted if not immutable truth for most people working in the industry and external observers of the medium. However, the most immediately destabilizing element surrounding the rise of cable TV was as old as human civilization: profit. The increasing number of homes wired for cable, combined with the growing number of pay channels available, created massive new revenue streams. Disputes over how that revenue was to be apportioned become a wedge that created a fissure throughout the entertainment industry. The first impactful example of this effort to acquire cable-created revenue can be seen in the extended actors' strike in the spring of 1980, which shut down the production of most mainstream TV and film studios. That strike having been settled somewhat favorably for the actors, it was inevitable that there would be other creative unions asserting their rights. The next attempt came quickly, as in the spring/ summer of 1981, the Writers Guild of America (WGA), which represented feature film and TV writers, asked for a greater share of the profits produced for future sales of their efforts to cable television. When its demands were rebuffed, the WGA went on strike in April of 1981.

The impact on the entertainment industry was evident in the slow-down and eventual ceasing of many film and TV productions. There were some WGA accusations that TV studios had stockpiled scripts and accelerated production schedules, which would dilute the efficacy of the strike. Nonetheless, these charges had little to do with the central issues of the work stoppage, a greater percentage of the profits from cable television sales and, to a slightly lesser degree, home video disc/tape profits. The strike would ultimately be settled in July, with the WGA winning what it called "truly historic" revenue-sharing agreements with producers. The thirteen-week strike produced just a three-week delay in the start of the TV season.[1]

While the impact of the WGA strike was not as significant as the 1980 actors' strike, the networks still had to fill original programming gaps with second and third reruns of series episodes, made-for-TV movies, and specials. Unlike the circumstances in the beginning of the 1980–1981 season there was not a glut of strike-exempt reality programs to shore up network schedules; going into the 1981–1982 season, there were just two reality shows with guaranteed time slots, *Real People* and *That's Incredible*. Though these reality shows were not substantially impacted by the writers' strike, they also adhered to the delayed schedule, with *Real People* not premiering until September 30.

Coming off of its most successful season to date, *Real People* made few substantive changes to the show's format and style. One of those small changes was the addition of two part-time hosts/reporters. Fred Willard, who had been one of the original hosts of season one, returned as a semi-regular host and field reporter. Willard had been wooed back by George Schlatter with the promise that he could choose the stories he would cover. Willard's forte would be "a salute to the people who dare to be different." His genius with this particular type of story was his ability to deliver a deadpan sincerity and inquisitiveness, no matter how unusual the subjects. If the segments had a mocking tone, it was likely the editing, or just the inescapable weirdness of the subjects, not snarkiness from Willard. The other new addition was also a somewhat familiar face, Peter Billingsley. As one of the hosts of the failed spin-off pilot *Real Kids*, the ten-year-old Billingsley had impressed George Schlatter, who made him a part-time correspondent, primarily covering stories on or for children. It comes off as a bit of gimmick, but *Real People* was trying to reach as broad an audience as possible.[2]

The audience participation element would continue to be a vital component of the show. Though the numbers and metrics changed from one

Real People cast photo, back row left to right: **Bill Rafferty, Byron Allen, Skip Stephenson; front row left to right: Sarah Purcell, Peter Billingsley, Mark Russell.**
NBC / Photofest © NBC

press interview or release to another, cast members and producers regularly suggested that there were thousands of letters coming in to *Real People*'s Burbank offices each week. Virtually all of these correspondents were sending in story ideas, funny pictures, advertisement typos, and opinions, all with the hope of getting their material on the air, so the hosts would say their name and hometown. Equally important, if their item did get on the air, they would be sent a *Real People* T-shirt, which was a rare and coveted, by some, cultural commodity because the shirts were not sold to the public, just earned. In May 1982, George Schlatter claimed a volume of twenty-one thousand letters per week, all of which were eventually answered.[3]

Late 1981 through 1982 was a dark economic time for many Americans, as the country experienced a recession the likes of which had not been felt since the 1930s. Viewer letters and audience comments expressed alternating currents of fear, anger, and hopelessness about the never-ending economic maladies of the day: high gas prices, unemployment, inflation, and government's inability to address these issues. These topics were not easy to address in filmed segments, because, quite honestly, a string of stories on unemployment, inflation, and gas prices would be depressing, not the escapist fare audiences expected from *Real People*.[4] However, the show had a quick and lighthearted way to deal with these hot-button issues. At the end of almost every show the hosts would deliver their parting shots, usually set to rhyme, and designed to strike the populist chord. Here is an example of a parting shot from 1981:

John Barbour: We're getting encouragement about unemployment, we're getting reassurance in gobs . . . that's what people have been getting, but what they really need is jobs!

Sarah Purcell: Gas and whiskey are getting so expensive, people are beginning to hoard it; just when those prices can drive us to drink . . . we find we can't afford it.

Skip Stephenson: Government economists keep explaining inflation, of explanations they are full, to them we say, our cow just died . . . so we don't need all your bull.

Byron Allen: It's true our country is facing problems, but when our flag is unfurled, I'd rather be an American than anything else in the world.

With that, the show signed off to thunderous applause from the studio audience.[5]

Though there was only one other prime-time network reality show for *Real People* to be measured against, there was a growing a number of syndicated reality shows, which, while not in direct ratings competition, did produce a scramble for interesting stories and people. In fact, there had already been similar stories that had appeared on multiple reality shows, including *Real People*. To fill the never-ending need for new subjects, George Schlatter had five film crews roaming the nation documenting people, places, and events. The process was necessarily streamlined, with one crew typically filming multiple segments in a given region. Those segments would then be viewed by George Schlatter and his associate producers to determine if they were worthy of broadcast, or if they fit into any of the proposed episodes. The hosts were utilized in two different ways when it came to filmed segments. For certain stories the hosts would actually go on location and interact with the subjects. For the other segments, the hosts would just provide voice-over narration for the film footage. The result was cohesion in style and presentation for each episode.[6]

Though committed to that standardized format, during season four *Real People* would experiment with a programming device it would use more regularly in the coming seasons, taking the entire cast and production on location. In the 1981–1982 season, the show presented a ninety-minute special from New York City. Setting a show in New York was logical for a variety of reasons. Practically speaking, there were a lot of unique people, places, and events in the city and surrounding areas, certainly enough to fill ninety minutes. Secondarily, from the beginning of the series, New York, and most coastal urban centers, had not been a ratings stronghold for *Real People*. Rather, the show performed consistently well in the interior of America, what some on the coasts called the flyover states. A show dedicated to New York, which ideally would draw a large hometown audience, was an opportunity to build a greater ratings base in the nation's largest market.[7]

In 1981, New York was still trying to bounce back from a mid-1970s fiscal crisis that had left it on the brink of bankruptcy, as well as the consequences of a pernicious drug culture and associated crime. But the episode was upbeat; the New York City Chamber of Commerce could not have done a better promotional job. The episode opened with Mayor Ed Koch introducing the show by saying, "Tonight the real people of the United States salute the Big Apple; where every race, religion, and philosophy are learning to live together in peace and harmony." Koch is also featured in a segment during which Sarah Purcell follows him throughout his long work day, where is he seen several times spouting his catchphrase, "How'm I doing?"

The rest of the show was a model of a typical *Real People* episode, with the exception of the show being a mixture of already broadcast New York–themed stories and a collection of new segments. There were the standard unique people: a dog walker, a cat doctor, a bird psychiatrist, the world's fastest painter, a vampire hunter, and a professional garbologist. There was also attention paid to more mainstream New Yorkers, such as steelworkers on a high-rise building; a colorful cab driver; stonemasons working on the Cathedral of Saint John the Divine; and female stevedores, trying to overcome male chauvinism. Of course there were inspirational stories for balance, with a track coach helping inner-city kids stay in high school and move on to college; Dance Theatre of Harlem; firefighters raising money for charity; and Charlie De Leo, a National Park Service caretaker at the Statue of Liberty, who loved his job and found inspiration for his poetry about the "lovely lady."

Throughout the show the hosts were engaged in iconic New York activities: riding a hansom cab, touring on the Circle Line with the show's guests, and marching down Fifth Avenue in a parade. As the show wrapped up, Frank Sinatra's "New York, New York" played over a montage of the skyline and the people of the city. It was reminiscent of a newsreel travelogue that would have been shown in a movie theater forty years earlier. Tom Shales, well-known TV critic at the *Washington Post*, grudgingly admired the hyperbolic optimism in his review of the show:

> One could easily fault the show's rosy view of New York as doggedly disingenuous, preposterous even . . . but the view point is put over in such a delirious and invigorating way that by the end of the special one may find oneself actually longing to be a New Yorker. Yes, a New Yorker.[8]

Though the dedicated special episode was a new and intriguing narrative possibility, *Real People* would still be heavily dependent on the scatter-shot anthology formula for most episodes. Regardless of the season, if one sifts through the various segments, most all eventually settle into the standard categories delineated in earlier chapters. In season four the eccentric lifestyle/hobby/collection still had a central role in the show, if for no other reason than it came to be expected, and it filled airtime. Nonetheless, the segments seemed to have been selected and presented in such a way as to avoid any overt indications of mockery, humiliation, or exploitation. Consequently, season four contained a measure of tempered eccentricity. Rather than just pure weirdness, many of the segments found comedy at the intersection of the seeming incongruence of person and proclivity. For instance, Disco Beulah, a sixty-five-year-old Illinois woman who recorded and performed disco songs; a Catholic priest who moonlighted as a stand-up comedian; a four-hundred-pound-man who raced mini-go-carts; a traditional funeral home that also had a drive-thru window for viewing the deceased; and a husband and wife who performed as male/female impersonators. The uniquely talented and/or inspired were represented by the world's fastest chess player; the world's champion chugalug beer drinker, who could swallow a mug in just a few seconds; a man who sold advertising on his bald head; a man devoted to "Pyramid Power," feeling that a pyramid ensured good health, intellectual expansion, and sexual prowess; a hypnotherapist who claimed to have been practicing for one hundred thousand years; "the most isolated woman in America," who lived alone in a northern Minnesota cabin; another Minnesota resident who dedicated years of his life to building a full-scale replica of a Viking ship; and a feature on Dr. Demento, a nationally syndicated radio host known for playing unusual or flat-out terrible music for his adoring cult of fans.

By the time production began on season four, *Real People*'s cultural prominence meant that the show would be invited to thousands of events, conventions, and contests across the nation. Though logistics, accessibility, and potential viewer interest played a role in where the show went, *Real People* had its pick of almost any event it liked; the result is a purposefully diverse collection of big, small, and often outrageous events. This lineup included fashion shows for dogs, cats, and frogs; "bike polo," a game of polo played on bicycles in New York's Central Park; inner-tube racing; a look at the emerging sport of snowboarding; a tattoo convention; sled-dog racing in the Yukon; contests in bird calling and dog howling; senior citizen and gay rodeos; and an annual reenactment of the route for the Pony Express. The above segments reaffirm *Real People*'s efforts to not just focus on big cities and urban centers, but to give at least equal, if not more, attention to small-town and rural lives.

For students of 1980s culture, *Real People* offers an accessible vantage point from which to view the ebb and flow of fads that eternally mark the decade. Season four had segments featuring popular activities like roller skating and disco music, and the combination of the two; but when you have disco Laundromats and senior citizen performers, the fad is clearly in its death rattle. Yet *Real People* was able to get much closer to the beating heart of emerging culture by featuring several segments on the assorted aspects of the punk rock movement, notably punk fashion, hairstyles, and ideology. At the other end of the cultural spectrum was the rise of "preppy culture" among the nation's young people. A season four segment looked at the clothing, style trends, and attitude of the "preps." It also made clear that not everyone liked the clean-cut, somewhat elitist preppy stereotype; one episode featured "anti-preps" who could not contain their contempt for their antagonists. Though they were not yet dominant national fads, a retrospective eye can see the early rumblings of rising trends like the fitness and aerobics fascination beginning to grip the nation, as illustrated by the popularity of Richard Simmons, who made a return visit to the show. One can also see future developments that would grab the attention of millions of young people around the world in the coming decade, including snowboarding and BMX bicycle racing and stunts.

Unlike cultural fads that rise and fall away, America's interest in sex never seems to dissipate. *Real People* understood this standard and regularly offered segments that ranged from classic jiggle TV to more overt T&A (tits and ass) material. Season four viewers were exposed to a New Jersey therapist who claimed he could increase the size of women's breasts using hypnosis; a review of male centerfolds; a man whose job was to take pictures of bikini-clad girls at Miami Beach for the chamber of commerce; female bikini oil wrestling; a truck stop where the menus were printed on bikini-clad girls; a cowboy who delivered strip-o-grams; and "Foxy Boxing," with scantily clad women in boxing matches.

Narrative contrast was the creative lifeblood of *Real People*. Within a single episode there could be a segment on an unusual job or pastime—

Promotional ad for *Real People*, September 30, 1981, *New York Times*, C23.

for example, Foxy Boxer—but there would often be a counterbalance in the form of a more serious job; for instance, an urban ecologist in New York City; a fifteen-year-old writer for *Newsweek*; a photographer from

Hollywood's golden age; or a female sports referee. More popular with viewers and an even greater shield against charges of exploitation and sensationalism was the heartwarming and inspirational story, at which *Real People* excelled. The 1981–1982 season had a strong collection of these stories in which people overcame disability; for instance, wheel-chair racing; a guitarist who played expertly despite having no arms; a feature on a blind boxing coach; a couple who taught horseback riding to children with cerebral palsy; and the work and achievements of the Junior Blind of America organization, which helped vision-impaired youngsters and adults. Also featured were age-defying accomplishments, such as a Florida grandmother who raced stock cars; a ninety-two-year-old radio talk show host; an eighty-one-year-old who taught ballet; and senior citizens who competed in rodeo events. Then there were those who were trying to make the world a happier or better place, including an eighty-five-year-old landlord from Venice, California, who had not raised the rent in fifteen years; a California teacher who helped young gang members by getting them involved in amateur boxing; a New York City police officer who started a community center to keep kids off the streets; and an aspiring cop who was fighting to become a Boston police officer even though he did not meet the minimum height requirement. In one of the more emotional segments of the season, there was a story on what was called the "adopt a grandparent" program in Prescott, Arizona. In the piece, children were visiting a senior citizens' community and spending time with their adopted grandparents. The scenes of young and old interacting were heartwarming, but the interviews were even more emotional, with the seniors beaming as they talked about the children; several suggested that the adoption program had improved their quality of life immeasurably, if not lengthened their lives. The segment was sappy and manipulative, but it worked as feel-good entertainment; and no other reality show did that as well as *Real People*.

Another story category for which *Real People* had no equal, either in quantity or in quality, was the patriotic, flag-waving "God bless America and her people" segment. In season four, *Real People* continued its campaign to celebrate the US military veteran, while the show markedly increased its advocacy for not just recognition of their service but also aid, comfort, and basic rights. Regardless of the tone, whether celebrating the veterans or scolding society for forgetting them, the segments were always bathed in feel-good patriotism. In that vein there was a segment on the WACs of World War II, specifically a unit of black women who served in that branch of the military. The piece focused on the relative obscurity of the black Women's Army Corps units, their segregated service and the lack of official recognition for their contributions. Like the veterans featured in many other segments there was no real bitterness coming from the women; rather, they were happy to be reuniting with each other and proud to have served. On November 11, 1981, Veterans Day, *Real People* presented an entire episode dedicated to military service. As the opening narrative intoned, "Tonight *Real People* presents a special Veterans Day tribute to all of the American heroes who have given of themselves to preserve this country and its freedoms." The hosts then read the Declaration of Independence, calling the document the "best letter of the week." The opening segment was a reunion of men who had served on the USS *Lexington* during World War II. The ship, nicknamed "the Blue Ghost," had seen extensive action, including a direct hit from a kamikaze attack. One interview is particularly emotional, reuniting for the first time in decades a man who had survived the Japanese attack with severe burns with the man who had saved his life. Most of the men interviewed had an overt mixture of pride and sadness, many of them choking back tears when talking about their lost shipmates and friends from forty years earlier. Tears flowed freely as a memorial wreath was tossed into the water while taps was played; and then again when the men of the *Lexington* were introduced to the studio audience.

Another tear-jerking segment was dedicated to the Navajo Code Talkers from World War II. During the war this specialized marine unit comprised over four hundred Navajo tribe members, who were used to send messages in their native language because the enemy could not decipher or decode the messages they sent. It was an ironic development given the extensive effort by the US government to force the Navajo to abandon their native language decades earlier. The vital utility of the Navajo Code Talkers often meant that they were the first into a battle zone and the last to leave. However, when the war ended they were largely forgotten. The *Real People* segment picked up in San Diego, California, as a group of young Navajo men were graduating from marine boot camp, with a number of former code talkers watching the ceremonies. John Barbour interviewed the young men, several of them sons and grandsons of the code talkers, and very firm in their commitment, saying, "I love this country," and "We're proud to be marines, it's what I always wanted." The code talkers themselves were equally proud and without resentment, neither for their treatment as Native Americans, nor for the lack of official recognition or commendation for their unique contributions. After introducing several code talkers in the studio audience, John Barbour made an assertive plea: "If you feel as we do that the members of the Navajo Code Talkers Association deserve a presidential citation, then do what we have done; write to President Reagan care of the White House, Washington, DC, and perhaps these men will get the recognition they should have gotten forty years ago."[9]

The most relevant and ultimately most painful segment of the episode was related to the Vietnam War. At the heart of this piece was Dr. David Westphal from Valverde, New Mexico. The doctor's son David was killed in 1968 on a battlefield in Vietnam. Almost immediately, Dr. Westphal began building a memorial to his son. After spending thirteen years and most of his life savings, Westphal had created a memorial chapel and garden. Even more amazingly, the memorial had become an emotional touchstone for other families who had lost loved ones in Vietnam. There was even a growing effort in the late 1970s to have Westphal's creation named an official memorial to those lost in the war. Once the word of the New Mexico chapel began to spread, a memorial for one turned into a memorial for many, as families began sending pictures of their loved ones to be posted on the walls of the chapel. The segment featured an interview with Dr. Westphal, who talked about his son and how much he missed him, the pain seeming so immediate, even thirteen years later. There were also very touching shots of people visiting and breaking down upon seeing their family member's picture. One emotional Vietnam veteran remarked, "It gives some knowledge that someone does have some love, and I'll never forget that." Another veteran was bitter: "I'll tell you one thing that really grinds me, is when they call it an immoral war; and I have yet to figure out which war they had in mind which was moral." The segment ended with a photo montage of those who were lost in the war, while the soundtrack was Roberta Flack's "The First Time Ever I Saw Your Face." It was a bit over the top, but as Tom Shales said in his review, it was "a case of bad taste in a good cause." When the filmed piece was over, the audience shots revealed a number of people misty-eyed, if not weeping openly. When this segment was broadcast, the official Vietnam Veterans Memorial in Washington, DC, had not been completed, nor had the nation fully embraced or reconciled with veterans from Vietnam. However, throughout the nation there was a growing desire to right the wrongs inflicted on Vietnam veterans; and *Real People* was at the leading edge of that movement.

The final feature of the veterans special was a hyperpatriotic segment exploring Arlington National Cemetery. The piece featured a look at the Tomb of the Unknown Soldier, particularly the Tomb Guard, an elite unit whose professional dedication and precise changing of the guard was an eternal draw for mourners and tourists. When one of the guards was asked to describe the importance of the cemetery, he said, "This is sacred ground because they laid down their lives to help us preserve our freedom." The end of the segment produced a rising crescendo, with Sarah Purcell walking through the cemetery and intoning:

> To fight in service of one's nation is the highest sacrifice a citizen can make. Not every soldier honored here may have totally agreed with or even fully understood the conflict they were involved in; but they served their country, and all of us should see they are not forgotten. The men who fought in war died for peace, we must remember and revere them, while embracing and respecting those veterans who still live. It is because of their sacrifice that the words to "God Bless America" still ring with truth and honor.

At that moment, Sarah began to recite "God Bless America," coming close to tears at several points.

As the episode was ending, images of the Tomb Guard and the waving American flag were accompanied by closing comments: "On this Veterans Day all Americans say to veterans everywhere that we care; our call you have heeded; you've been there when needed, you've made sure our flag was still there." Clearly, the episode had some aspects of hyperbolic patriotism and narrative manipulation of the heartstrings; but the people featured were real, as was their service and sacrifice. One would have to be truly hardhearted not to feel some strong emotions while watching these segments. Tom Shales further lauded the show when he said, "*Real People* should never be confused with *That's Incredible!* or other video freak shows. When it is good, it is very very good; and tonight it is good."[10]

Real People was NBC's highest-rated show for the 1981–1982 season. In any other year for any other network that distinction would have likely translated to a top ten show in the Nielsen ratings. However, the

1981–1982 season was the worst in the history of NBC, as it finished a distant third to CBS and ABC, respectively. *Real People* finished a disappointing twenty-third in the ratings. The explanation for the relatively poor performance is manifold. First, *Real People* had reasonably strong competition in its time slot from *The Greatest American Hero*, a show geared toward young people. The show's theme song, "Believe It or Not," had become a number one hit on the pop music charts in the summer of 1981, likely providing more viewer interest. Second, there was a growing volume of reality content, particularly in syndication, which may have hurt the unique quality of *Real People*. For example, in the same season that the show visited Arlington National Cemetery, both *PM Magazine* and the syndicated *The New You Asked for It* both presented segments from Arlington. Third was the overall terrible performance of NBC, which offered little opportunity for promotion of the show across the network. TV viewing is habitual, and when viewers get out of the routine of watching a network at certain times, it can have a ripple effect throughout the schedule. NBC's total viewership was down almost 7 percent from the previous season; this acted as a ratings anchor around the neck of *Real People*. Although twenty-third was not as strong as earlier ratings, as the number one show at the network, *Real People* was secure in its scheduling; but there was clearly much room for improvement in 1982–1983.[11]

The volume of critical interest in *Real People* and reality in general began to decrease in 1981–1982. *Real People* was still receiving a good amount of attention, including a *TV Guide* cover featuring the entire cast, and a lengthy story inside the magazine. An early advocate for the show was Tom Shales, one of the preeminent TV writers in the country. Shales would continue his advocacy for *Real People* into the 1981–1982 season, with deep insight into the cultural impact of the show as well as a firm grasp on its character. In one review, in November 1981, Shales perfectly framed the show:

> The *Saturday Evening Post* no longer arrives in the nation's mailboxes; it makes its way indoors through the TV screen each week on George Schlatter's *Real People*. The NBC series that is loved by no one except the public is not only the *Saturday Evening Post* of its time, but also the *Life*, the *Look*, the March of Time newsreels and Pete Smith's old shorts.

> *Real People* can be as shamelessly corny as a Norman Rockwell cover, but then, like those covers, it can also hit home in a blunt, beguiling, universally accessible way. There is probably less distance between *Real People* and its audience than there is with any other prime time network show.

Though there was not the critical cacophony of the early years of the reality wave, there were still indictments of *Real People* to be found. Several sources, including the *Alfred I. DuPont/Columbia University Survey, 1979–1981*, noted the incursion of shows like *Real People* into the traditional news realm, which ultimately led to "the softening of the news." As observed in earlier chapters, George Schlatter was willfully active in this incursion. In season four, one segment is particularly representative of the slide into news, as *Real People* did an exposé on children who had run away from home, only to end up living on the streets of Los Angeles. The feature had no laugh track; there was no attempt to find comedy; there was no inspirational happy ending. It was a gritty informational piece, it was not entertainment. With ratings starting to dip midway in the series run, *Real People* would delve into the news realm a number of times to reframe or rebrand the show to keep it on the air. [12]

OTHER REALITY PROGRAMMING

The major networks' failed experiment with expanded reality programming in 1980–1981 had somewhat tempered executives' and programmers' enthusiasm for the genre. Nonetheless, there were several unique offerings from the networks. NBC had a dual problem as the 1981–1982 season ended; its ratings were poor, and consequently its revenues were down, from daytime to late night. To counter these concerns, NBC attempted to work both ends of the problem by raising the ratings with programs that were more cost-effective in production. Thus, ideally, even a minor ratings boost would significantly increase revenue, given the lower production costs. Reality programming was the perfect genre to accomplish this, if a network had the right show. In June 1982, NBC tested out a unique reality show pilot called *Wedding Day*. This half-hour late-morning show was an incomprehensible mixture of intimate reality with a game show element. At the heart of each show was a couple who agreed to have their wedding and the events associated with it broadcast in front of a live studio audience and viewers across the nation. It was an experiment with the concept of presenting personal events for public consumption. *Wedding Day* was described in the show's introduction as "a brand-new television event that brings you a different love story every day." The show's format was framed by NBC publicity as "selected couples exchanging marriage vows and sharing other events surrounding that special occasion with the television audience." Those other events included "the traditional bridal shower, the humor and good fun of the groom's bachelor party, and the warmth and spirit of the reception for family and friends." It was a remarkable shuffling of people and props in roughly twenty-five minutes, with a quick introduction, a bridal shower, a bachelor party, a real wedding with a genuine religious or secular official, and a quick reception with a first dance. These events were punctuated by the revelation of intimate personal details, hugging, kissing, and crying, and included comments by hosts Mary Ann Mobley and Huell Howser and, of course, five minutes of commercials. Even more incongruous, at each step along the way the couples could win gifts like a Jet Ski, kitchen appliances, and vacations. From a programming perspective it was a brilliant fusion of two daytime staples, the soap opera and the game show. The few critics who bothered to review the show apparently only did so because they were dismayed by the shameless absurdity of the show, and the seeming desperation of NBC for airing the show. Not surprisingly, the reviews were uniformly negative and insulting. Mike Drew in the *Milwaukee Journal* suggested, "In the sad history of TV stinkeroos, perhaps nothing equals *Wedding Day* for pure noxiousness." NBC ran five episodes in a week-long trial run, with a plan to evaluate the show's performance for a possible full season in the future. Unfortunately for NBC, *Wedding Day* did not live up to expectations, nor did the critical panning bode well; and resultantly, *Wedding Day* was never seen again after its initial pilot week. Putting negative reviews and a short run to the side, it is very easy to view *Wedding Day* as an early antecedent to later reality shows that wallow in the intimate details of their subjects' personal moments (*Bridezilla*, *A Wedding Story*, *A Baby Story*, *Teen Mom*, etc.). However, although clearly a narrative precursor, this show appears highly truncated, antiseptic, and tame in scale and scope when compared to its distant progeny.[13] Coincidentally, a month after the *Wedding Day* experiment, approximately 750 million people around the world were enthralled with another real-life wedding, that of Diana Spencer and Prince Charles of England.

NBC's primary reality competitor, ABC, experimented with two pilots in 1981–1982, which revealed a new subgenre, the reality crime show. The first of these was *Shoot, Don't Shoot* (May 1982), hosted by well-known TV actor Peter Falk. At the core of the show was an effort to debunk the sensationalized depiction of TV police shows, particularly the use of deadly force. The pilot featured nine scenarios in which viewers had to make a split-second decision whether to discharge their imaginary weapon. In some cases the use of deadly force was justified; in others it would have been excessive, as with a male who repeatedly refused to stop walking and then reached for something quickly; as it turned out the man was hearing impaired. It was just as sensational in its own way as any TV cop show, but it did get the viewer closer to the reality of being a police officer. It was the type of point-of-view narrative that a later crime reality show, *Cops* (1989–), would turn out for more than two decades.

The second crime reality experiment, *Counterattack: Crime in America*, ran for four weeks in May 1982. Host George Kennedy oversaw a multipurpose program that was designed to provide crime prevention tips, but also to elicit help in solving unsolved crimes across the nation. ABC publicity described the show as "a reality crime prevention series based on We-Tip, a national anti-crime organization operating a toll-free hotline by which citizens can anonymously report criminal activity." Each episode would feature reenactments and reports on crimes or wanted fugitives, with the We-Tip phone number prominently featured. It was real stories, real criminals, and an opportunity to help real people make a difference. Unfortunately, *Counterattack* was aired in the Sunday 7 PM time slot opposite ratings powerhouse *60 Minutes*, which contributed to a ranking at the very bottom of the Nielsen charts. Though *Counterattack* would not be picked up for the fall schedule, you can once again see the blueprint for future successful reality crime shows like *America's Most Wanted* (1988–2011), *Unsolved Mysteries* (1987–2008), and *Rescue 911* (1989–1996).[14]

Counterattack was the second attempt by ABC to challenge *60 Minutes* with a reality program. In April 1982, the network had a month-long trial run for a series called *Inside America*. The show was hosted by TV icon Dick Clark, with contributions from soap opera star Michael Damian, movie critic Rex Reed, football star Lynn Swann, and 1980 Miss

Universe Shawn Weatherly. The show resembles a chef's salad of elements that had appeared on other reality shows in the previous three years. As Dick Clark described it, "Our forte is—well, you might call it fluff. It's an amalgamation of *Real People, Entertainment Tonight, Two on the Town, Look at Us*, and *People* magazine." *Inside America* had lower-tier TV celebrity participation, as well as typical stories on lifestyle and cultural trends. The series also polled public opinion on issues ranging from semi-serious to the completely ridiculous: Should the government restrict the importation of foreign cars? If you could, which one of the Ten Commandments would you eliminate? Who is sexier, Burt Reynolds or Tom Selleck? And even though it was aired on Sunday nights at seven, the show did have some jiggle TV and risqué elements, usually including Shawn Weatherly, and segments such as a test to determine "how good a lover you are." *Inside America*, and *Counterattack* for that matter, skirted the bounds of a Federal Communications Commission mandate that required the first hour on Sunday evenings to be "designated for children, public affairs programs or documentary programs." Those considerations would matter little, as *Inside America* finished as one of the lowest-rated shows for the entire season, leaving no chance for future airings.[15]

Despite the multiple failed pilots and series, ABC still had one of the two successful prime-time reality shows, *That's Incredible*. In its third season, *That's Incredible* was no longer a top ten show, but it could still land respectably in the middle of the Nielsen ratings each week. However, just like NBC, ABC could not break through with a second prime-time reality show success. The other major network, CBS, essentially abandoned its reality efforts, with one exception. The Tiffany Network attempted to capitalize on the achievement of *60 Minutes* by airing a half-hour daytime newsmagazine show called *Up to the Minute*. The show had a rotating cast of hosts from *60 Minutes* and CBS News, with some serious subjects combined with celebrity interviews, feel-good stories, lifestyle trends, and current events. It was not *60 Minutes*, but it was not *PM Magazine* either. The show lasted for four months, and slowly faded away when local affiliates balked at running the show in the late afternoon when they could air more appealing syndicated programming.[16]

The local CBS affiliates who chose not to air *Up to the Minute* did so because of the booming syndication marketplace, which offered a great variety of programming from which to choose. In 1981–1982 the reality genre continued as a major force in syndicated television with several new offerings. *Look at Us* was a weekly half-hour program created and produced by George Schlatter and hosted by veteran character actor Richard Crenna. Not surprisingly, the program was modeled on *Real People*, with a mixture of semi-serious segments and superficial fluff. On the serious side, there were stories on the controversy over the side effects of Agent Orange; sexism; homelessness on Skid Row; acid rain; the epidemic of shoplifting; the rising tide of violence in American life; sexual surrogates; and the controversial Reverend Sun Myung Moon's Unification church. On the lighter side there were segments on female body builders; the life of a Las Vegas showgirl; the world's happiest man; the world's weirdest zoo; the largest American flag; and various contests, conventions, and other unique accomplishments.

The show's promotional material made a clear link with *Real People*, and sounded like it could have been lifted from NBC publicity:

> If you think prime-time "reality" television is something only the networks can afford to produce, think again. . . . Introducing *Look at Us*, new from George Schlatter, the man who practically invented the form. . . . Here is the humor and spirit of America. A national magazine that can take a hard hitting look at subjects of vital interest, then turn around and laugh with the best of them.

Look at Us was syndicated to over 120 stations across the nation, usually airing in early evening on Saturday or Sunday. The initial season comprised twenty-four episodes, each of which was repeated once. Unfortunately, the imprimatur of George Schlatter and a reliable creative formula were not enough, as *Look at Us* did not perform well in local ratings. When the time came for local stations to purchase a second season of the show there were not enough interested buyers to make it profitable to produce another twenty-four episodes.[17]

In September 1981, one of the most successful programs in the history of syndicated television, *The People's Court*, premiered on over one hundred stations across the country. *The People's Court* applied the reality formula to small claims court disputes. Producers Stu Billett and Ralph Edwards found real-life small claims suits and asked the people involved if they would like to have their cases aired on television and agree to abide by the decision of the retired judge. Aside from the often petty disputes, the centerpiece of the show was Judge Joseph A. Wapner. Episodes opened with a staccato theme song and a voice-over detailing the cases of the plaintiff and defendant, while attaching a witty title to each dispute, such as "The Frat Boy v. the Young Lady," "The Vanished Volkswagen," "The Case of to Hell and Back in a Limo," and "The Case of Pop Goes the Porsche." These court cases featured bickering families, disgruntled lovers, angry customers, intractable business owners, and others who defy categorization. Promotional advertisements emphasized the centrality of the reality component, suggesting the show will "take you inside a courtroom where real plaintiffs and real defendants argue real cases in front of a real judge."

The promotional ads were stating what was very obvious when watching the show. The people featured were inescapably real; they were inarticulate, inconsiderate, angry, obnoxious, selfish, sincere, honest, and respectful. In short, they were all the various things people are at given moments in their lives; they were real; it just so happened to be in front of a TV camera, on a stage-set courtroom. In many ways it was the ideal reality show; the production was fixed in a studio, the "performers" came to the show, the costs were standard for each episode, and there was an endless source of people from which to draw. In economic terms it was a money-making machine, if it could take hold in a competitive daytime television market.

Almost every critique of *The People's Court* linked it with what many mistakenly thought was a dissolving reality trend, which had begun with *Real People* and *That's Incredible*. The reviews of the show ran the gamut, with some calling the show "an educational experience" and "terrific entertainment." Legal experts even weighed in, some lauding *The People's Court*'s ability to increase public awareness of court proceedings, while others worried that the "quick money" and pettiness of some of the cases would drive up the number of frivolous legal suits. Other critics, like John J. O'Conner in the *New York Times*, unknowingly presaged the main vein of early twenty-first-century American culture when *The People's Court* inspired him to say, "People will agree to anything evidently for a few moments in the television spotlight." *The People's Court* was an immediate success, heading to the top of local daytime ratings, beating out the entrenched game shows and talk shows. With the 1981–1982 season, *The People's Court* began a twelve-year run as a syndicated stalwart. Judge Wapner became a well-known reality celebrity during the 1980s, famously serving as a plot device in the 1988 film *Rain*

Promotional ad for *The People's Court*, November 4, 1981, *Newsday*, 69.

Man, in which Dustin Hoffman's character has to watch "Wapner" at a designated time every day or risk a behavioral breakdown. Equally noteworthy is the collection of narrative clones that followed *The People's Court* over the subsequent years and decades.[18]

The 1981–1982 season included the revival of a 1950s reality-themed program, *You Asked for It*. The reborn show was not so originally entitled: *The New You Asked for It*. The series was a thirty-minute daily, or for some stations weekly, program hosted by comedian and impressionist Rich Little, with a collection of field reporters and a special segment with Jack Smith, a host of the original show, who introduced classic segments from the past. As with the original, the new show relied on viewers writing in to request specific segments. For their efforts viewers received $50, a mention of their name and location, and on occasion an appearance on the show. The style and setting for the show would feel very familiar and comfortable for viewers, with Rich Little on a stage, hosting and introducing the stories in front of a studio audience. The unusual wrinkle was Rich Little, a renowned impressionist, slipping into impressions of figures like John Wayne, Johnny Carson, and Dean Martin, to name a few. Although the allegedly unique premise was viewer-generated stories, the segments were very similar to those seen on *Real People*, *That's Incredible*, and *PM Magazine*. The segments were a broad mix of topics from locations around the world, including a modern-day Tarzan; "Japan's Human Bomb"; the world's strongest traveling salesman; Austria's trout circus; "Kung Fu Movie Star" Jackie Chan; the world's only wild-boar circus; India's ten-ton bellyache; Cambodian tongue spiking, a form of religious martyrdom; chainsaw sculptors; the Japanese juggler king; a house made of junk; various unique occupations; and many others. The show ran in syndication for two years, but in the second season the scope of the show and its budget, alleged to be $10 million in season one, were scaled back, and Rich Little was replaced by Jack Smith.[19]

The elasticity of reality TV was clearly on display in syndication, with a melding of *Real People* and a professional advice column in the form of a show called *Couples*. Premiering early in 1982, this half-hour daily show featured Dr. Walter Brackelmanns, a practicing psychiatrist who specialized in family relationships. The show's creator and executive producer Arnold Shapiro, an Emmy and Academy Award winner, had originally produced a failed pilot for a similar program in 1978, before the reality wave hit. It was not until after *Real People* and its cohorts thrived that *Couples* was picked up for syndication in just over twenty markets around the country. The premise of the show was fairly basic: a couple would appear in a small studio and reveal intimate, if not embarrassing, details about the conflicts that plagued their relationships. The term "couples" was used in a liberal way, as the couples represented people who were married, dating, divorced, or had some other familial relationship, such as a wife and her mother-in-law, or a step-parent and children; and there even was an episode with a gay male couple.

More often than not, the couple's problem revolved around sex, trust, or money, the issues that shape most relationships. A sample of the topics addressed in the first season includes a young unwed mother and her lover arguing about infrequent sexual activity; a husband with uncontrollable jealousy toward his wife, who happened to work as a nude dancer; a physically abusive alcoholic husband; a man who was no longer attracted to his wife after she had gained weight; a woman who suggested her husband was an inadequate lover; and a continual string of quarrels over sex, fidelity, and finances. The format of the show was fast-paced, with the couples introduced, their issues revealed, the advice offered by Dr. Brackelmanns, and a quick happy-ending resolution—all of which occurred in twenty-five minutes. The alacrity with which people's concerns were addressed led to criticism from the medical community to the effect that the show simplified psychotherapy, creating the impression that some emotional or psychological problems can be fixed quickly and easily. Brackelmanns tried to shield himself by suggesting that what he did on the show was "counseling" as opposed to professional therapy. In fact, the show was very clear in what it was offering during its daily introduction:

> For many of us facing problems, counseling is still frightening, embarrassing, or mysterious. We hope to remove the mysteries of what actually goes on behind the doctor's door. We hope you can benefit from the real encounters you are about to see—as couples struggle to resolve their conflicts. Remember, these people are not acting, what you are about to see is real.

In truth, it was the real stories and intimate details that were the draw for viewers, not a desire to better understand psychotherapy. As for TV and cultural critics, they continued to link almost every reality-themed show back to *Real People*, while simultaneously marveling at the lengths to which people will go to get on TV. As John J. O'Conner of the *New York Times* opined, "The willingness of ordinary people to expose themselves in whatever manner before television cameras is little short of astounding."[20]

The realm of relationships, or rather potential relationships, was the basis for another syndicated reality show, *Singles Magazine*. This show focused on the world of single Americans, sixty million of them, according to the show's promotional material, in the search for love. The series was hosted by Paul Ryan and was typically intended to be aired on weekends, ideally in a late-night time slot. In each half-hour show, four single men and women were given the opportunity to present what was in essence a televised personal ad. Each subject was allotted approximately two minutes to define their outstanding attributes and state what they desired in the opposite sex. Predictably, the people on the show emphasized their intellectual, emotional, and, for some, physical gifts. As for what they found appealing in the opposite sex, some were appropriately superficial; for example, "Hi, I'm Randi, and if you can bench-press two hundred pounds, write me care of this station," or "Hi, I'm Marjorie, I fly and model and act for a living. If you're a guy who likes dancing and knows how to take care of a woman, write me care of this program."

In addition to the personal ads, *Singles Magazine* also had featurettes focusing on celebrity singles, which the show called singlebrities, and self-help tips for dating, such as how to dress for a date, how to kiss with confidence, and general sexual etiquette. The intended appeal of the show was evidently the sexual atmosphere, but the fact that real people were used made the featured singles and dating lifestyle appear much more accessible. *Singles Magazine* would run on stations across the country for one season of original episodes, but it left no lasting cultural impact. Nonetheless, the reality-themed dating show would proliferate by the end of the 1980s and early 1990s, making *Singles Magazine* an evolutionary stage in this emerging subgenre.[21]

The sexually themed reality show had content potential that could not be fully explored within the restrictions of free broadcast television. However, the blossoming cable television world offered unique opportunities to stretch the bounds of adult reality. In 1981–1982, there were two of these shows broadcast on pay TV, *Everything Goes* and *Candid Camera*. *Everything Goes*, aired on the nascent adult-entertainment-themed Playboy Channel, was essentially a game show with one unique component, real people stripping off their clothing. The show featured one male and one female contestant, who appeared in theme costumes (pirate, Victorian, 1920s, etc.), as well as a cast of three celebrities. The non-celebrities had to match the celebrity answers; when they failed to match, the contestants had to remove a piece of clothing, all the way down to skimpy underwear. There was also a special round where beautiful models would parade on set and stand behind a portioned wall with removable cutouts that would reveal their breasts and buttocks. The contestants would have to match body parts to the models they had seen. Of course the winner was really not important, and it certainly was not why viewers tuned in. It was the nudity; particularly, it was the draw of seeing real people, maybe even the people next door, strip down.

A similar enticement must have prevailed for *Candid Camera*, which was reborn as a periodic special program on Home Box Office (HBO). Obviously, *Candid Camera* was an old show, but it had a premise that could be revitalized. The show's creator, Allen Funt, had produced a *Candid Camera*–themed motion picture entitled *What Do You Say to a Naked Lady?* (1970), which featured *Candid Camera*–style scenarios with strategic nudity designed to fluster, frustrate, or confuse the unsuspecting subjects. The HBO version utilized that formula, but with a little more nudity and more sexually suggestive scenarios. For example, there were segments using a topless window washer; an actress playing a hearing-impaired woman undressing in front of a man who came to believe she thought he was doctor, leaving him to explain that he was not before she was naked; and an alleged hidden-camera commercial where costumers were asked to use a new contraceptive. The real people subjects in these setups were not naked, but in the 1990s HBO would go on to specialize in producing sexually explicit material featuring real people, most notably *Real Sex*.[22]

As mentioned in earlier chapters, the reach of reality media was so broad that even the more thoughtful and intellectual Public Broadcasting Service (PBS) found some of its programming being lumped in with the reality wave. Such was the case in 1982, with the PBS production of *Middletown*. This six-part miniseries aired in March/April on most PBS stations across the country. The film was a document of the town of Muncie, Indiana, inspired by the groundbreaking study of Robert and Helen Lynd. Cameras followed various citizens of Muncie using a "fly on the wall" perspective designed to provide some genuine insight into the lives they lived. It was intimate documentary filmmaking, and it was also reality TV, but it was closer to early twenty-first-century reality, on par with modern shows that allegedly depict the daily lives of its subjects. It was also more realistic than any other reality show in the early 1980s or any on the air in the twenty-first century. In fact, it was so realistic that one of the episodes was withdrawn from broadcast because PBS had developed reservations about the graphic depiction of high-school teens using profanity, smoking marijuana, engaged in frank sexual discussions and an interracial relationship. It would be years before that episode would be broadcast unedited by PBS. [23]

By 1982, the annual assessments of the state of network television had evolved into an exercise in managing disappointment, and exploring the ways the big three networks were trying to stem the tide of audience erosion. These concerns were not industry secrets; major publications like *U.S. News and World Report* and *TV Guide* were writing about viewer loss and posing questions like, "Is the Network Heyday in TV Coming to a Close?" Collectively the networks had lost approximately 10 percent of their viewers since 1977. Ironically, even though the networks were losing viewers, industry polling suggested that overall, people were watching more hours of TV than ever before. Even more troubling was that the problems were not subsiding or leveling off; in fact, each year saw new challenges emerging. In August 1981, Music Television (MTV), a channel dedicated to music videos, premiered on cable stations across the nation. This development was guaranteed to cost the networks viewers in the vital thirteen-to-twenty-five demographic. That factor, combined with new home video game consoles and declining costs for those systems, meant the networks were starting to lose viewers at an escalating pace. At the same time, older viewers were being peeled away by the growing volume of local independent station programming; the increasing selection of pay TV options, including adult programming; and the continued spread of videocassette recorders and rented Hollywood films. [24]

In 1981, the major networks faced a challenge that was not nearly as easy to quantify or assess statistically. Morality monitoring and even censorship were not unique in the creative arts, but network television faced an emerging threat that eddied up from the emerging neoconservative movement of the early 1980s. The driving force behind this threat was Donald Wildmon, an evangelical minister from Mississippi. As a committed Christian and father of four, Wildmon had become deeply concerned about the volume of sex, violence, and encouragement of nontraditional values. In response, in 1977, he created an organization called the National Federation of Decency. The organization, based in Mississippi, had 450 members who volunteered to monitor and fill out reports logging immorality or offensive themes on network TV. By early 1981, Wildmon's grassroots operation had gained enough popularity that he was invited to join forces with Reverend Jerry Falwell, the mind behind the Christian organization known as the Moral Majority. In 1981, the totalitarian-sounding Federation of Decency was exchanged for the Coalition for Better Television (CBTV), which Wildmon claimed had affiliation with 1,300 religious and civic organizations around the country. The CBTV was on the lookout for general immorality, but it also had a specific list of issues that its members continually monitored. Not coincidentally, the themes that raised the greatest concern were those that were important to Christian evangelicals and the cohort increasingly referred to as the New Right, including drug use; homosexuality; sexual promiscuity, both adult and youthful; abortion; adultery; and that amorphous realm of anti-American opinion.

The CBTV, having failed to gain entry into the corridors of network headquarters, decided to force its way into the discussion by threatening a boycott of programs containing offensive material. This was not a mild threat if you believed that millions of the CBTV/Moral Majority members would actually adhere to a broad boycott. Wildmon claimed to have spoken with major television advertisers who were planning to withdraw their sponsorship of tainted shows. One of the largest television sponsors, Procter & Gamble, had already begun modifying its commercial spending in advance of the proposed boycott. Needless to say, Wildmon was not well received in the television industry, being called "a Hitler with a hit list" and "the Ayatollah of the airwaves." However, the threat of a network-wide boycott never fully materialized in 1981; and in early 1982, the Moral Majority publically bowed out of any organized TV boycott. Nonetheless, Wildmon carried on in his crusade, ultimately targeting NBC quite specifically in March 1982, calling for a viewer and sponsor boycott. The most inflammatory program for the CBTV on NBC was *Love, Sidney*, a show that featured an openly homosexual character, played by Tony Randall, who in the show had some responsibility for raising a child. The CBTV also cited shows such as *Hill Street Blues* and *Saturday Night Live*; and certainly Donald Wildmon would not have been happy with the more jiggly or sexually suggestive segments on *Real People*. It is ironic that *Real People*, which was a promoter of some of the

New Right ideals (patriotism, small towns, anti-elitism), now had a different branch of the neoconservative movement boomeranging back at it by attacking the show's home network.

The CBTV boycott lasted throughout 1982, but NBC chairman Grant Tinker dismissed the effect of the boycott, saying "it had no discernable impact," and "actually, our ratings are up a little since before the boycott began." No self-respecting artist concerned about their creative legacy is going to admit to voluntarily acquiescing to a pressure group; and that was certainly the case with executives and producers at NBC and the other networks. Nonetheless, industry observers noticed a marked decline in sexual content and other allegedly offensive themes. This change in world view was particularly evident at NBC, which began a network-wide campaign against drug use by young people. *Real People* was not immune to these pressures, but the adjustment for an anthology reality show was much easier than for scripted fare; and the show was already slowly moving toward more feel-good news, public advocacy, and infotainment by the end of the 1981–1982 season. [25]

4

SLIDING DOWN THE TV FOOD CHAIN: SYNDICATED REALITY

1982–1983

Most television seasons begin with great optimism for all the major networks and the participants in the prime-time schedule. That hopeful confidence manifests itself in various ways depending on where a series is in its artistic life cycle. New shows earnestly strive to break through the mass of options to establish themselves as viable series; the top-rated shows work to maintain their audience share and guarantee as long a series run as possible; and older, declining shows attempt to recapture some of the magic that produced the initial success. Entering its fifth season, *Real People* found itself slowly sliding into the latter classification. Although the show had come into the new season as the National Broadcasting Company's (NBC) highest-rated show from the previous season, it had fallen from its earlier ratings peak to outside the top twenty shows, and the relative weakness of a distant-third-place network meant that *Real People*'s highest-rated designation was something of a hollow accomplishment. *Real People* would need a strong season to solidify its position and ensure a longer life.

The prospects for a successful year were shaded in doubt, due in large part to the most significant cast change in the history of the series. In January 1981, John Barbour was relieved of all responsibilities when his contract was not renewed by George Schlatter. It was a substantial move. Barbour was not just an original host from episode one forward, but he was also pivotal in the creation of the show, as well as a coproducer and writer. However, George Schlatter owned the show, and when the two men could not coexist, Barbour was removed. The reason for the spilt was speculated upon in the entertainment press, with several writers conjecturing that it was a clash of two prodigious egos, neither of whom was timid about speaking his mind. Schlatter and NBC intimated that Barbour had become distracted by other projects, notably his efforts to produce and sell into syndication a reality-themed game show, as well as shopping around a potential feature film idea. Barbour responded succinctly, "That's a bunch of bull." The former host also suggested that the show was now doomed to failure because he would be impossible to replace: "That show was my vision. Most of the best shows I wrote and edited." In what became a very public spat, Schlatter sarcastically countered by saying, "I'm in awe. His talents are almost as awesome as his modesty." Schlatter further dismissed Barbour's claims by noting that 150 people worked on the show, and therefore no one person could claim that much credit. Barbour fueled the feud with a snarky retort: "A lot of guys contributed to painting the Sistine Chapel too. One guy mixed the paints; one guy held ladder—well George held the ladder while I painted. Now I'm gone and he's still holding the ladder." Barbour was right about one thing: he had lost whatever battle of wills existed between the two. However, he was a loser who left with a smile on his face, as he was reported to be entitled to 10 percent of *Real People*'s future syndication earnings.[1]

George Schlatter responded to the elimination of Barbour by adding new talent and shifting the established hosts. To replace Barbour, Bill Rafferty was moved from "roving reporter" and made a permanent studio host. The studio hosts would be Sarah Purcell, Skip Stephenson, Byron Allen, Fred Willard, Bill Rafferty, and Peter Billingsley part-time. To fill Rafferty's slot as dedicated field reporter Schlatter chose Kerry Millerick. It was an interesting but revealing choice, as Millerick had previously been a correspondent on reality competitor *That's My Line*, and a "light news" reporter on a local Los Angeles TV station. It was a small indication of how transitive the worlds of news/infotainment and reality had become. When pressed by reporters about whether participating in reality represented a degraded professional status, Millerick mirrored the looming demise of television news, saying, "News has become entertainment, especially after the first five minutes. How can you say you're doing news when you're giving makeup tips and cooking hints. They've watered down the news now so that it's acceptable to everybody." What Millerick did not mention was that *Real People* and its reality brethren had helped to facilitate the decline of television news. In fact, season five would have *Real People* sliding into even more traditional "harder" news stories.[2]

Despite the personnel maneuvering, the creative formula of season five was very similar to earlier seasons. There were still video segments introduced by the studio hosts; and there was audience participation in the form of opinions on topical issues, witty comments, and viewer mail, including funny photos and newspaper typos or absurdities. In most respects, the shuffling of the hosts had very little impact on the presentation or content of *Real People*.

One of the more successful and well received episodes of season four had been the ninety-minute special dedicated to New York City. For the new season, George Schlatter expanded upon that premise by taking the cast on a long-distance train trip from Los Angeles to Chicago. The results of the trip would be broadcast as a trilogy over the first three episodes of the season. The special featured the hosts on an Amtrak train named the Real People Express, where the cast would introduce pre-taped stories. In essence, the train's dining car acted as a mobile studio. Often, the stops along the route were coordinated with the locations of the pre-taped segments. Joining the hosts on the train were some of the subjects featured in the stories, who would be briefly interviewed. It was a brilliant idea, in that the arrival of the train and the associated local media stories were strong promotion for the show, but it also illustrated so much of what *Real People* had come to represent. It was a nostalgic slice of Americana. The whistle-stop train tour brought to mind politicians from William Jennings Bryan to Harry Truman stopping at big and small towns and speaking to crowds of all sizes, in a time before radio and, later, television. Not surprisingly, that is just what the *Real People* cast did, stopping at locations of various sizes and having their pictures taken by local newspapers and television stations, while mingling with their assembled fans. Many Americans likely remembered earlier cross-country train tours to promote Hollywood films, or to encourage the sale of war bonds or food drives to feed needy people around the world. The Real People Express tour also celebrated small-town America—the areas that the interstate highways bypassed, particularly the western and midwestern communities, those separated both geographically and philosophically from the elitist coastal cities; two narrative elements upon which the show had consistently relied for content over the previous four seasons.

The first leg of the trip, detailed in the ninety-minute season premiere, took the Real People Express from Los Angeles to Fort Worth, Texas. At stops along the route local towns turned out with high-school bands, cheerleaders, politicians, and keys to the city. In San Antonio, Texas, almost twenty thousand people were waiting to meet the train at 5 AM, a result that was repeated at several stops along the way, including El Paso, Texas, and Phoenix and Tucson, Arizona. In a nod to history, during the opening episode the cast was shown being accosted by train "desperadoes" acting out a Wild West standard. There were also the characteristically unique personality studies, such as Hub Cap Annie, who roamed the rural highways looking for lost hubcaps, which she sold to make a living; Red Neck Granny, a woman who talked to lonely truckers on a CB radio throughout the night; Pamela Wingo, a female train engineer in a male-dominated profession; and a karate team that used kicks, punches, and chops to demolish a full-sized house in twenty minutes. There were also visits to small communities like Buffalo Gap, Texas (population: 389), where the town had an all-female volunteer fire department; as well as the unusually named town of Why, Arizona, thusly named because of its location at a "Y" intersection of a rural state highway.[3]

The second leg of the trip followed the Real People Express from Texas into the center of the nation toward the outskirts of Chicago. The whistle-stops included Dallas, Texas; Saint Louis, Missouri; and Little Rock, Arkansas, where ten thousand people turned out in 85-degree heat at 2 AM. The segments ran the gamut, including the "Most Perfect Body contest"; the singing M&M Girls, a senior citizens music group ranging from sixty to eighty-seven years old; the famous Budweiser Clydesdales; an Abraham Lincoln look-alike contest; and a serious segment on a lunch program for disadvantaged children.

The third portion of the season-opening trilogy was an hour-long episode dedicated to Chicago, Illinois, and surrounding communities; essentially a remake of 1981's New York episode. The city opened its arms to the show, with the cast greeted by a marching band and a parade. The hour-long episode was staged in front of a crowd of several thousand people in the cavernous lobby of the Hyatt Regency hotel. The featured segments were typical of the *Real People* canon. A day in the life of

Mayor Jane Byrne was prominently featured, including legislative sessions, constituent service, and several festivals and block parties. There were other segments with a Chicago flavor; for instance, a feature on Morey Greenblatt, the "swimsuit king of Chicago"; the Billy Goat Tavern, made famous in *Saturday Night Live*'s "Cheeborger-Cheeborger" sketch; a visit to Wrigley Field, home of the Chicago Cubs; a group of Chicago police officers who dressed as clowns to entertain sick children; and a visit with the Chicago Bears.[4]

The Real People Express was clearly a programming gimmick designed to reconnect with viewers and spur ratings, but it did not come off as a hokey contrivance or populist pandering; rather, it was what the show had always been from its inception. However, in a portent of its future, the ratings for the three-part road trip did not rise substantively; the season's opening episode did not even win its 8 PM time slot. Nonetheless, the seemingly eternally optimistic George Schlatter put a positive spin on the effort: "It was wonderful! Great! Everybody in television ought to do it. There's a lot of love alive in this country, and I think we may be in better shape than we think."[5]

After the season-opening trek across the heartland, *Real People* settled back into the familiar surroundings of a Burbank studio, with the hosts presiding over the standard variety of segments. The eccentric and unique, from human to animal, were liberally sprinkled throughout the season. There was a family who lived in a county jail because the husband/father was the sheriff in the community; a man who maintained and lived alone in an isolated lighthouse; a couple with a passion for the color purple, whose house, clothing, furnishings, and everything else in their lives was colored purple; a college professor who claimed he could create nutritious food out of garbage; a four-year-old body builder with a shockingly muscular body; and a man who had transformed his automobile into a vehicle that looked like a hippopotamus, with a segment in which the car was shown drawing slack-jawed incredulous stares as it drove down the street. There was an extended segment on the "crazies and cuckoos" from Key West, Florida, with visits to bars, festivals, haunted houses, and various other intriguing spots. An old favorite from earlier in the series, Captain Sticky, made a return appearance; this time the superhero consumer advocate was getting married, with *Real People* there to film the festivities. The wedding had a collection of guests, well-wishers, and fans who turned out to see the 350-pound Captain in his skintight costume, as well as his female assistants, the Stickettes, and of course his vehicle, a customized stars-and-stripes specially equipped Sticky Mobile.

The unique—some might say obsessed—collector was represented by a massive hat collection; a history-themed telephone collection; and a man with a massive sports memorabilia collection, which coincidentally was becoming a hugely popular and potentially lucrative pastime for millions of people in the 1980s and beyond. Among the more continually reliable and popular segments on the show were those that featured animals with unique qualities or skills. During season five, there was a dog who ran errands for his owner, with the dog shown going from place to place in their small town, an outing that included the dog drinking several beers; there was a full-sized pig who acted as a watchdog; there were dogs who participated in hang-gliding and scuba diving, though these activities were clearly more about the owners' desires, and might even be classified as animal abuse in a later, more sensitive era; there was an allegedly talking cow, who never actually talked, though Fred Willard hilariously did an "interview" with it; and there was a slightly sad segment about a seventy-year-old man and his pet worm.

Running parallel with and occasionally intersecting the eccentric subjects was the crazy contest, the whacky event, and the conventions of those whacky and crazy. *Real People* visited the Peabody Hotel in Memphis, Tennessee, to record a group of ducks that were essentially the mascots of the upscale hotel, as they made a daily march through the lobby to the fountain where they swam. Animals also featured prominently in the National Pig Day celebration, which showcased pig races, beauty contests, calls, and other recreational activities. In the realm of the unknown, there was a feature on the possible existence of Scotland's Loch Ness Monster, a well-worn tale seen on any number of reality-themed and science fiction shows.

There were numerous segments that defy explicit categorization. There was a comic look at a male wet-shirt contest; a San Francisco barber shop that specialized in haircuts and hairstyles for infants; a visit to a midnight screening of the emerging cult film phenomenon *The Rocky Horror Picture Show*, replete with elaborate costumes and sing-alongs; and the Las Floristas Headdress Ball, a Beverly Hills, California, charity event in which wealthy and famous women promenaded while wearing elaborate, even outlandish costumes, all for the benefit of disabled children. Rounding out this subcategory were the seemingly never-ending competitions and contests at which the American people excel. To wit, there were cardboard box races; adult tricycle racing; a wild turkey calling contest; players who shot pool with their noses rather than a cue stick; underwater shopping cart races; a race between teams of construction workers to see which could build a house more quickly; the Chili Hall of Fame inductions; respective championships for Kung Fu martial artists and mechanical bull riders; a stuntman's rodeo; golf played in the snow; and a national championship for college cheerleading teams.

The third prong of *Real People*'s triptych of eccentricity was the unusual occupation or avocation. The "crazy/absurd" occupation likely resonated with many viewers because there was a deep vein of personal independence in the lives of people who did these jobs. While not everyone would want to be a garbologist or a rodeo clown, many people have an unattained dream lifestyle, possibly outside of the mainstream, that has never materialized. Though many of these segments produced raucous laughter, for some in the audience there would be veiled admiration for those who lived their lives the way they wanted—not something that many people could claim. The panoply of jobs and enterprises encompassed a biplane pilot who spread the ashes of the dearly departed from three thousand feet; a man who dressed like King Kong for the entertainment of others, particularly at the Empire State Building; a classical violinist who played for her cows to produce better milk; a trick shot golfer; the fastest bartender in the West; a collection of professional female impersonators; a love witch, who acted as an alternative Cupid; a professional artist in the medium of jelly beans; a florist who delivered dead flowers to willing customers; a senior-citizen couple who operated a mobile disco party business; and a man who rented himself out as a costumed extraterrestrial, comically shown walking the streets of Manhattan in a sci-fi costume offering his services with the novelty song "Flying Purple People Eater" as a soundtrack.

In October 1982, *Real People* featured an extended segment on arguably the most prominent and for many the most annoying cultural fad of the 1980s, the Valley girl. Born in California's San Fernando Valley, the Valley girl phenomenon gained national exposure with the 1982 hit novelty song "Valley Girl," performed by Frank Zappa and his daughter Moon Unit. The fad was marked by a distinctive lexicon of catchphrases, such as "I'm sure," "grody to the max," "gag me with a spoon," "totally tubular," and "totally awesome." The song is in fact a scathing critique of the superficiality and consumerism of the 1980s, embodied in young women affecting this persona. However, many people seemed not to comprehend what was essentially an insult. *Real People* producers looked past this as well, in organizing the "Ultimate Valley Girl Contest." In one of the epicenters of "Val speak," the Sherman Oaks Galleria in the San Fernando Valley, a panel of judges (Sarah Purcell, George Christy of the *Hollywood Reporter*, Fred Willard, Byron Allen, Moon Unit Zappa, and former Miss America host Bert Parks) sifted through over one thousand young girls who hoped to make the top five and compete for the title in a later studio segment. The gathering of the Valley girls and their parents in a mall was the epitome of the 1980s, and no other cultural fad is more linked with that decade. The one person who seemed to sense the alleged ugliness of it all was the person most closely associated with the phenomenon, Moon Unit Zappa, who said, "It's like a nightmare. It's ridiculous that anyone would consciously try to imitate this style, dress up and be proud of it. As far as I'm concerned, it's a bad idea. I just get mad because I'm identified with this thing."[6]

One standard element that appears to have diminished slightly in volume was the sexually themed segment. Though it is hard to confirm because neither George Schlatter nor anyone at NBC would admit to it, the efforts of Donald Wildmon and his supporters may have had a chilling effect on the show's content. Nonetheless, there were several segments that at the very least had some jiggle in them; for instance, the "Most Perfect Body Contest," both male and female; the "swimsuit king of Chicago," who was seen fitting suits for attractive young women; a nude centerfold model who was also a mother of two; a male beauty pageant; the "Miss L.A. Best Body Contest"; and Jell-O wrestling featuring bikini-clad young women. Sexual themes were never an integral aspect of the show, just a tool to draw a certain segment of the audience. But the willingness to reduce that type of content reveals a series that was capable evolving, even if it was out of necessity.

That evolution had *Real People* increasingly reliant on more serious stories, infotainment/news, and the inspirational feel-good genres. As the show had done in previous seasons to counter the more superficial occupation/avocation, it featured more serious jobs, like the female locomotive engineer overcoming inequality in a male-dominated profession; an all-female volunteer fire department; search-and-rescue dogs and their handlers; the work of the American Avalanche Institute, which saved lives and practiced avalanche prevention; and a look at the work of a Los Angeles narcotics squad. The segment on the narcotics squad straddles the line between infotainment and hard news, a barrier breached by *Real People* with increasing frequency during the 1982–1983 season. Exemplars include a segment on Lenny Skutnick, a man who risked his life to rescue victims of an Air Florida crash in the frigid waters of the Potomac River; and a visit to Little Rock, Arkansas, where there was a free breakfast program for disadvantaged children, a segment that also examined the plague of poverty and childhood hunger. Additionally, a large portion of the season finale was dedicated to the issue of child safety, particularly the prevention of child kidnapping and sexual assault. The inspiration for the segment was the tragic case of Adam Walsh, a six-year-old Florida boy who was kidnapped and murdered in July 1981. Since the loss of his son, Adam's father, John, had been on a crusade to increase awareness of child protection and recovery of missing children. With that in mind, *Real People* dedicated a sizable portion of the episode to providing tips on how to protect children, including having children fingerprinted so they could be more easily found if kidnapped. Relative to other *Real People* segments, the missing children story was dark, foreboding, and somewhat depressing. It is also difficult not to feel a twinge of cynicism, as NBC was producing a made-for-TV movie on the Adam Walsh story to be aired in the fall of 1983. Given the usual fare of the series, it is not illegitimate to at least question whether the child safety content was motivated not exclusively by public interests, but also by the promotional opportunities of the segment. Nonetheless, *Real People* would produce similar segments steeped in "news qualities" in its next and final season. [7]

As fundamental as the whacky and wild story was to the success of *Real People*, many in the viewing audience had come to expect and likely appreciate the inspirational or feel-good story regularly featured. The most frequent of these inspirational themes involved someone overcoming perceived obstacles or impediments. Stories pivoting around extremes of age, whether old or young, were an effective way to tug at people's heartstrings. During the 1982–1983 season, senior citizens continued to be popular subjects; for instance, an eighty-eight-year-old nun who ran a safe haven for abandoned or injured animals; a seventy-five-year-old man who was a newlywed and an ultra-long-distance runner; the oldest active Kelly Girl (temporary office worker) in the country; an over-seventy ski club; a look at the Gray Panthers, a sometimes militant advocacy group for senior citizens; a colorful character named Dancing George, an eighty-year-old man who performed all the popular current dances; and an eighty-five-year-old waitress who also had her own rural Oklahoma radio show, which she broadcast from a public telephone booth. Those overcoming more immediate obstacles included a man who ran marathons despite having a pacemaker; a woman with a hearing impairment who was training a "hearing ear dog"; and a feature on the Wheelchair Games, an athletic competition for people confined to wheelchairs. Then there were the heartwarming/feel-good stories, such as a professional dancer who taught ballet to young kids who would never have been exposed to that art form; a woman's tackle football team, where the husbands acted as cheerleaders; the Flippo Morris Tumblers, an acrobatic troupe that helped poor or at-risk children; the Volunteers of America, who collected, fixed, and distributed Christmas toys for disadvantaged families; and a piece on a former homeless man who returned to Skid Row to help the current denizens survive and, ideally, get off the streets.

Patriotism was on display in season five in a number of unabashed flag-waving segments. In Fox Lake, Illinois, Skip Stephenson visited the hyperpatriotic Puppet Bar, an establishment with patriotic animatronic puppets and live parrots, in which every evening the jukebox would play "God Bless America," while patrons sang along and waved small American flags and sparklers. When Skip asked one man why he sang the song, he replied, "Do you believe in America? Do you believe in what it stands for? Did you sing when it was on? That's why I sing, I enjoy it, I get a good feeling inside." The patron described the proceedings perfectly, and much of early 1980s America as well; it was feel-good, reaffirming, and often superficial patriotism, which could conceal genuine problems. Sarah Purcell presented a reverential piece on the highest-ranking female cadet at West Point; particular attention was given to the difficult accomplishment of being a woman at the military academy, not to mention a woman in a position of authority over male cadets. The segment highlighted the difficulties in a somewhat comedic way, but in total it was an encouraging promise of the American dream, and a salute to those willing to serve, male and female. A more somber acknowledgment of recent military service was seen in the story of Tassos Chronopoulos, a man who tirelessly raised money for a memorial to eight servicemen who died in April 1980, while trying to free the American hostages in Iran. Because it was an embarrassing failure for the United States, there was not as much support as might have been expected. Ultimately, Chrono-poulos persevered and an eight-foot white marble memorial was erected in Palos Heights, Illinois, in July 1980.[8]

The remembrance and celebration of veterans had become a trademark of *Real People*, a distinction in which the show reveled, and which it promulgated with another entire episode dedicated to celebrating Veterans Day 1982. The episode was staged in the standard Burbank, California, studio, but the audience was filled almost exclusively with service members and their families. The show opened with a story on the "forgotten few," a term used to describe the servicepeople presently stationed in the demilitarized zone (DMZ) in South Korea. To bolster the spirits of the soldiers, the Dallas Cowboys cheerleaders visited the DMZ during Christmastime to perform and create some holiday cheer and a "little piece of home." The segment was tinged with some sadness that the soldiers were away from home during the holidays, in one of the few "hot spot live fire zones" for the entire American military; but the soldiers seemed happy to see the cheerleaders and also to deliver recorded messages to their loved ones.

The episode made an attempt to insert some goodhearted military-themed humor by featuring funny photos, signs, and short stories designed to illicit laughs from veterans. There was also a filmed segment on a man named Boss Markham, from Dayton, Ohio, who impersonated General George S. Patton. The somewhat cartoonish character was seen dressing and talking like Patton while riding around in a military jeep. There was also a piece on George Baker, who was well known for his widely read *Sad Sack* cartoons, which he created during World War II.

Nonetheless, the episode took on an increasingly and wholly appropriate reverential tone. There was a segment on the Women's Army Corps (WACs), who served during World War II but had received little official recognition, nor were they entitled to the same benefits as male soldiers. The piece appealed for both of those injustices to be remedied, and also introduced surviving WACs seated in the studio audience. There was also a feature on the USS *Laffey*, which served in World War II, surviving a Japanese Kamikaze attack in 1945 and going on to serve for thirty more years. The story revolved around a restoration of the vessel by people who were closely associated with the ship: former shipmates, their husbands and wives, and even widows of deceased sailors. Once again, there were emotional moments and memories from the sailors and their families, some of whom were introduced in the studio audience. Another bittersweet segment introduced Douglas Albert Munro, a young man who died at the Battle of Guadalcanal while saving the lives of a marine unit. For his sacrifice, Munro became the first coast guard serviceman to earn the Congressional Medal of Honor. Many in the audience were brought to tears while loud applause rained down when Albert's mother was introduced in the studio audience.

Though the special episode was dedicated to, and featured, veterans from various American wars, the Southeast Asian wars were prominent. Two segments dedicated to the Vietnam War resonated deeply with viewers at that time, and quite likely still would for contemporary viewers. Appropriate for that contentious conflict, the emotions were more varied in the Vietnam segments. The groundswell of support for Vietnam veterans, and an emerging national guilt for how they were treated, was evident at the moment the episode aired, as that same week the Vietnam Veterans Memorial was officially opened on the National Mall in Washington, DC. It had been a slow and controversial path to that moment, but many Americans were happy the memorial was finally open. However, *Real People* seemed to recognize that a memorial would not fully salve all the wounds of Vietnam veterans, nor would it immediately erase all the sadness, bitterness, and anger felt by many veterans and their families.

The first Vietnam segment acknowledged this truth in the introduction to the piece. Mark Russell and Sarah Purcell, sitting at a desk, highlight these feelings: "Until this memorial, perhaps the least honored veterans of any war are the servicemen from Vietnam. Lacking sympathetic ears from the public and with no government agencies to turn to, they did the only thing they could, they turned to each other." The segment examined the reunion of the "River Rats," a group of fighter pilots who served in the Red River Valley in Vietnam. The men at the reunion have fond memories of their service, talking about the hundred-plus sorties each member flew, and some of the close calls they experienced. But there were also memories of men who had been shot down and killed or taken prisoner of war. A Sarah Purcell voice-over emphasized the genuine bitterness felt by many Vietnam veterans, noting that they "weren't greeted as heroes, rather, they were blamed for fighting in the war by some, blamed for losing by others." The River Rats piece ended in an uplifting way, with a dinner party in which the surviving pilots took up a cash collection for a college scholarship for the children of their deceased comrades.

The other Vietnam-related story had no happy moments in it, just some measured hope for an unlikely future. At the heart of this piece were servicemen who were still considered missing in action (MIA) in Vietnam. It opened in Whittier, California, with the mother of an MIA visiting the cemetery in which she had placed a memorial marker for her son, even though he was not officially dead. In an interview with the mother, one can see the pain and conflict in her face as she describes her son and voices her anger with an American government that has never adequately explained where, why, or how her son went missing. Even more gut-wrenching and revelatory of how toxic that war was to American values are some of her comments about her son and other MIAs: "These boys came from very patriotic families, and you obey the law. My son went to Vietnam because you obey the law; I wish to hell he'd gone to Canada." It is a jarring comment to come from a middle-aged, middle-class mother, who seems to have given up on patriotism. The lack of answers about her son only compounded her bitterness.

The second portion of the segment was a visit to a gathering of MIA families. In an effort to receive and promote collective comfort, as well as to put pressure on the government, these families had forged a bond, determined to work until all of the 2,500 MIAs had been accounted for and returned home. Many in this group were convinced that their loved ones were still alive, and angry that the government was not doing more to find the MIAs. Several of them bitterly admonished the public and media for forgetting 2,500 people; some painfully noted the amount of attention given to the American hostages in Iran, compared to minimal media coverage for MIAs. *Real People* took this call to heart, and used this segment to push people into action. During the segment Sarah Purcell tearfully accepted a bracelet with the name of an MIA on it, and said that it was almost certain that there were some men alive in Vietnam. She issued a call to action for the audience: "The only way to help free them is to convince the Vietnamese we have not forgotten these men, and that we still care." She then provided the address for the Vietnamese UN mission in New York and pleaded with people to write letters making their feelings clear. "They fought for us, now perhaps we can fight for them."

The show came to an end with a rousing ovation from and for the assembled military studio audience. As the picture slowly faded to black, a waving American flag was shown while the "Battle Hymn of the Republic" played. The ending was fairly melodramatic, and would possibly seem satirical if it were used in a different venue. But it was more genuine than not, for a show like *Real People*. As if to put their money where their mouths were, the day after the veterans episode aired, which actually was Veterans Day, Sarah Purcell, Bill Rafferty (a Vietnam veteran himself), Byron Allen, Peter Billingsley, and George Schlatter joined three thousand people riding the Staten Island Ferry to visit the Vietnamese mission in Manhattan. With a film crew in tow, the cast and representatives of the MIAs visited with the Vietnamese ambassador and formally requested information about the unaccounted-for servicemen. The meeting produced minimal results beyond generating some publicity for the MIA cause, but the event was overshadowed by the opening of the Vietnam Veterans Memorial in Washington, DC, as well as the announcement of the death of Soviet Premier Leonid Brezhnev. However, within a year the MIA issue took hold in American culture, with films, television shows, and a social consciousness that would thrive into the late 1980s.

Though the MIA campaign did not produce immediate results, it is reflective of what *Real People* was attempting to become. When asked about some the recent out-of-character efforts of the show, Sarah Purcell summed up season five perfectly: "I'm thankful the show had evolved. Many shows never get the chance. Only this year have we recognized that our possibilities are endless. We've gotten into what I call 'cage rattling' with the MIA and missing children segments."[9] Unfortunately, the changes to *Real People* did not translate into higher ratings; in fact, the show fell further down the Nielsen rankings to number thirty for the season. A major challenge for the series was its 8 PM competition on the American Broadcasting Company (ABC), *The Fall Guy*, starring Lee Majors. It was an action show about a stuntman turned bounty hunter, who is often surrounded by beautiful women. It was not a show that was unique in theme or setting, but neither was *Real People* four years into the reality wave. It is difficult to determine whether it was the success of *The Fall Guy* or some failure of *Real People*, but what is clear is that *The Fall Guy* averaged almost two million more viewers than *Real People* once the two shows were head-to-head; even *That's Incredible* had a higher season rating than *Real People*.

Equally disconcerting was an apparent declining relevance and recognition in the press. The season-opening trilogy garnered some attention from TV writers, as did a few individual stories, like the MIAs and the child safety segments; but in general, *Real People* was not a topic of conversation or interest in the American media. Nonetheless, *Real People* was still the fourth-rated show on NBC, which was still the distant third-place network. Being the fourth-ranked show on a struggling network ensured the series at least one more season in 1983–1984. However, NBC was on the rise, with a stable of scripted programs (*The A-Team*, *Family Ties*, *Cheers*, *Hill Street Blues*, and *The Cosby Show* on the way) that would come to dominate prime-time television, leaving little room for a poorly performing reality show. *Real People* would have one year to reestablish itself and extend the series run. [10]

In the fall of 1982 *Real People* reached an important milestone for any national TV series, particularly significant for a reality show: it began airing reruns in syndication in over one hundred markets across the country. For *Real People* producers it was a financial boon, as the accepted wisdom in the television industry held that the major profits were found in syndicating a show and getting paid for each airing on every station. The syndication of the show was also significant because many industry observers thought that repeats of a reality show would not be as popular as those of scripted shows. Though that assumption would be tested, there were high hopes in the show's production offices. George Schlatter repacked the hour-long *Real People* episodes into a half-hour series called *More Real People*, which would be aired five days a week in local markets.

In the summer of 1982, a controversy emerged that posed the question of what category of show *Real People* belonged in; was it entertainment or documentary? Two local stations, WEWS in Cleveland and WXIA in Atlanta, planned to air *More Real People* in the prime-time access period of 7–8 PM. The Federal Communication Commission's (FCC) Prime-Time Access Rule had established 7–8 PM as a period designated for programming of local origin or documentary and educational programming. The rule also prohibited local network affiliates in the top fifty national markets from airing reruns of network entertainment shows in the 7–8 PM time slot. The two network affiliates were seeking an exemption for *More Real People*, claiming it was a documentary program. A challenge was filed with the FCC by the National Association of Independent Television Producers and Distributors, who benefitted from creating programs for the access hour and feared losing that hour to network reruns of reality programs categorized as documentaries. Ultimately, the FCC refused to take action, essentially noting that it was just two stations, and was not likely to damage the Prime-Time Access Rule. However, it was universally acknowledged by virtually everyone, networks and syndicators included, that *Real People* was in fact an entertainment show. In the larger reality milieu, there were now three and a half hours of *Real People* aired in over one hundred markets across the nation.[11]

NBC continued to tinker around the periphery of reality programming, attempting to find a formula that would work the way *Real People* had four years earlier. In February 1983, the network called upon reality guru George Schlatter, who came up with a show entitled *Magic or Miracle*. The central premise of the program was the investigation of paranormal or psychic abilities. The narrative structure presented a true believer and practitioner, Uri Gellar, pitted against skeptic and debunker James "The Amazing" Randi. The hour-long show featured allegedly gifted psychics being challenged and summarily discredited by Randi and his "investigative style." Schlatter described the special as "the next level of reality programming . . . not a documentary or variety show . . . an entirely different form that presents a lively debate between the psychic community and the scientific community, the believers and the doubters." It was an interesting premise, but it failed miserably as a pilot, finishing as the sixtieth-ranked show out of sixty-one programs aired that week. Not surprisingly, *Magic or Miracle* was not given a second chance to secure a permanent spot on the schedule.[12] In the spring of 1983, NBC experimented with a sports-themed reality show entitled *America's Heroes: The Athlete Chronicles*. Aired in the Sunday 7 PM time slot, it was another attempt by a competing network to chip away at the power of the Columbia Broadcasting System's (CBS) *60 Minutes*. Producer Don Ohlmeyer described the special as "a people oriented show with drama and intrigue." The results were a feature on young children who entered a high-pressure Florida tennis camp designed to produce world-class players; a look at Mark Fidrych, a former Major League Baseball star who was now struggling in the minor leagues; and a speculative piece on what would have happened if Jim Thorpe had been able to win his Olympic medals in 1984, as opposed to having them stripped seven decades earlier for violating his amateur status. This one-hour pilot, hosted by pro football star Joe Theismann, finished last out of sixty-seven shows for the week, and never appeared again. [13]

ABC had slightly better success challenging *60 Minutes* with a reality-tinged program. The ABC effort was an hour-long program named for and based on the classic comic strip created by Robert L. Ripley, *Ripley's Believe It or Not*. The show premiered in September 1982, and was hosted by the slightly offbeat and eerily intense character actor Jack Palance. What made *Ripley's Believe It or Not* a strong reality candidate was that essentially all of the segments on the show were true; remarkable and unbelievable, but true. The show had a more global, exotic feel than *Real People*, but at its core most of the segments were about the odd and unusual practices and achievements of people. The show utilized Palance to introduce filmed segments, which included stories about spectacular events and odd rituals, amazing animal stories, and reenactments of historical events or classic tales from the old *Ripley's* comic strip. Stories from season one included a real-life Dr. Jekyll and Mr. Hyde; walking on hot coals; extreme death rites; Japanese men racing down a mountain on a log; archeological discoveries; crazy weddings; flying snakes; vampire bats; and unique artists. In comparison, *Ripley's* was more like *That's Incredible* than *Real People*, but it fit nicely in the reality genre. Unfortunately, *Ripley's* was up against *60 Minutes*, the number one show on television; consequently, it finished at the bottom ten of the Nielsen ratings almost every week of the season. Despite that deficit, *Ripley's Believe It or Not* would run for four seasons, outlasting both *Real People* and *That's Incredible*. [14]

By 1983, the scope of cable television had broadened quite significantly; with each new cable outlet the demand for original programming accelerated. One of the emerging networks was WTBS (TBS), a local station from Atlanta, Georgia, which had successfully transformed into a "Superstation" available on a large number of cable systems across the United States. TBS' original format relied heavily upon syndicated reruns of classics TV series like *The Andy Griffith Show*, *The Beverly Hillbillies*, and *Leave It to Beaver*. However, by 1983 the Superstation was attempting to incorporate its own brand of programming to differentiate itself from other broadcast cable networks. TBS did not have the cultural cache nor the financial resources of the major networks, so it would have to create original programming with lower production costs while not employing high-priced talent, which of course made reality shows a viable option. To that point, in January 1983, TBS premiered *Portrait of America*, hosted by actor Hal Holbrook. The network's promotional materials framed the series thusly: "On *Portrait of America*, where you'll discover a whole new world of things about our country you never knew before. Each month, host Hal Holbrook profiles a different state, uncovering fascinating things about people and places that make America so unique." The ads also had evocative photos of two young boys walking a country road with fishing rods, featuring a rural train station platform and the bright lights of a city skyline. *Portrait of America* was a mix of *Real People* and Charles Kuralt's "On the Road," and it would run for fifty-four episodes over five years, garnering an Emmy Award for Hal Holbrook.[15]

Portrait of America joined an already existing reality-themed show on TBS, *Nice People*. This half-hour weekly series, which began in 1981, was a reality show in which all the segments were about nice, heartwarming, and happy people, places, and events. It was essentially the equivalent of a news program that only presented good or happy news, rather than bad news. In this case, it appears that the "bad news" was represented by the more sensational or salacious stories on *Real People* and *That's Incredible*, or on local news. Nonetheless, *Nice People* was filled with segments reminiscent of the feel-good inspirational segments often seen on *Real People*. The *Nice People* segments included an adoption agency for children from India; a school for hearing-impaired children; coffee and friendly conversation at Vivian's Café; an orphanage for baby seals; a swimming program for disabled children; and many other uplifting stories. The show ran for three years on TBS, but it made little impact on American culture. However, in the long view of the history of reality TV these two series are early exemplars of original cable reality programming, which by the turn of the twentieth century would be driving the modern saturation of the reality genre on networks such as MTV, Bravo, VH1, Discovery, etc.[16]

The year 1983 also featured a retrospective look back at a proto-reality show, *An American Family*. In August, Home Box Office (HBO) aired an hour-long special on the ten-year anniversary of the 1973 series, entitled *American Family Revisited—The Louds Ten Years Later*. The production was not a re-creation of the original; rather, it was essentially a "where are they now" feature, with some attention paid to what the show meant to American culture, as well as the Louds, and how they felt about it ten years later. As it turned out, most of the family members seemed to have come to terms with their experiences, and moved on with their lives. Though several reviewers compared this special and the original series to the state-of-the-art reality television in 1983, often by referencing *Real People*, *An American Family* still appears very different from any reality-themed show that had aired in the previous five years, save for the 1978 NBC series *Lifeline*. In his review of the program, John Corry of the *New York Times* raised a question about reality programming's past and future: "Where does reality go now? How do you top *Real People*? Its people are real because they can hold their breaths underwater for long periods of time, or do other curious things. The camera pays attention to them just as it paid attention 10 years ago to the Louds. In the new documentary, however, they seem just like plain folks. Television has passed them by." Ironically, ten years after this Corry quote, television would come back around to the *American Family* approach, with shows like *The Real World* shaping the genre. It took twenty years for *An American Family* to be imitated successfully, at in least in format, though certainly not in quality, much to the detriment of American culture. [17]

The biggest hit in the syndication market of the 1981–1982 season had been *The People's Court*. This reality court show ranked near or at the top of syndicated ratings for most of the season, while being broadcast on over two hundred stations across the nation. In the highly competitive and equally unoriginal arena of television, the success of *The People's Court* initiated a spate of new "court shows" for syndication. Many local stations were hoping to schedule a "court block" of programming, pairing *The People's Court* with another court-based reality show. Several options were available for syndication in the 1982–1983 season. *Custody Court* was a series based on the gut-wrenching realm of contested child-custody cases. The show had a mix of reality and reenactment; the cases were real, the judges and attorneys were authentic, but the defendants, plaintiffs, and children were actors. The cases were heard by the judge and argued by the attorneys, while the actors added the drama, often yelling, crying, and emoting effusively. A similar show, produced by Ralph Edwards, one of the producers of *The People's Court*, was *Family Court*. There were several differences in this show. All of the principal players were authentic, including the plaintiffs, defendants, judge, and attorneys, who engaged in real cases. There was also more diversity in the potential cases, as a family court could deal with issues ranging from child custody to juvenile delinquency to alimony/child support. Another hybrid show in this subgenre was *Police Court*, where nonprofessionals acted out cases in front of a real judge; essentially, they were real cases but not the actual principals. These reality court shows were enabled by the elasticity of the form, coupled with people's seemingly insatiable desire to watch other people's problems and misery.[18]

Though it was not explicitly a courtroom reality show, *Lie Detector* utilized one of the tools of law enforcement and the legal profession, the polygraph. This half-hour daily series was hosted by prominent and notorious attorney F. Lee Bailey. The show's promotional material framed it as "reality programming at its most compelling because it deals with deep human emotion." The series' opening narration was even more dramatic, saying the subjects were "putting their stories, their very lives on the line." In each episode the featured subjects, usually between one and three, were introduced and had their narratives, essentially the reason they were appearing on the show, explained to the audience. For the most part, they were there to establish their version of the truth through the use of a lie detector. The mechanics of the show had Bailey asking the relevant questions of the guests to provide some exposition. Following that initial segment, the subjects were ushered into a small glass booth, in which a polygraph examiner, Ed Gelb, hooked people up to the machine and asked the same questions again. After a short commercial break Bailey delivered the results.

The guests on the show varied; there were celebrities, public officials, and average citizens, quizzed on issues that ranged from serious crime and corruption to superficial, even silly subjects. Featured guests on the show included Zsa Zsa Gabor, who was asked if she always married for money; alleged Howard Hughes heir Melvin Dummar, who was proclaiming his legitimacy; Harry Drucker, Ronald Reagan's barber, who truthfully claimed that the president did not dye his hair; professional wrestler Cyclone Negro, who was deemed untruthful when asked whether his occupation was real or fixed; and Major League Baseball player Gaylord Perry, trying to prove he did not throw an illegal spitball. The more serious segments engaged such topics as marital infidelity and embezzlement, and in several episodes murder cases were explored. Exemplars of this variety included Caril Ann Fugate, trying to prove she had been an unwilling accomplice of Charles Starkweather in a 1958 mass murder spree; former Johnson administration official Bobby Baker, who wanted to refute his conviction for corruption; and a collection of others who were accused, convicted, or witnesses in a criminal case.

Lie Detector was syndicated with high hopes for success; it was sold to eighty-three stations across the nation, including twenty-four of the twenty-five largest markets. However, the television critics' assessment of the show was decidedly negative. Tom Shales suggested, "The most a show like *Lie Detector* can hope to be is irresistibly awful, and while it's awful alright, this new syndicated program may prove highly and fatally resistible." Other critics noted the deleterious social consequences of the frivolous use of the polygraph, or they just did not like Bailey, calling him unctuous, pretentious, and tawdry. Equally problematic for *Lie Detector* were several lawsuits, primarily for defamation, filed against the show's producers. Adding to the litany of difficulties, the ratings for *Lie Detector* were disappointing; just four months after it premiered, local stations began canceling the show. By September 1983, there were not enough stations willing to air *Lie Detector*, leading producers to end the production of new episodes. As it turned out, the lawsuits generated by *Lie Detector* lasted longer than the series itself.[19]

The 1982–1983 syndicated season featured a block of game shows that were tinged with reality. The first of these to garner a lot of attention was *That Awful Quiz Show*. This series had an immediate and widely promoted link to *Real People*. The executive producer was John Barbour, late of *Real People*; and the hosts were John and Greg Rice, who had appeared on Barbour's previous series because they were twin dwarves who had made a fortune in real estate. The other reality link was found in the identities of the contestants, all of whom were selected because they had unusual jobs, hobbies, or skills. They included a collector of used game show tickets, a pet psychiatrist, members of the Flat Earth Society, an attractive female Frisbee champion, a professional roommate finder, a song therapist, a professional laugher, a one-man band, and the world champion beer chugger. Not coincidentally, a number of the contestants were former subjects of *Real People* segments.

As for the competition in the show, two-person teams were given $500 to start the competition and allowed to bet on satiric trivia questions. At the end of the show the team with the highest money total was able to play for a grand prize. It is hard to determine exactly from whence the comedy emerged; was it the comical questions, the whacky contestants, or the diminutive hosts, dressed in matching suits and standing on boxes to be eye-to-eye with the contestant teams? The show struggled from its inception: having difficulty signing up the necessary stations to air the show, barely obtaining enough to make it profitable. The title even appeared to be an issue, with a change occurring just before the premiere, in which the *Awful* was dropped, leaving *That . . . Quiz Show*. The series lasted just a few months before stations began canceling their contracts.[20]

As inimitably unusual as was a show with twin dwarf hosts, it was not the most unique or incomprehensible reality-themed show of 1982. That distinction has to be awarded to *So You Think You've Got Troubles*. Remarkably, the host of this show was Jay Johnson, a moderately popular ventriloquist who worked with a dummy named Bob. Jay and Bob had some measure of fame based on their roles in the ABC comedy series *Soap*. This daily half-hour program found its ration of reality in the contestants who came on the show to seek advice for the troubles in their lives. Before they got the advice they were comically debriefed by Bob and Jay. The troubles were not life-threatening, but rather more of the quirky and annoying, and only occasionally of the serious, variety. For instance, there was a couple who wanted advice on how to create a lasting marriage, even though the husband was on his ninth wife; a couple in which the husband was a TV addict and the wife had a transplanted heart, and they had divorced each other once before remarrying; a couple who met while the man was in jail; a psychic who talked to dead celebrities; a man who was regularly visited by ghosts and wanted to stop it; and on the serious side, a girl who wanted to lose weight so badly she wanted her jaw wired shut, and when that failed she turned to bulimia. The experts offering advice were a psychologist, Dr. Joyce Brothers; a minister, Dr. Robert Schuller; and an astrologer, Ruth Revson. After each expert offered their advice the audience would vote on which piece of counsel they liked the best. At that point, the guests came back and guessed which expert the audience had chosen; if they chose correctly they won a collection of prizes. As improbable or ridiculous as the premise of this show was, it was one of the most widely purchased programs in syndication. However, the show never captured a large audience and it disappeared after one season.[21]

NBC also attempted a reality-infused game show entitled *Fantasy*. This daily, hour-long daytime series was hosted by game show stalwart Peter Marshall and well-known actress Leslie Uggams. The central principle of the series involved viewers writing into the show requesting the fulfillment of a fantasy. The "winners" on this show seem to have been chosen based on the combined factors of having an engaging story to tell and a request that was not cost-prohibitive or logistically impossible. According to press reports this show received eighty thousand letters per week, many of which asked for the fulfillment of small fantasies, like a bus ticket, a set of work tools, and winter clothes. But there were also larger fantasies, like a family reunion in Israel, a new kitchen for a viewer's house, and a large family reunion. Reviewers and TV writers attempted to frame *Fantasy* in relation to earlier programs; one scribe called it "a cross between *Real People* and *Strike It Rich*," while another suggested it was a "combination of *Queen for a Day* and *This Is Your Life*, with a dash of *Fantasy Island*." Once again, in these three distinct game shows the elasticity of the reality form is evident; however, as with most genres, finding a truly successful show was difficult. *Fantasy* would not be that hit either; it would run only one original season with summer reruns before it was removed from the NBC schedule.[22]

In the late 1970s and early 1980s, *The Phil Donahue Show* was the leading talk show in daytime television. It featured a daily variety of stories, most of them dealing with the day-to-day issues that daytime viewers were theoretically dealing with in their lives. The topics ranged from broader issues like single parenthood, child rearing, family budgets, and cultural fads to more nuanced topics such as environmental pollution, consumer protection, government fraud, and larger domestic and international social and political issues. Many of the segments straddled the line between news and infotainment/reality, though the show would not be explicitly defined as reality programming. Nonetheless, the trademark of the show is what caused it to exhibit reality tendencies. In every episode Donahue would flit through the studio audience eliciting commentary and personal perspectives from the assembled viewers. It was real people being allowed to voice opinions and engage in the topics. Essentially, it was a more reasonable and measured version of *Speak Up America*. Phil Donahue rode a wave of popularity that made him a national celebrity and the epitome or stereotype of the modern sensitive man. In the late 1980s and beyond, Donahue would be surpassed by Oprah Winfrey, who further personalized, and many would say perfected, the format.

In 1982, there was an effort to match the sensitive reasoned discussion show format with *Tom Cottle: Up Close*. Cottle, a licensed psychologist, hosted this daily half-hour syndicated series, during which he engaged in pseudo-therapy with "average people" who had problems like marital infidelity, family dysfunction, addiction, life-altering phobias, anxiety, and depression. The show's promotional materials described Cottle as "Warm. Caring. Sensitive. Tom Cottle is a man for the 80s." Another component of the show was celebrity interviews, largely with stars from television. By the time the show left the air, the real person element was overshadowed by the celebrity content. However, the reality-based TV talk show would come to play a large role moving forward, and it is clearly evident that in the mid-1980s "real people" guests with increasingly sensational narratives were becoming the key element. [23]

For every show that makes it into syndication there are many proposed syndicated series that never made it past the pilot stage. Nonetheless, the volume and variety of failed shows shed light on the appeal and evolution of specific genres. Reality themes were widely represented in this failed pilot category. In the reality talk show class there was *Getting Personal*, a confessional show where intimate revelations were allegedly legitimized by the presence of a therapist on the set. The show's host, veteran character actor Joseph Campanella, extracted the confessions/conflicts from matched pairs of guests, including married couples, parents and children, boss and employee, and boyfriend and girlfriend. The intimate details were presented in front of a studio audience, who clapped, booed, or hissed at the revelations. Eventually, the audience was asked to vote on who they thought was right, and what direction the couple should take. Intermittently, the show's "guest psychologist" offered advice, insight, and opinion. *Getting Personal*'s promotional material promised, "TV audiences will watch with fascination as pairs of individuals with conflicting attitudes on personal issues air them on this new reality series." The promotional ads were partially accurate. TV audiences would be fascinated by people airing painful and embarrassing problems on a talk show, but it would not be on *Getting Personal*; audiences would have to wait several years before the exhibitionist, sensationalist talk show format exploded, with series like *Sally* (1985), *The Jerry Springer Show* (1991), *Maury Povich* (1991), and *Jenny Jones* (1991). [24]

The dating reality show was represented by a proposed half-hour show called *Singles Only*. In this program single men and women would enter their "stats" (physical traits, hobbies, likes/dislikes, etc.) into a computer, after which they would be matched and sent on a date. The second half of the show would include a recounting of their date. Though this show would not spread across the nation in the 1982–1983 season, it would be retooled by producer Eric Lieber and made available in 1983–1984 as the much more successful series *Love Connection*. There was even an effort to reboot the classic proto-reality show *Queen for a Day*. The promotional campaign promised "an updated and enlightened Queen," but clearly the format of even an enlightened "misery show" would produce a string of sad if not embarrassing revelations. [25]

The syndication of independently produced non-network programming would become an increasingly vital element in the television industry. The value of syndicated fare would become evident as the number of cable networks swelled, thus increasing the demand for content of any kind. The need for programming accelerated throughout the 1980s, particularly after the Reagan-era deregulation of the television industry. The FCC incrementally allowed broadcasting entities to have increased autonomy. The result was an increase in the number of independent stations a single corporate entity could legally own. This allowed for established corporations to expand their holdings, creating new stations that likely would not have existed without the relaxing of FCC rules. Further deregulation in the 1980s eliminated guidelines as to how much commercial time a station could air in an hour, as well as eliminating the "fairness doctrine," which had compelled stations to air a balanced point of view on some topics they broadcast. [26]

Particularly in non-cable broadcasting, reality programming was already beginning to become a preferred option by 1983. Across the nation, local and network-affiliated stations were likely airing thirty-five-plus hours of reality-themed programming each week in their markets. It was not just smaller cities that utilized reality; the largest market in the nation, New York City, had a substantial amount of reality-themed programming. For example, on a random but representative day (Monday, January 31, 1983), there were seven hours of reality across the daily schedule:

9 AM: *So You Think You've Got Troubles*
11 AM: *Hour Magazine*
11 AM: *Candid Camera* (repeats of classic episodes)
11:30 AM: *The New You Asked for It*
12 PM: *Tom Cottle: Up Close*
3 PM: *Fantasy*
4:30 PM: *More Real People*

4:30 PM: *The People's Court*
8 PM: *PM Magazine*
8 PM: *That's Incredible*
11 PM: *Lie Detector*[27]

Given the mass of reality programs filling the airwaves, *Real People* was no longer unique on television. In season six *Real People* would have to offer up not just reality, but a more engaging brand of reality; something to set it apart from the rest and restore its ratings prowess. However, that would not be an easy goal to accomplish.

5

EBB TIDE

1983–1984

Real People entered it sixth season in a desperate state. The show's ratings had declined for each of the previous two seasons; it was facing strong competition in its time slot; and it was no longer a unique programming entity. Consequently, there were several changes made for the 1983–1984 season. Most notably, there was an alteration in the cast of hosts. Fred Willard and field reporter Kerry Millerick were not returning. Willard was not replaced, while the new field reporter was TV character actor David Ruprecht. Fortunately, the show was able to avoid the fate of many faltering shows; it was not moved to another time slot, thus allowing fans to tune in at the familiar time of Wednesday at 8 PM. The basic mechanics of the show remained largely the same as they had been since season one. The hosts, Byron Allen, Peter Billingsley, Sarah Purcell, Bill Rafferty, and Skip Stephenson, introduced the film clips, bantered back and forth, and interacted with the audience. The audience participation element remained very similar to what it had been in previous seasons: viewer mail, whacky photos, typos, and opinions on topical issues, which changed slightly over time depending on current events.[1] *Real People* opened the sixth season the way it had the fifth, with a cross-country trip on the Real People Express. This time the cast was traveling on a train from Chicago to Washington, DC. A ninety-minute season premiere was the first of a trilogy of episodes depicting the events of the whistle-stop tour. On the train with the cast were a number of the subjects featured in the filmed segments. Once again, the train was not just an exercise in nostalgia or fabricated Americana, it was a way for the show and its cast to go beyond the big cities into the heart of the country's small towns. Like the earlier train tour this trilogy presented stories based in locations along the path of travel. The first leg included segments from Ohio, Michigan, and upstate New York. The subjects included a futuristic car that could communicate with the driver—a real-life effort to match the National Broadcasting Company's (NBC) action-adventure show *Knight Rider*; the Silver Belles, a team of precision ice skaters; a sixty-nine-year-old female racquetball champion; a look at the various sports teams from Michigan; a visit to a café where the cook tossed pancakes to his customers; Jerry "Mr. Softball" Burton, who could throw a softball over 100 MPH; and a commentary by Mark Russell exploring the allure of Niagara Falls, including stories of people who voluntarily went over the falls in a barrel.

The second leg of what NBC's promotional material called "television's greatest traveling show" took the cast into upstate New York (Utica, Amsterdam, and Albany) and New England (Pittsfield and Boston). Though the show was on location it still bore the earmarks of its standard anthology format. For instance, there was an eighty-eight-year-old woman who dedicated her life to the protection of the beaver; a reenactment of the Boston Tea Party; a dancer and therapist who insisted that stress and anxiety could be tap-danced away; a theology student who worked part-time as a male stripper; and a punk rock club run by senior citizen Evelyn "Granny" Knoll. The final installment of the Real People Express trilogy took the show into the big cities of New York, Philadelphia, and Washington, DC. In Philadelphia, there was a tour of Independence Hall and a profile of the Philadelphia Bell Ringers, who had been working the city's special occasions for thirty years; and a Temple University professor who stressed the value of learning new languages. There were also personality pieces on New York disc jockey Don Imus and a bikini-clad hot dog vendor, and a feature on investigative reporters and the type of stories they cover. Unfortunately, the whistle-stop tour did not resonate with viewers as NBC would have hoped, as the three episodes finished thirty-fourth, twenty-third, and forty-first in the Nielsen ratings. [2]

Nonetheless, the appearance of the Real People Express and the cast was a popular event for the local citizenry. The arrival of the train was often met by thousands of cheering fans, including five thousand in Albany, New York; ten thousand in Utica, New York; and allegedly thirty-five thousand in Cleveland, Ohio. When asked by a local reporter why he took the show on the road, producer George Schlatter played up the heartland, down-home ethos: "It's a way of getting out and touching people. Television is geared to talking at people. We like to sit down and talk with them." Schlatter then let his pride in the show shine through. "We have had a lot to do with raising the self-esteem of people. We have had a lot to do with raising the level of patriotism in this country. I think it's more than just entertainment."[3]

Real People would return to the road later in the season with a new location and alternative mode of transport in the form of an old-fashioned steam paddle boat traveling down the Ohio and Mississippi Rivers. The boat stopped at Cincinnati, Ohio; Saint Louis, Missouri; Louisville, Kentucky; Paducah, Kentucky; Evansville, Indiana; and Cairo, Illinois, where the cast was greeted by twelve thousand people. Segments featured in the show included a visit to Hannibal, Missouri, Mark Twain's hometown; a tour of Graceland, Elvis Presley's mansion in Memphis, Tennessee, accompanied by recollections from his high-school classmates; a motorcyclist whose sheepdog rode along with him everywhere he went; the "Eagle Lady," a woman who dedicated twenty years of her life to protecting the American bald eagle; a paralyzed man who kayaked down the Mississippi River from Minnesota to Louisiana; and the cast performing a short spoof of *Gone with the Wind*. In an unusual quirk of production, the cast and crew were filmed at the annual German Maennerchor Festival in Evansville, Indiana. However, the actual date of the event was set three weeks before the *Real People Mississippi Queen* steamboat was to arrive. To accommodate the production, the city of Evansville would restage the festival to be filmed several weeks after it originally occurred. The city visitors bureau recognized it was well worth the extra expense to restage the festival, calculating, "To buy a minute on national television costs several hundred thousand dollars. This is free. Absolutely it is worth it." The willingness of an entire town to engage in a "do-over" illustrates the potential for manipulation in reality TV, as well as affirming the overwhelming promotional power of any exposure on the three national networks.[4]

There was one other location-specific episode in the sixth season, which took the show to the Hawaiian Islands. In September 1983, the entire cast and crew boarded the SS *Constitution* and sailed for several ports of call, including Kona, the big island of Hawaii; Kahului, in Maui; and Kauai, Honolulu. The SS *Constitution* had a reputation for romance, as it was featured in the classic Cary Grant/Deborah Kerr film *An Affair to Remember*. It also played a role in the real-life fairy-tale romance of Grace Kelly and Prince Rainier of Monaco, with Kelly using the ship to travel to her grand wedding ceremony in 1956. The romantic legend of the *Constitution* was fitting, as one of the central themes in the episode was the wedding of Sarah Purcell to Robert McClintock on board the ship. In 1983 it was not a common occurrence for TV stars to have their nuptials broadcast for the general public; yet thirty years later it would seem very normal for a reality star to have her wedding ceremony filmed for the world to experience.

The wedding of Sarah Purcell was not the singular focus of the episode; there were a number of stories exploring the exotic locations. Presenting the flavor of Hawaii were segments on world champion sand sculptor Joe Maize; a female outrigger canoe team; Skip Stephenson getting hula lessons; pro surfboarder Buttons Kaluhiokalani giving Sarah Purcell surfing lessons; the cast participating in a traditional luau; comedian Andy Bumatai; the fifth annual Underwater Pogo Stick Championships; and a 1,100-pound pet pig. There were also passing glances at well-known Hawaiian landmarks like the Pearl Harbor Memorial and Volcanoes National Park. For whatever reason, whether it was the eternal appeal of Hawaii or the novelty of watching a celebrity wedding, sixteen million viewers tuned in for this special event, making it the highest-rated episode of the season at number seventeen in the Nielsen ratings. Elements of the Hawaii trip were also incorporated into the annual Valentine's Day episode.[5]

A prevalent unifying theme of season six was the use of dedicated episodes focused on a single topic. This was not a completely new approach. From the first full season of the series there had been special holiday episodes celebrating Halloween, Christmas, and Valentine's Day. The final season had each of those holiday episodes as well as several other single-theme specials. One of those episodes was entitled "A Salute to Women." The theme of the episode was the celebration of women's accomplishments, with a mild, oftentimes comedic feminist tinge. Even the viewers' letters, audience participation, and scripted banter were all geared toward the principle of female achievement and empowerment. For instance, there were segments on a hearing-impaired young woman from New York who was teaching a dog to understand sign language; a female auto racer from Virginia; a wife and mother who was also the shift boss of a mining crew, with particular emphasis placed on the difficulty of the job, notably having to deal with male chauvinism; a 108-year-old bowler; Sarah Purcell free-falling with an all-female sky-diving team; and Skip Stephenson being overwhelmed when he visited a class that taught women the art of flirtation. Essentially, the women's episode was composed of segments that normally would have been spread throughout the season, but were culled to create a theme that might appeal to female viewers. Ideally, the women viewers would be drawn to the special episode and return for future episodes. Unfortunately, like most of the producer's efforts at ratings renewal in 1983–1984, it did not work, as the episode ranked thirty-third in the weekly ratings.[6]

Another dedicated episode was driven by a ratings imperative, though somewhat indirectly. Nineteen eighty-four was an Olympic year, with the Winter Games being held in Sarajevo, Yugoslavia, and the Summer Games in Los Angeles, California. Given the boycott of the 1980 Summer Olympics in Moscow, combined with the US location, there was a good deal of anticipation and excitement for the coming games. Though neither of the seasonal games was going to be broadcast on NBC, *Real People* producers hoped to capitalize on the public interest by presenting an episode entitled "A Salute to Olympians Past and Present." The tone of the episode was purely celebratory and inspirational. The quality of the hour-long program was established by the use of film footage from Bud Greenspan, a renowned Olympic documentary filmmaker. Most segments were a mix of sports, relationships, and personal lives. Included in the presentation were 1968 gold medal boxer George Foreman; a piece on Jesse Owens' brilliance at the 1936 Berlin games; the close friendship of Rafer Johnson and C. K. Yang, who were intense competitors in the Olympic decathlon; Shun Fujimoto, a gymnast who continued to compete despite a broken leg; the underdog track-and-field victory of Dave Wottle in 1972; gold medal diver Pat McCormick and her daughter Kelly, who was hoping to compete in Los Angeles; Al Oerter, who was seeking a fifth gold medal at age forty-seven; and a look at the origins of the "Truce of God" march, which had become the closing procession of athletes at every Olympic Games since 1956. It was a thoughtful and well-produced episode; one that George Schlatter called "the best most unusual episode ever."[7]

The remaining single-topic episode was one *Real People* viewers had come to expect, the Veterans Day salute. The 1983 Veterans Day episode differed from earlier efforts in that it was staged outside of the Burbank studio. The setting of the program was the outdoor Sylvan Theater on the grounds of the National Mall in Washington, DC, with an audience of several thousand. The iconography was applied with a heavy hand, as a fife and drum corps played the *Real People* theme and the cast was introduced by a uniformed veteran. The presence of the large crowd, many of whom were service members and their families, created an unusual atmosphere of reverence mixed with entertainment. For example, the introduction of the hour-long special proclaimed, "We are pleased to be here to celebrate Veterans Day. For many years television has ignored Veterans Day; and some servicemen have felt that the media has done as much for the veterans as Liz Taylor has done for designer jeans." It was a cheap joke related to the renowned actress Elizabeth Taylor's well-publicized struggles with weight gain.

Nonetheless, the episode shifted gears immediately, becoming deeply serious and issue-oriented. The program's most powerful segment was a portrait of Roy Benavidez, a Green Beret sergeant who earned the congressional Medal of Honor in 1981. Benavidez received the medal for saving twelve men in a combat zone, including carrying injured men to a chopper, even though he was wounded as well. It took thirteen years for Benavidez to receive the medal because the events occurred in Cambodia during a period when the US was not supposed to be in that country. Less than two years after being presented with his medal by Ronald Reagan, Benavidez was informed that his government disability payments would be discontinued. It was at that point that *Real People* became involved in the story. The show's cameras filmed a parade for the hometown hero in El Campo, Texas, and then followed him to the White House, where he had a meeting with presidential aides. At the meeting he was promised "private sector" support, but he insisted that he only wanted what he was entitled to, not "charity." Furthermore, Benavidez would become an advocate for other veterans in similar circumstances, as would *Real People*. Eventually, Roy Benavidez would testify before a congressional committee, after having his benefits restored. [8]

Another segment focused upon the Women Airforce Service Pilots (WASPs) of World War II. These female pilots delivered airplanes across the country and flew experimental aircraft, and thirty-eight died in the process. The piece detailed the WASPs' struggle for official recognition and elicited reminiscences from surviving pilots. One woman recounted a story in which she lost a friend after flipping a coin to determine who would fly a particular plane during a mission that went wrong. As she tearfully said, "I landed but she didn't; it's my biggest sorrow . . . the flip of a nickel." World War II was featured in several other segments. There was a piece on the 508th Parachute Infantry Regiment that landed in France on D-Day. This group lost one-third of its membership in the European theater. At a filmed reunion of the Red Devils, the men recounted their feelings of pride, sadness, and survivor's guilt, while still remembering and reciting their regiment fight song. There was also a reunion of those who served on the USS *North Carolina*, in Wilmington, North Carolina. In 1960, the ship had been decommissioned and designated for scrapping. But it was saved by North Carolina schoolchildren who collected money to save the ship, with the intention of creating a naval museum. One of the veterans interviewed likely summed up the feelings of many of his former shipmates when he said, "I wouldn't want to go through it again, but those memories I wouldn't sell for a million dollars."

The contemporary military was examined in a piece on the USS *John F. Kennedy*. The daily lives of sailors aboard the ship were featured, as were the poignant moments when families said goodbye to their loved ones, and then months later the joy as the servicepeople and their nearest and dearest were reunited. The other modern military segment was more comedic in nature. Bill Rafferty was featured trying to complete the standard tasks at marine boot camp, including a zip line, parachute jump, and obstacle course. In several of the contemporary segments, servicepeople were asked why they enlisted, and they provided genuine insight into the socioeconomic realities of 1983 and beyond: "I joined because there weren't hardly any jobs out there. It's better than washing dishes." In another lighthearted, arguably sexist piece, there was a focus on the legendary pinup girls of World War II, Korea, and Vietnam. Featured were women such as Jane Russell, Rita Hayworth, Betty Grable, Joan Collins, and Raquel Welch. As was the show's wont, there was a crude joke slipped in:

Byron Allen: During the Korean War there were four outstanding pinups, Marilyn Monroe and Bridget Bardot.

Sarah Purcell: Byron, that's only two.

Skip Stephenson [to Sarah]: You count your way and we'll count our way.

The episode ended with a moment of dedication and memorial for the 2,500 veterans still missing in Southeast Asia. After a rousing ovation from and for the assembled veterans in the audience, "America the Beautiful" began to play as a voice-over intoned, "As world tensions mount, more courageous Americans are once again being asked to give their lives. For their sakes we must never forget them." These were not empty words for *Real People*; the show consistently advocated for veterans and their issues. After having exposed the shame of ignored POWs/MIAs in earlier seasons, the show continued to agitate on the issue, featuring several updates on their offscreen activities. Of the many things history has forgotten or ignored about *Real People*, its sincere advocacy for the military is arguably the most glaring. It is particularly notable given that when *Real People* started its military-themed segments and episodes, celebrations of veterans were not common on television or in larger American popular culture. This was especially true of the Vietnam War and its veterans. It would be difficult to argue that *Real People* was singularly responsible for the growing acceptance of Vietnam veterans; nonetheless, a show that was drawing sixteen to twenty million viewers per episode (20–25 percent of the entire TV audience) can claim some credit for rehabilitating the perception of a cruelly forgotten cohort of veterans.

Unfortunately, though not completely unfairly, the legacy of *Real People*, for those who even remember it, is that of a whacky, weird, vacuous time killer. Season six has done its part in building that flawed memory. To wit, Skip Stephenson was shipped in a full-sized envelope to Mill Valley, California; there was a psychic who claimed to have antennae in the back of his head; a warlock who sculpted aliens; a seventy-five-year-old stripper who lived in a nursing home; a family who lived underground in an abandoned missile silo; a man who covered his van in thousands of ornaments; a woman who made art out of dryer lint; a tollbooth operator who yodeled while he worked; and a man who wore a gorilla suit and lived in his spaceship. The real animal kingdom in all its weirdness was represented by stories such as a man who provided obedience training for pigs; a dog who had his own pet pig, which he raised; a fashion show for "glamorous dogs"; a soccer-playing horse; a baby goril-la raised in a house like a family member; and a woman who sang opera to increase the milk output of her cows.

The unique way in which Americans have fun and compete with each other was also on display in pieces on the National Arm Wrestling Championships; an eleven-year-old barrel racing champion; a sardine-packing contest; a mosquito festival; and a look at San Diego Comic-Con before it became an international event. The uniquely talented or employed had consistently offered a trove of stories for *Real People* producers during previous seasons. In season six there were a variety of these features; for instance, a former ballerina who taught skating techniques to professional hockey players; a man who crusaded against excessive regulation and safety laws; male strippers who also taught aerobics; Los Angeles TV horror hostess Elvira, Mistress of the Dark; the world's fastest cartoonist, Sergio Aragones; a photographer who took his photos from the ledges of New York City skyscrapers; a man who "free climbed" mountain peaks with no equipment; and the official skunk trapper of North Syracuse, New York.

The broad view of the previous five seasons compared with the offerings in the final season reveals an obvious effort to present more serious, informational, or inspirational stories than had been featured in earlier seasons. This move was no doubt motivated by the need for a failing show to rebrand itself, or possibly draw new viewers. *Real People* would never be mistaken for newsmagazines like *60 Minutes* or *20/20*, but in the 1983–1984 season there were several segments that could have appeared on either of those esteemed shows. For example, there were pieces on a husband and wife, both of whom worked for the California Highway Patrol; a man who had dedicated his career to stopping the slaughter of baby seals and whales for commercial use; a program that fed the needy and homeless by collecting food that would have been thrown out by supermarkets and restaurants; and the growing use of flight simulators to train pilots and improve air safety.

Season six also featured one of the more painful and disappointing stories in the history of the series. The piece, introduced by Sarah Purcell as the "Forgotten Children of War," explained the often sad state of Ameri-Asian children, those born to Southeast Asian mothers and American military fathers serving in that region during the 1960s and early 1970s. The segment depicted the tenuous lives of these children who still lived in their home countries, where they were deemed "the in-between people," who were not accepted by their own cultures, yet had no way to reach out to their American fathers. As Sarah said, they were "shunned by the land of their mothers because they are half-breeds, while ignored by the land of their fathers." The filmed segment showed the Ameri-Asian children living in the streets and panhandling to survive. The more hopeful element of the piece focused on Alfred Keane, a minister who worked to place Ameri-Asian children in foster homes in the United States. There was particular attention paid to one family, which had six adopted Ameri-Asian children, all of whom appeared happy and well adjusted. The goal of the feature was to make an appeal to the American government to take action, and to a lesser degree to dole out some guilt or possibly motivation to those American fathers who willfully ignored their children. It was aired with no jokes or lighthearted touches; it would have fit nicely in an episode of *60 Minutes* or any serious newsmagazine.

Numerically, the feel-good and inspirational stories were among the most prevalent of the final season. People helping people was the most frequent theme in this category; for instance, a Juilliard School of Music student who traveled to New Guinea to introduce and teach the work of Mozart to the local people; a California program in which abandoned pets were taken to convalescent homes to brighten the spirits of the residents; a Santa Claus who used sign language with hearing-impaired children; a twelve-year-old boy who had saved a young girl's life; a woman who operated a travel company that specialized in Hawaiian tours for the elderly and handicapped; an Idaho man who took disabled people on white-water rafting trips; the Make-A-Wish Foundation, which tries to fulfill dreams for seriously ill children; and Mother Waddles, a seventy-year-old woman who had dedicated her life to helping poor people.

Except for the occasional newspaper or magazine article on a specific story, or a profile of one of the hosts, *Real People* was essentially ignored by the larger media. Of course, this is not a unique position for any show suffering a decline in ratings and cultural relevance. Ironically, the series won its only Emmy Award during the 1983–1984 season, in the category of Outstanding Live and Tape Sound Mixing and Sound Effects for a Series. Tellingly, *Real People* was not nominated for Outstanding Informational Series, a category for which it had been nominated in 1980, 1981, and 1983, though it had never won.[9]

For *Real People* the immutable force was the continued degradation of its Nielsen ratings status. For the 1983–1984 season the series finished as the fortieth-ranked show, while regularly losing to its 8 PM competition on the American Broadcasting Company (ABC), *The Fall Guy*, which finished as the sixteenth-rated show of the season. Few shows in television history have survived a decline in ratings for three consecutive years, particularly if they were on a perennial third-place network. Other factors working against the renewal of the series included the loss of momentum or interest in prime-time reality programming across the three networks. Additionally, NBC had found what it considered a thematic replacement in the programming niche filled by *Real People*; it was a show called *TV's Bloopers and Practical Jokes*. This Dick Clark creation featured the bloopers (flubbed lines, dropped props, and general silliness) of prominent TV stars, who would introduce their show's blooper reel. The show also featured orchestrated practical jokes involving TV personalities and occasionally non-celebrities. Though it may have had some similar elements, it was not a reality show, but it was inexpensive to produce and scored high enough ratings to win a permanent spot on the 1984–1985 schedule.

Finally, Brandon Tartikoff, the president of NBC Entertainment, had a creative vision that favored the development of scripted programs. Though NBC had again finished last in the Nielsen ratings, Tartikoff had created a stable of shows that would quickly come to dominate television, including *The A-Team*, *The Cosby Show*, *Hill Street Blues*, *Family Ties*, *Cheers*, *Night Court*, *Miami Vice*, and *Highway to Heaven*, which took *Real People*'s time slot. *Real People*, a fortieth-ranked show, had no place in a lineup of emerging Nielsen powers. The official cancelation announcement came in early May 1984, and the last episode aired on July 4. Fittingly, it was a repeat of the 1983 "Salute to Veterans" special; the show got to leave prime time with one of its pinnacle achievements. Around the time *Real People* aired its last episode there were press reports that Metromedia Productions was considering a continuation of original episodes in syndication, but it never materialized. [10]

NETWORK REALITY 1983–1984

In producing and scheduling the 1983–1984 season, network television appeared willing to keep tinkering with reality shows to find another potential hit program. However, those efforts were not of the risk-taking, groundbreaking variety that had made *Real People* appear so innovative just four years earlier. NBC continued to be more active than its network competitors in the reality realm. In March 1984, NBC offered a reboot of the Art Linkletter–hosted show from the mid-1950s, *People Are Funny*. The new half-hour version featured Flip Wilson as host, and a Saturday 9 PM time slot. The format was basic, with man/woman-on-the-street scenarios, occasionally with hidden cameras a la *Candid Camera*. Scenarios included a pizza deliveryman being asked to deliver an order to a "contaminated" radioactive room; passersby being asked to retrieve a wallet from a car's backseat in which there was a vicious-looking dog; a man in a supermarket taking items from other shoppers' carts; a woman in a nightgown attempting to have random pedestrians take her to lunch; and a man with a hole in his pants trying to get people to walk close behind him to shield him from embarrassment. In each episode Flip Wilson was tasked with accomplishing odd tasks with the public; for instance, trying to find one hundred celebrities on the streets of Los Angeles; creating a comedy team of random people; and finding one person who shared Wilson's real first name, Clerow. The ratings for *People Are Funny* were initially promising, as the show's premiere won its time slot against ratings stalwart *The Love Boat* on ABC. This was likely due to the heavy promotion of the show and the popularity of Flip Wilson, a major TV star from the previous decade. In fact, one reviewer summed up the likely appeal by saying, "The show is just silly enough to provoke a chuckle now and then, particularly if you like Flip Wilson. Maybe *only* if you like Flip Wilson." Unfortunately, after the initial ratings success, the Nielsen numbers declined, which disappointed Brandon Tartikoff. *People Are Funny* ran into July, but would not be added to the fall 1984 schedule. [11]

NBC also experimented at the murky periphery of reality programming with a daytime magazine show entitled *Personal and Confidential*. This hour-long program was a hybrid drawing from several genres: celebrity fluff, self-help/informational, and personal stories made public. The show was hosted by Steve Edwards and Christine Belford, with filmed excerpts and studio segments. A typical show included short celebrity pieces; a segment on a South Carolina woman who shot her husband after years of domestic violence; a story on sexual enhancement seminars; a feature on a husband-and-wife paparazzi team; and a story on "test tube triplets." The content was undeniably superficial, sensationalistic, and even a bit sleazy. In his review of the show Tom Shales of the *Washington Post* suggested, "It makes *Real People* look like the *Times of London*." Further burnishing, or, depending on one's point view, tarnishing the show's reality credentials was the producer, Alan Landsburg, who was known for *That's Incredible* and various syndicated reality shows; a man who Shales labeled "one of Hollywood's lowlier sleazemongers." The show had a short pilot run in August 1983, but would not become a regularly scheduled show. Ironically, just a few years in the future, *Personal and Confidential* would seem relatively tame compared to many other daytime programs across television. [12]

NBC made a more traditional and some might say respectable effort to produce a reality-tinged newsmagazine with *Summer Sunday U.S.A.* The hour-long show, hosted by Linda Ellerbee and Andrea Mitchell, was committed to giving voice to the mass of people across the country. Over its nine-week run in the summer of 1984, the show would be broadcast live and with local flavor from North Carolina; San Francisco; Houston; Los Angeles; Woodstock, New York (for the anniversary of the music festival); and Baltimore. The show had a strong mix of hard news, soft infotainment, and commentary with a populist tinge. However, it was plagued by technical difficulties caused by the live broadcasts from across the country, a lack of interest from affiliates, and the "instant death" time slot opposite *60 Minutes*. The result was a consistent placement as the worst-rated show of the weeks in which it aired. [13]

The Columbia Broadcasting Company's (CBS) efforts in prime-time reality staked out safe and familiar ground with the return of Charles Kuralt's "On the Road" segments. In June 1983 CBS began ten weeks of half-hour *On the Road* episodes. The segments were typical of those that Kuralt had been presenting on the CBS Evening News since 1967. In this mini-revival of his classic format, Kuralt did what he had always done, traveling the back roads and small towns looking for stories that were quirky, heartwarming, and often bathed in Americana. Kuralt talked with three men who had helped build the Golden Gate Bridge; a North Carolina man who fixed broken bicycles for needy kids; traveling shoe salesmen; a woman who opened her private library of books to the public; a man who built massive models made of toothpicks; a freight train engineer who built and drove his own steam engine; sheepherders in Idaho; and the participants in a whistlers' convention, to name but a few. These were stories that could have and in some variety had appeared on *Real People*, the difference being there were no jokes, no laugh track, scripted comic banter, or salacious segments featured; and Kuralt had the cultural imprimatur of CBS News to shield him if needed. That news branding kept *On the Road* from being labeled entertainment or infotainment, or other less flattering terms, as *Real People* and other reality shows had been regularly marked. Kuralt and his work were also very popular with television critics, though he was not a ratings winner in this abbreviated summer series.[14]

Kuralt was given another chance in March 1984 with *The American Parade*, a studio show that featured filmed segments from across the country. This show tilted more overtly to soft news/infotainment; so much so that respected TV journalist Bill Moyers declined to participate as co-anchor, in what was something of a public embarrassment for CBS. The theme of the show was uplifting "good news" stories mixed with feel-good American boosterism, though not arrogance—not unlike many *Real People* segments. As Howard Rosenberg in the *Los Angeles Times* described it, "The program is patriotic without being nationalistic. It never says America is better, only unique." Tom Shales was effusive if not hyperbolic in his praise of the show: "The future of network television depends on the success of *The American Parade*. More or less. If this serious, diverting, ambitious new CBS news magazine cannot find an adequately enormous audience, that could be a true last straw—the last time anybody tries to do anything daringly decent in prime-time." Shales had been an early advocate of *Real People*, and prescient in assessing the potential for informational/unscripted programming becoming the dominant genre in the TV industry. In that context his concerns over the fate of this Kuralt effort are more understandable. His apprehension was well founded, as *The American Parade* was a ratings disaster. After just four weeks the show was taken off the air and retooled, with Bill Moyers joining to manage a transition to more of a *60 Minutes*–style presentation.[15]

With the cancelation of *Real People* and *That's Incredible* there was only one reality-themed show, *Ripley's Believe It or Not*, still airing in network prime time. The experiments in prime-time reality would continue, but the genre was shifting away from diverse anthology shows to more specific or narrow content. In essence, the categories on *Real People* would be spun off to create the reality subcategories that came to dominate the genre over the next twenty years.

SYNDICATED REALITY, 1983–1984

Though it may have appeared that reality TV was slowly fading out in prime time, the genre still had a firm and expanding presence in syndication. As the 1983–1984 season began there were already several highly successful reality shows in the middle of, or settling into, long syndication runs (*PM Magazine, Hour Magazine, The People's Court*). Ironically, *More Real People* was not one of the syndicated success stories, as it faltered in local ratings, though it was still being aired. A survey of the most successful syndicated reality series indicates a clear preference on the part of viewers for original reality content, not reruns of previously seen episodes. This predilection clearly hampered *More Real People*, as it would another successful prime-time reality show, *That's Incredible*, when it was syndicated in 1985. [16]

One of the more popular reality programming subgenres in the late 1980s and early 1990s was the dating show utilizing real people and their experiences. The 1983–1984 season witnessed the premiere of a milestone in that emerging category, *Love Connection*. This daily half-hour daytime program offered a variant on the video dating formula by expanding the personal ad component and allowing a bachelor or bachelorette, with the help of a studio audience, to choose a prospective date from three candidates shown on video. After the date, the couple would reappear to be interviewed by host Chuck Woolery, who would elicit details of their time together and have them discuss their opinions of each other—a practice one reviewer called "smarmy, pseudo-intimate confrontations." These opinions ranged from effusive attraction, to politely dismissive, to extremely cruel. Invariably, the studio audience, and presumably the home viewers, enjoyed the biting comments more than the humility and politeness. *Love Connection* was syndicated by Telepictures Productions, which had found ratings success with *The People's Court*. In fact, *Love Connection* and *The People's Court* were often sold together as a programming block and aired back-to-back on local stations. *Love Con-*

nection would run for eleven years with over two thousand episodes produced, proving to be one of the most successful reality-themed shows in the history of the genre. An additional video dating show, *Finders Seekers*, was produced in the 1983–1984 season. This series featured the use of video classified ads, though with more of a salacious intonation. *Finders Seekers* was evidently viewed by many local stations as a lesser option than *Love Connection*, thus the series did not make it to full-scale syndication.[17]

A television classic was rebooted in syndication in 1983, with *This Is Your Life* making a brief return. The show was best known for surprising celebrities with reminiscences of their lives, punctuated with appearances by important people from their past. Though celebrities were the main draw, there were many lower-profile non-celebrities featured on the series. In the updated version, producer and former host Ralph Edwards created a syndicated package that included 130 of the best episodes from the original series in the 1950s, to be shown weekdays on local stations. There was also a full season of new episodes based on the original format and hosted by Joseph Campanella, to be aired on weekends. The weekend version's ratings started off strong in its first two months, including finishing number one in its time slot in New York and Los Angeles, and near the top in several other cities. Nonetheless, the novelty appears to have worn off quickly, as the ratings declined and the news series was not put into production for a second season.[18]

In 1983, the court-based reality show genre was joined by *Miller's Court*. The titular centerpiece of the series was law professor Arthur Miller. The setting was a makeshift courtroom with a studio audience. The cases were based on real events, and often argued by practicing lawyers, including celebrity counselors such as F. Lee Bailey and Marvin Mitchelson, though the principals were usually portrayed by actors. The TV jury and audience members would determine the outcome of the case, after which Miller would dissect the "trial." *Miller's Court* would evolve over its series run to include topical discussions with audience members and guest experts on issues such as the death penalty, right to die, censorship, the First Amendment, journalistic ethics, and various contemporary legal events of consequence. The show's promotional materials framed the show as "real life cases, including murder, divorce, porn, malpractice, and many other topics . . . debated by America's top lawyers, before an audience jury, for a climactic final verdict." Though never as popular as

The People's Court, Miller's Court would run for five increasingly sensationalistic seasons.[19]

In the mid-1980s, a new style of reality program, one based on reenactments of real events, began bubbling up from the creative caldron of independent TV production. *The People Versus* was a proposed courtroom series that would reenact well-known or compelling legal cases from the past to contemporary America. *Survive* was an anthology series that reenacted life-and-death situations involving real people and events. Each weekly episode was designed to present an extraordinary dramatization of an act of survival; or, as the promotional ads proclaimed, "true stories that touch everyone in an unforgettable way." *Wanted by the FBI* was a crime-based reenactment series that featured dramatizations of the criminals populating the FBI's Most Wanted list and their crimes. As an added component, the audience was encouraged to report any information they might have on the wanted fugitives. Though none of these series found an enduring place in syndication, they would provide a template for future successful reenactment series such as *America's Most Wanted* (1988), *Unsolved Mysteries* (1988), and *Rescue 911* (1989).[20]

The 1983–1984 season also featured a successful revival of an early TV standard: the talent show. Treading the same creative ground as Ted Mack's *Original Amateur Hour* (1948) and *Arthur Godfrey's Talent Scouts* (1948), *Star Search* premiered in syndication on over 170 stations across the country. This weekly hour-long program was hosted by TV veteran Ed McMahon. Each episode featured unknown or amateur performers competing in several categories (male/female vocalist, junior vocalist, dancer, spokesmodel, and comedian). In a tension-filled "reveal" after the performances, the winner, chosen by entertainment professionals, would be announced to a large live theater audience. The winners would continue performing and competing until they lost, with some winning large cash prizes for their efforts. *Star Search* was not populated by the oddities seen on *The Gong Show*, nor the uniquely or barely talented characters on *Real People*. Rather, *Star Search* had truly talented performers whose ability was generally closer to that of professionals than amateurs. Nonetheless, the appeal of undiscovered talent or the draw of seeing people's "friends and neighbors" striving for stardom fit nicely into the reality formula. Over twelve seasons the series would introduce a sizable cohort of future stars and became one of the most successful shows in the history of syndicated television. Viewers of twenty-first-century reality television would find *Star Search* very familiar, as the amateur talent show (*American Idol* [2002], *Last Comic Standing* [2003], *So You Think You Can Dance* [2005], *America's Got Talent* [2006], *The Voice* [2011]) is a standard of network television schedules.[21]

In the mid-1980s, reality programming was going through a settling process. Network television was moving away from the anthology format popularized by *Real People* and *That's Incredible*, to more narrow, single-topic shows like *Unsolved Mysteries* (1988), *America's Most Wanted* (1988), *Rescue 911* (1989), and *Cops* (1989). Meanwhile, in the syndicated market, reality stalwarts like *The People's Court*, *Love Connection*, and *A Current Affair* were beginning extended runs. Consequently, there were not as many new reality-themed shows premiering every year. Nonetheless, the volume, or total hours, of the genre was not declining. In fact, on local stations by the end of the 1980s reality programming, in all its diversity, began to crowd out programming staples such as reruns of network shows and older movies (both feature films and made-for-TV). Reality programming had forged a presence in American popular culture that would only increase over the subsequent two decades. Writing in the *Christian Science Monitor*, Arthur Unger presaged the view many would come to have on the ubiquity of reality TV: "As the human memory of actual events fades, the vividness of television reality too often takes over and is perceived as the only reality. Thus, without consciously applying for the role, many of us have become actors in an endless electronic drama."[22]

As the 1980s progressed, the big three networks, and an emerging fourth in the nascent FOX Network, would find no answers to their most pressing concern, loss of viewers. Ironically, while network viewership was declining, the total number of hours being watched by the average American was increasing. This dichotomy is easily explained by the defection of network viewers to alternative programming options, wherein people did not stop watching television, they just stopped watching as much network programming as they had in the past. By early 1985, viewers wired for cable TV could choose from networks such as A&E, C-Span, Cinemax, CNN, Disney, ESPN, HBO, Lifetime, The Movie Channel, MTV, Showtime, and a number of locally originating channels. To this array could be added the superstations (WGN from Chicago, WOR from New York, and TBS from Atlanta) and a small collection of experimental programming options; for example, the early stirring of home shopping channels. As if these challenges were not enough, by the end of the decade networks would be competing with and often losing ground to home video movie rentals, home video game consoles, and even the burgeoning home computing industry. The economic consequences of viewer erosion and the loss of advertising revenue would further drive networks to pursue the lower-cost/greater-profit-margin option of reality-themed programming. In point of fact, once the utility, if not necessity, of the reality genre was firmly acknowledged, both the broadcast networks and non-network entities would engage in a saturating frenzy of reality programming, the likes of which even the most ardent of the genre's early proponents would not have likely imagined.[23]

As for *Real People*, after the final broadcast in July 1984, the series began to recede from the collective cultural memory. Except for diehard fans or possibly those who knew someone who had appeared on the show, the series is largely forgotten. It barely has a presence on the Internet, which acts as a repository of nostalgia or video archiving for many TV series. Certainly compared to other hit shows of the early 1980s, it appears not to resonate culturally. It can be easily argued that contemporary reality shows such as *That's Incredible, The People's Court*, and *Love Connection* are more widely and fondly remembered than *Real People*. The potential causes of this almost uniform ignorance of the series are manifold. To begin with, by initial design there were no major stars, either in the cast or as recurring characters in the series. Additionally, *Real People* was not known for the big spectacle or sensationalism for which shows like *That's Incredible* are remembered. Further marginalizing the series was its failure in national syndication. Within two years of leaving the NBC schedule it was off the air completely. Unlike scripted hit shows that run for years in syndication and develop an audience who never saw the show in its original network run, *Real People* disappeared quickly without adding any additional fans.[24] Finally, though not a strong candidate for such consideration, *Real People* has never been released into the home video market, either on VHS, DVD, or streaming service. By way of contrast, from the 1980–1981 TV season, in which *Real People* finished as the twelfth-rated show, thirteen of the other top twenty shows have had some type of home video release.

Whatever the cause, *Real People* has been deposited on the scrap heap of popular culture. If remembered at all, it is usually a flawed memory of whacky characters, canned jokes, or possibly jiggling bodies. Equally likely is a cursory dismissal of the series as just another time-killing show for people to watch. Though it may have been a time-killing exercise for many viewers, its legacy in the course of television history deserves more attention and acknowledgment. Ideally, this study has aided in clarifying *Real People*'s seminal role in popularizing the reality genre, as well as its centrality in establishing the creative potential and economic viability of a format that continues to dominate the contemporary medium at every level.

EPILOGUE

From *Real People* to *The Real World*

Though the early 1980s frenzy of reality TV had eased, as symbolically evidenced by the cancelation of *Real People* and *That's Incredible*, the genre would continue to thrive and ultimately saturate American popular culture by the early twenty-first century. There were several factors that would accelerate the dominance of reality programming in the coming two decades.

Nineteen eighty-five is one of the more impactful years in the history of American television. However, this designation was not the result of a string of groundbreaking shows or the birth of legendary careers; rather, it was the machinations at the corporate level that altered the course of television history. During that year the future of all the big three networks and network television in general was indelibly transformed. In March 1985, the American Broadcasting Company (ABC) was purchased by Capital Cities Corporation; in December 1985 General Electric swallowed up the National Broadcasting Company (NBC); and in the summer of 1985 the Loews Corporation began aggressively buying the stock of the Columbia Broadcasting System (CBS), eventually leading to the network being controlled by Loews in 1986. These corporations were not experienced television producers; they were global conglomerates that had a variety of business interests, of which broadcasting would be a lesser concern, at least creatively. The result at each of the networks was a corporate ethos stressing the bottom line; not quality programming, but profit. The immense pressure now placed on the networks to turn a sizable profit made the lower production costs of reality TV very attractive.

The obvious counterapproach to relying on the reality genre would be to lower the production costs of scripted programs. However, that option was less viable, particularly given the escalating salaries for the creative artists (actors, directors, writers) on successful series. Reinforcing the increasingly expensive and complicated nature of television production was a writers' strike that lasted for five months in 1988. Not only would the settlement of this strike ultimately raise the budgets of scripted television shows, but it would also reveal an inability to control production and distribution of content when there were labor unions with which to contend. These are not impositions that global corporations were used to accommodating in their business practices. As detailed in earlier chapters, reality shows not only have lower costs, but they also are not subject to many of the craft union rules that might shut down a production in the event of a strike. Given the confluence of these factors it is not surprising that networks would look to reality programming in the future. Nineteen eighty-five was also remarkable for the founding of a fourth major network in the form of FOX Television. As a fledgling network FOX was not only conscious of costs, but to draw viewers it also had to take programming chances that the established networks might avoid. Consequently, FOX would be an active contributor to the reality genre in the late 1980s with shows like *America's Most Wanted*, *Cops*, *Totally Hidden Video*, *American Chronicles*, and *Yearbook*.[1]

Two other structural factors drove the reality genre into the 1990s. The first was a steady increase in the number of local TV stations. Reagan-era deregulation of the communications industry had enabled corporate entities to own multiple television stations across the nation. These stations, being in need of original content, consistently filled much of that demand with syndicated reality shows of all kinds. The second development was the continued evolution of a number of cable TV networks. As some of these networks jockeyed for position in an increasingly competitive industry, they diversified their program offerings by presenting original content. Once again, the lower-cost reality productions were a preferred option. Most notable in the larger history of the genre is Music Television's (MTV) reality franchise, *The Real World*. Premiering in 1992, *The Real World* would initiate a rising tide of imitations and permutations of the reality format into the 1990s and beyond. In 2007, on the occasion of the series' twentieth season, MTV's president of entertainment Brian Graden noted this legacy with pride when he claimed *The Real World* was "quite simply the undisputed granddaddy of modern commercial reality television." Of course Graden, as do many others, either ignores or is unaware of the reality TV trend that was thriving over a decade before 1992. In fact, as *The Real World* premiered, the legacy of *Real People* was still evident even if it was no longer on the air.[2]

In the years following the cancelation of *Real People* up to the premiere of *The Real World*, the reality genre progressed and diversified unabated. During this period a new subcategory of reality emerged in the form of video captured by average people on their personal video recording devices. The most prominent of these shows was ABC's *America's Funniest Home Videos* (1989). This weekly series hosted by Bob Saget featured short video clips submitted by viewers. At the end of the show a cash award was presented to the funniest video. ABC would later produce a spinoff series, also featuring viewer-submitted home video, entitled *America's Funniest People* (1990). FOX offered up *Totally Hidden Video* (1989), which melded hidden-camera practical jokes with videos submitted by viewers. Of these home video reality show offerings the most compelling, or for some most disconcerting, were FOX's *Code 3* (1992) and NBC's *I Witness Video* (1992). Both of these shows utilized video footage, occasionally news video, of people in harrowing situations such as a house fire, flood, car accident, natural disaster, etc. To many critics these shows felt like pure exploitation being passed off as benign infotainment.[3]

The already abundant court-themed reality show category continued to grow into the early 1990s. In national syndication there was an updated version of *Divorce Court* (1986) as well as the new series *Superior Court* (1986) and *On Trial* (1988). Of these three, *On Trial* was the more prescient because it was utilizing video footage from real court cases in real courtrooms across the nation. The use of genuine courtroom video was an emerging trend in television; NBC had its version with *Trial Watch* (1991), while the CBS entry was entitled *Verdict* (1991). The courtroom camera provided arguably the purest form of reality programming; there was no editing, no script, and no actors, just the legal system in action. So appealing and cost-effective was this form of reality programming that it spawned an entire cable network, Court TV (1991), dedicated to live coverage of prominent legal cases around the nation.[4]

From the late 1980s into the early 1990s one of the most successful varieties of reality series was that which relied on reenactments of real events. The use of dramatization provided elasticity for producers, who could present stories from almost any place in any period of time. The settings, whether in a studio or on location, were relatively inexpensive, as were the unknown or even amateur actors used in the filmed re-creations. Thus, these shows had the draw of "true stories" combined with narrative flexibility, while still maintaining the lower production costs. The exemplars in this field include FOX's *America's Most Wanted* (1988), which focused on apprehending fugitive criminals; on CBS there was *Rescue 911* (1989), a show featuring police or medical emergencies, and *Top Cops* (1990), which highlighted police investigations of prominent or sensational crimes. However, by far the most successful of this reality subcategory was NBC's *Unsolved Mysteries* (1988), which presented stories on topics such as unsolved murders and crimes, missing persons, and unexplained phenomena. The series finished in the top twenty rated shows for five consecutive years, outpacing *Rescue 911*, which finished in the top twenty twice. [5]

National syndication offered opportunities to programs that would have never aired on the networks, particularly those that were more intimate or sensationalist in their content. Included in this category would be shows like *Strictly Confidential* (1987), a talk-show-style format featuring a psychotherapist, Dr. Susan Forward, who hosted what the show's publicity called a "provocative new show that probes the bitter conflicts unraveling the fiber of modern marriage." Also in this category was a dating show called *Studs* (1991), a daily late-night show that featured risqué, if not sleazy, banter about the dating matchups of contestants. If *Love Connection* was rated PG-13, *Studs* was clearly R-rated content. However, the most disconcerting development on the periphery of the reality realm was the emergence and growing popularity of daytime talk shows. Included in this cohort are *Geraldo* (1987), *Sally Jessy Raphael* (1989), *Jenny Jones* (1991), *The Maury Povich Show* (1991), *The Montel Williams Show* (1991), and *The Jerry Springer Show* (1992). Though several of these shows began with relatively high-minded ideals akin to Oprah Winfrey or Phil Donahue, ratings imperatives eventually drove them toward the lowest common denominator in programming. The result was a pattern of exploitative, degrading, and trashy entertainment; in many ways the worst that television and American popular culture could offer.[6]

Though trashy shows like *Studs* or the various daytime talk shows produced a good deal of hand-wringing over the state of American culture, an equally if not more damaging development emerged in the 1980s. Since the initial days of the reality wave in the early 1980s, there had been consistent rumblings, particularly from network news divisions and TV critics, that reality themes were "softening" the news and helping to transform television journalism into infotainment. These jeremiads seemed quite rational after the appearance of three syndicated "news" series: *A Current Affair* (1986), *Hard Copy* (1989), and *Inside Edition* (1989). Collectively, these shows wallowed in the most sensational or exploitative elements of the stories they aired. This produced segments on sex scandals, murders, political corruption, crime, and anything relatively salacious, with an occasional effort at a cloying feel-good piece. Critics were relentless in their attacks on these tabloid series, calling them "a mongrel lot," "dishonest," "junk news," and "the lowest of the low." Although these series bear little resemblance to *Real People* or other early 1980s reality shows, both the shows themselves and critics regularly referred to them as reality TV. Despite the criticism, these shows performed well enough in the ratings to thrive for years to come—all the while damaging both the state of television news and the reputation of reality television.[7]

As reality broadened its narrative scope in the late 1980s, drama and action themes became very popular elements. Undoubtedly, TV producers recognized that the daily lives of first responders (fire, police, rescue) could provide abundant doses of the desired action and drama. Unlike the reenactment format, there were several shows that actively followed and filmed these public servants as they performed their duties. The trailblazer in this reality subcategory was the FOX series *Cops*, which premiered in 1989. The narrative structure of this weekly half-hour show utilized camera crews following police units in specific communities as they engaged the local populous, encountering a diverse array of crimes, criminals, and victims. It was "fly on the wall" intimacy that standard documentary rarely achieved and scripted drama could never fully re-create. Featuring a similar format was a syndicated series called *On Scene: Emergency Response*, which centered on the often dramatic activities of fire rescue crews across the United States. Stretching the narrative boundaries of this category were two other syndicated series, *Group One Medical* (1988) and *Emergency Call* (1991). Setting these two shows apart from the others was an effort to develop and explore the personalities and private lives of these first responders and doctors. On *Group One Medical* both doctors and patients were engaged in a genuine intimacy that was rarely seen on television. The show's promotional material promised, "For the first time on a regular television series, viewers will have the opportunity to observe medical examinations, diagnoses, and in some cases subsequent treatments." Evidently, the producers of this series had forgotten or were unaware of NBC's *Lifeline*, which had done exactly the same thing ten years earlier. Nonetheless, this level of intimacy became obligatory in reality television by the early 2000s. [8]

Although not nearly as dramatic or heroic, FOX aired a short-lived series featuring the daily lives of a group of Illinois high-school seniors. This series, entitled *Yearbook* (1991), followed the trials and tribulations of a group of students as they moved toward graduation. This included lighthearted events like the selection of a homecoming queen, but also more personal moments, such as a discussion between a student and a school psychologist and an intimate conversation between a teen and his pregnant girlfriend. Predating *The Real World* by almost a year, *Yearbook* is an early indication of the direction in which reality TV was heading. [9]

Even though *Real People* had been canceled because of its low ratings, the show's anthology reality format had not been invalidated by that action. Consequently, in the late 1980s and early 1990s there were several shows that bore some resemblance to *Real People* in format and content. *All about Us* (1985) and *It's a Great Life* (1985) were two daily syndicated programs featuring short video pieces on interesting people and places. *All about Us* tread similar ground to that of *Real People*, with an early exemplar episode featuring an orchestra filled with senior citizens, a profile of a hardworking emergency room nurse, and a piece on an "Eastern guru" who taught people to walk on hot coals to build emotional strength. *It's a Great Life* was narrower in focus, as it was a lifestyle show, dedicating much of its time to vacation resorts, fine dining, fashion, travel, and celebrity profiles. It was similar in tone and context to another and better-known series on the periphery of reality TV, *Lifestyles of the Rich and Famous* (1984). [10]

In the network reality realm a *Real People* derivative was found in the CBS offering entitled *High Risk* (1988). This weekly series hosted by TV star Wayne Rogers borrowed from *Real People* by exploring events, occupations, or hobbies, but the segments were infused with action and drama because these activities were imbued with danger. A typical episode might feature a motorcycle race without the use of brakes; jumping from a helicopter onto the wing of a plane; people challenging their phobias; or various law enforcement officials detailing or acting out the riskiest aspects of their jobs. In 1990, FOX presented *American Chronicles*, a creation of feature film and television visionary David Lynch. This weekly half-hour series was a documentary-style show in which each week was dedicated to a single topic and the associated people, places, and events. For example, there were episodes dedicated to a Texas beauty pageant, a twenty-fifth high-school reunion in Illinois, a day in the life of Manhattan, the last day of baseball at Chicago's Comiskey Park, Mardi Gras in New Orleans, and a biker convention in Sturgis, North Dakota. Even the original *Real People* clone, *That's Incredible*, made a return appearance. In 1988 *Incredible Sunday* premiered, airing on Sunday nights opposite *60 Minutes*, with only one holdover host in John Davidson, but with a similar format of daredevil stunts, unusual habits or abilities, and some supernatural phenomena. The reboot ran for just one season, garnering very little attention culturally or in the Nielsen ratings. [11]

A final, more immediate linkage with *Real People* was evident from 1985 to 1992 with the participation of the show's principals (hosts and producers) in further reality-themed programming. In 1985, Sarah Purcell became the centerpiece of a highly anticipated syndicated daily series entitled *America*. With a major investment of $22 million, *America* was intended to be a hybrid that would include pieces on unique people, places, and events; heartwarming stories; lifestyle segments; and celebrity interviews and content. The general acceptance of reality themes combined with Sarah Purcell's success and name recognition from *Real People* seemed to hold the promise of widespread audience appeal. Unfortunately, the show was a colossal failure, barely lasting a few months on many local stations across the country. Fred Willard also hosted a short-lived syndicated reality/lifestyle series, called *What's Hot? What's Not?* (1985), which examined cultural and social trends in American life. In March 1986, John Barbour was given an exceptional opportunity by ABC. For two weeks he hosted an experimental late-night series entitled *The Barbour Report*. Airing at midnight, it was hoped to be a challenger for Johnny Carson's *Tonight Show*. The thirty-five-minute show featured *Real People*–style stories such as the watermelon seed spitting championships; a blind wine-tasting contest between a cheap wine and a pricey French import; and man-on-the-street interviews. In pre-broadcast publicity, Barbour described the show as "Phil Donahue meets Johnny Carson on *Real People* with $1.50 to spend." Apparently, that mix of elements was not enough to impress viewers or ABC executives, as *The Barbour Report* never made it past the two-week tryout. [12]

In the summer of 1988, *Real People* creator/producer George Schlatter tried to revitalize the formula of the original series by engaging in a six-week pilot run for a new show entitled *George Schlatter's Funny People*. With a mix of videotaped segments from around the country, in-studio commentary, and skits, several critics called it a marriage of *Real People* and *Laugh-In*, or "son of *Real People*." Schlatter agreed, "I think it has its roots in *Real People*, as does a lot of television today," adding, "We did a lot of funny stories in *Real People*, but this is all about people who are funny. Some who are funny on purpose, some who are not intentionally funny and some of the people behind the funny people." Despite the strong pedigree, unlike with *Real People*, a six-week trial did not result in a full season run. [13]

On October 1, 1991, NBC broadcast the *Real People Reunion Special*. In truth, it was not much of a reunion, as only two of the original hosts, Fred Willard and Sarah Purcell, were utilized in this hour-long show, which featured a retrospective of older stories mixed with several new segments. The new stories were classic *Real People*, with pieces about an elephant who painted on canvas; an artist who created "butt sketches" on the backsides of beachgoers at Venice Beach, California; and Sarah driving a Sherman tank. The older stories highlighted the diversity of the series by revisiting some of the whacky eccentrics, while also promoting the feel-good and inspirational segments. In some of the pre- and post-broadcast coverage of the special there were allusions to the possibility that the series could be reborn, not an unreasonable consideration given the prevalence of reality programming on TV in 1991. However, that possibility evaporated quickly when the weekly Nielson ratings were released. The *Real People Reunion* finished as the seventy-fifth-ranked show. As it turned out, *Real People* finished behind eight other reality shows, including its timeslot competition *Rescue 911*.

Nonetheless, among some critics the reunion did generate a reconsideration of the series and the state of the reality genre. A number of newspaper articles noted the influence of the original in "fathering reality television," while others called it "the father of infotainment" or "the daddy of what became a slew of reality-based television shows." However, critics also noted the show's alleged complicity in enabling the darker side of reality TV. Mike Drew writing in the *Milwaukee Journal* claimed that *Real People* inspired "today's casual relationship between news and entertainment" and was "partly responsible for that mix of life-style features, localized tele-movie themes, police blotter, happy talk and let us help you pandering that passes for TV news." Still proud of his creation, George Schlatter bristled at the negative legacy being promoted by some critics. Schlatter rejected the linkage with the contemporary tabloid-style and reenactment reality themes. As he said, "We were and are a celebration of the little guy . . . we acknowledged their achievements, enjoyed their eccentricities and attempted to raise the self-esteem of individuals who were not always winners." When pressed on *Real People*'s link to the trashy reality or the violent and exploitative reenactment shows, he asserted, "There's a connection, yes. You can blame me for *A Current Affair* if you really want to reach. You can bet I didn't say to use it that way . . . that would be like blaming Henry Ford for automobile accidents. Yeah he did the cars, but he said be careful how you drive them." Ironically, the state of reality TV in 1991 made one reviewer reassess the original series. Rick Sherwood in the *Hollywood Reporter* opined, "Funny thing. In the days of dramatization and sleaze, this show doesn't seem half as bad as it once did. In television as in life all things are relative." It is impossible to know, but it is easy to imagine many TV viewers who remembered *Real People* having a similar reaction. [14]

Like a devoted parent, George Schlatter preferred to accentuate the positive, while downplaying the negative aspects of his creation. Nonetheless, the influence of *Real People* as the father of reality TV, whether it is viewed as a positive or negative, is clearly evident if one is willing to look closely.

APPENDIX A

Real People Episode Guide

SEASON ONE: SPRING 1979, WEDNESDAY, 8 PM

Hosts: John Barbour, Sarah Purcell, Bill Rafferty, Skip Stephenson, Fred Willard
Special Correspondents: Jimmy Breslin, Mark Russell

Episode One

Original Airdate: April 18, 1979
Featured Segments: Lesa "yo-yo" Worley, a female trucker from Tennessee; John "Sherlock Bones" Keane, a private investigator from San Francisco, California, who finds lost pets for his clients; Frank McNulty, an Irish Sweepstakes winner who spent five years in jail for refusing to pay taxes on his prize money; a visit to the smallest television station in the United States, operated in Miles City, Montana, by a husband and wife; a satirical look at the US Internal Revenue Service, including some children attempting to decipher the standard tax forms; an Italian man who invites destitute families to move in with him and his wife; a survey of television news bloopers; Jimmy Breslin's commentary on the high price of sneakers ($40); a bogus soft drink "taste test"; Mark Russell looks at the nation's Department of Fraud, Theft, and Waste.

Episode Two

Original Airdate: April 25, 1979
Featured Segments: Car dealers who do their own local commercials; patrons of a health food restaurant who eat dirt with their meals; professional panhandler "Omar the Beggar," who helps train other street beggars; male and female weight lifters and body builders at World's Gym in Santa Monica, California; Tom Clay, a ninety-seven-year-old newspaper editor from Nevada, who is fighting a crusade against legalized gambling; Kelly Everett, a New York City woman who strips for God; Carl Brashear, the first black American to became a US Navy deepwater diver ("frogman"), despite the loss of one of his legs; people who have contacted outer space; a piece on kudzu, the wild weed swallowing Georgia, with President Jimmy Carter seen in a short clip; Mark Russell on the building of a new Senate office building in Washington, DC; a Greek man living in Germany, who goes to great lengths to adopt children.

Episode Three

Original Airdate: May 2, 1979

Featured Segments: "Space Ship Ruthie," who claims that aliens have landed on Earth; Ed Vanelsen, who claims that there are aliens visiting his Wisconsin home, and who is also building a spacecraft shaped like a banana; a visit to Chippendales, a male strip club; a man who lives in a truck for four years to save money; a club for self-professed ugly people; a basketball game played while riding on donkeys; an exclusive tap-dancing school in Washington, DC; a hobo named Walking George, who plays Beethoven on the piano and dates beautiful women, while also living in a crate.

Episode Four

Original Airdate: May 9, 1979

Featured Segments: A Queens, New York, doctor who runs the Vampire Research Center; a woman who teaches karate classes for men; a Minnesota college professor who hugs as many people as he can, saying it brings people together; a Neurotics Anonymous meeting in Washington, DC; a basketball game played on unicycles; a rowing team composed of women over seventy; an eight-year-old boy who prefers to live with his grandmother rather than his mother; Jimmy Breslin looks at the workplace of flight attendants.

Episode Five

Original Airdate: May 16, 1979

Featured Segments: A visit to the erotic lingerie store Frederick's of Hollywood in Los Angeles, California; Smokey Rolland, a man who drives and lives in a passenger airliner he converted into a mobile home; a man who lives in a desert shack; a hog named Waterhole Ike; a high-rise funeral home; Cliff Vargas and his "Circus Vargas," billed as the largest circus big top in the country.

Episode Six

Original Airdate: May 23, 1979

Featured Segments: Students at an Elmira, New York, high school compete to see how many kids they can stuff into a compact car; sixty-seven-year-old "Disco Harry," who wears hip clothes and dances at discos; a class of senior citizens learning the latest dances; Omar the Beggar and his school for panhandlers; an artist who paints gas pumps to look like animals and insects; a former NASA scientist, now private citizen, who is building his own one-man spacecraft; a visit to a pizza parlor, proclaimed to be the world's largest; the remnants of the US Cavalry fort at Fort Chickamauga, Oklahoma; Jimmy Breslin explores why court cases take so long to come to trial.

SEASON TWO: 1979–1980, WEDNESDAY, 8 PM

Hosts: Byron Allen, John Barbour, Sarah Purcell, Bill Rafferty, Skip Stephenson
Special Correspondents: Jimmy Breslin, Mark Russell

Episode One

Original Airdate: September 5, 1979
Featured Segments: A family named Nielsen provides their TV ratings; Sarah Purcell visits the Dallas Cowboys cheerleaders; John Barbour attends a convention for bald people in North Carolina; a piece on the fastest oil painter in the world, who runs a New York City art school and gallery; high-school cheerleaders in Ohio; the search for America's ugliest person.

Episode Two

Original Airdate: September 12, 1979
Featured Segments: A hollering contest in North Carolina; a party for former male centerfolds in *Playgirl* magazine; an Arizona bar where patrons, men and women, drink and box each other; the Johnny Carson replacement contest; the world's smallest real estate agents, twin dwarves John and Greg Rice of Florida; Ted Giannoulas, who stars as the San Diego chicken, a famous sports mascot; a wall made of chewing gum in San Luis Obispo, California; the TV viewing habits of Fred Nielsen, a

bachelor living in Harlem, New York City; a woman who owns more than one hundred Saint Bernards; a commentary on the gas shortage.

Episode Three

Original Airdate: September 19, 1979

Featured Segments: A farm where the intelligence of animals is rated; roller disco at a roller rink in Marina del Rey, California; Skip Stephenson talks to senior citizen cheerleaders in Sun City, Arizona; a senior citizen couple who scratch out a living as gold prospectors in the desert of Death Valley, California; a five-year-old pool hustler in Sacramento, California; John Barbour interviews the country's tallest Nielsen ratings family; a Southern California low riders car club; a Tampa, Florida, woman who lives out her food fantasies; a veterinarian befriended by a pelican; belly bumping fights; the nation's tallest buildings; the return of the woman who owns over one hundred Saint Bernards.

Episode Four

Original Airdate: September 26, 1979

Featured Segments: A report from Las Vegas, including a tourist who wins $280,000 on a slot machine, a profile of "high rollers," horse-racing fanatics, and Gamblers Anonymous; a female fan finally gets to meet her favorite baseball team, the Boston Red Sox; the explosion of jogging across the nation; Byron Allen goes to a roller coaster convention in Cincinnati and rides the nation's best roller coaster, known as the "Beast"; a family of five hundred Nielsens in Utah; Jimmy Breslin comments on "TV cops"; an energy-efficient car that gets sixty-five miles per gallon; trained-turkey races; a husband and wife both undergoing sex change procedures; a California man who collects lizards; people with unusual names; whacky weather reports; a visit to a factory where tiny working replicas of famous cars are made.

Episode Five

Original Airdate: October 10, 1979

Featured Segments: A visit to a restaurant in an Indiana nudist resort; a Minneapolis, Minnesota, millionaire who gives away silver dollars; from Brooklyn, New York, Fred Thompson, a successful businessman who takes his own time to train a track team of disadvantaged youths, with the hope of having them earn college scholarships so they can escape their circumstances; a Nielsen family in Delta, Utah; a road ranger who has outfitted his car as a rescue vehicle for stranded motorists in San Jose, California; a ventriloquist convention in Fort Mitchell, Kentucky; a mind reader named "The Astonishing Neal"; a Mark Russell commentary on events in Washington, DC, leading up to the 1980 election; skateboarding; "Buddy the Wonder Dog," a canine who can drive a car; the "Men Watchers" beauty pageant.

Episode Six

Original Airdate: October 17, 1979
Featured Segments: Sarah Purcell attends the twenty-fifth-anniversary party for *Playboy* magazine, at Hugh Hefner's Playboy Mansion, in Holmby Hills, California; Byron Allen performs with a knife thrower in San Diego, California; families gather for a ghost town reunion in Contact, Nevada; a hollering contest in Spivey's Corner, North Carolina; a convention of Edsel car owners in Concord, California; a man who offers editorial and artistic critiques of religious services; animal behaviorists at the Animal Behavior Institute.

Episode Seven

Original Airdate: October 24, 1979
Featured Segments: Byron Allen profiles a ten-year-old disc jockey from Coshocton, Ohio; Sarah Purcell rafts down the Colorado River with guide Georgie Clark; a barbershop quartet convention; a reunion of Tuskegee Airmen, a decorated black fighter pilot squadron that fought in World War II; Stan Lemkuil, the human noisemaker; a backward bike rider; Pleni Wingo, also known as "Mr. Backward," a man who walks backward; a Mark Russell commentary.

Episode Eight

Original Airdate: October 31, 1979

Featured Segments: A Halloween-themed episode, including auditions for the Ringling Bros. "Clown College," a school for future clowns; Byron Allen profiles Laurie Cabot, the official witch of Salem, Massachusetts; the town of Cassadaga, Florida, inhabited by mystics, psychics, mediums, and other occultists; a documentary look at a "real" haunted house (location concealed); Ben Scorra, from Palos Hills, Illinois, a unique inventor of his own mechanized house and a personal servant robot named AROK; Joe Jenkins, from Santa Clara, California, who believes he is the reincarnation of George Washington; a jugglers convention in Boston, Massachusetts.

Episode Nine

Original Airdate: November 7, 1979

Featured Segments: A visit to a wrestling school in Massachusetts; Andre the talented performing seal; a lobster hypnotist in Philadelphia, Pennsylvania; female boxers; a beauty pageant for pigs and a hog calling contest; a convention of jugglers; "dime a dance" girls, sometimes referred to as taxi dancers, a throwback to the 1930s; a man building his own rocket ship; fancily dressed chickens; an opera house in the Mojave Desert, in which the audience is painted in place; a female barbershop quartet; people with UFO experiences.

Episode Ten

Original Airdate: November 14, 1979

Featured Segments: Michael Lord, a twelve-year-old evangelist; a water-skiing squirrel; a horse that drives; an ugly dog contest; lifeguards from Long Island, New York, including newly permitted female lifeguards and a ninety-three-year-old lifeguard; a sandcastle-building contest in Nantucket, Rhode Island; tap-dancing at a Delaware beach; a couple raising a chimp and their own child; underwater music with "Ironing Board Sam"; a hotel catering exclusively to honeymooners; a Mark Russell commentary.

Episode Eleven

Original Airdate: November 21, 1979

Featured Segments: Special episode entitled "Real People's Family Reunion," including a retrospective of earlier guests: the world's fastest oil painter; "Space Ship Ruthie"; the San Diego Chicken; the official witch of Salem, Massachusetts; a six-year-old pool player; evangelist Ma Bean; female weight lifters; the Dallas Cowboys cheerleaders; a cow that thinks he is a horse; *Playgirl* magazine centerfold models; Dianne Grosskopf, *Playgirl* magazine editor; a modern-day vampire hunter; "Mr. Backward" (walks and rides a bike backward); "Sherlock Bones," a lost-pet detective; a ten-year-old disc jockey; Omar the Beggar and his school for panhandlers.

Episode Twelve

Original Airdate: November 28, 1979

Featured Segments: Bill Butcher, a Tarzan memorabilia collector from Sacramento, California; goat racing in Aberdeen, South Dakota; bathtub races in Fulton County, New York; turtle races in Marina del Rey, California; traveling hot tubs; rocket builders in Saratoga, California; Famous Amos, the chocolate chip cookie king; a toilet-trained cat; a pet pelican; a commentary by Mark Russell; a critic who reviews and ranks church buildings.

Episode Thirteen

Original Airdate: December 5, 1979

Featured Segments: Skip Stephenson travels to Phoenix, Arizona, to interview scientists who are making a serious investigation into reported UFO sightings; Bill Rafferty visits "Susie Skates," who delivers messages on roller skates in San Francisco; Sarah Purcell examines how a family of loggers live and work in Eugene, Oregon; a monkey that guards a pigpen in Fairway, Kansas; Skip Stephenson learns how to throw a Frisbee from an expert at the pastime; the annual hobo convention in Britt, Iowa; a school for vacuum cleaner salesmen; people who make music with a stick and rope; a school in Newbury, Ohio, where students learn to ride unicycles; the residents of Chickamauga, Oklahoma, talk about the cavalry that used to be stationed there; the only parking meter attendant in Nome, Alaska.

Episode Fourteen

Original Airdate: December 12, 1979
Featured Segments: A man who makes his belly button whistle; downhill "outhouse racing"; a school for female wrestlers; a church given a summons for praying too loudly; a man who washes coins for a living; a volleyball instructor; a man who used to install Nielsen ratings meters; a trained walrus and his handler.

Episode Fifteen

Original Airdate: December 19, 1979
Featured Segments: A Christmas-themed episode, including Robert George, the nation's official Santa Claus since the Eisenhower administration; a visit to a school in Los Angeles where students are taught how to be proper Santas; a factory in Kansas City, Missouri, where Santas are made in all sizes; a Sidney, Ohio, woman who gets dressed up as a Christmas tree; hand puppets tell the story of Chanukah; Eskimos in Alaska, singing Christmas carols; a charitable organization that helps the disadvantaged celebrate Christmas; a train trip through Alaska.

Episode Sixteen

Original Airdate: January 9, 1980
Featured Segments: Camel racing in Virginia City, Nevada; Joe Wright, a Chicago man who uses his body as a drum; a visit to the cruise ship *Queen Mary*, permanently docked in Long Beach, California; a Los Angeles nightclub that features men impersonating female celebrities; Andre the seal; a horseradish factory in California; people with exotic and/or extensive tattoos; a female canoeist and trail guide in Alaska.

Episode Seventeen

Original Airdate: January 16, 1980

Featured Segments: A water-skiing dog; a Las Vegas showgirl who teaches Sunday school; a laughing contest; an ambulance service for animals; a Nielsen family of senior citizens; Carol Johnston, a California college student who became a champion gymnast and Olympic hopeful, though she only has one arm; a visit to the Kilauea Volcano in Hawaii; speed board racing in Oregon; skateboard racing; a trained walrus performing with a dog; a review of the events of 1979, with Mark Russell.

Episode Eighteen

Original Airdate: January 23, 1980
Featured Segments: A hot-air balloon race in Albuquerque, New Mexico; husband and wife disc jockeys; a duck race in Pearblossom, California; a Los Angeles woman who travels everywhere with her coffin; a consumer report on what to look out for when dealing with lawyers, with consumer advocate Herb Denenberg; the mayor of Moscow, Ohio, a town planning its own Olympics, in light of the US boycott of the 1980 Summer Olympics in Moscow, Soviet Union; a bar in San Francisco that specializes in giant margaritas.

Episode Nineteen

Original Airdate: January 30, 1980
Featured Segments: In Oakland, California, 10 cent taxi dancers; a wild race at Lake Calhoun, Minnesota, featuring boats made of milk cartons; psychics and mediums in the town of Cassadaga, Florida; an ugly dog contest in Petaluma, California; Sarah Purcell takes a tour of Nome, Alaska, and meets some local characters; the Miss Physique contest in Tampa, Florida; beach dancing at Bethany Beach, Delaware; a man in Monterey, California, who makes roughhewn wooden furniture resembling Neanderthal man and other natural figures; Ontario California Speedway, where people-powered vehicles race.

Episode Twenty

Original Airdate: February 6, 1980

Featured Segments: A man from Ogden, Utah, who dons a giant top hat and applies makeup on his stomach to make it appear as though his belly button is whistling; a visit to the US Olympic volleyball team tryouts; a prison rodeo in Texas; a military school in Harlingen, Texas.

Episode Twenty-One

Original Airdate: February 13, 1980
Featured Segments: A Valentine's Day theme, including Harry, a man who can be seen in New York's Midtown Manhattan, where he angrily espouses "husband's lib" while handing out literature and wearing signs deriding "women's lib"; Captain Sticky, of San Diego, California, a three-hundred-pound-plus consumer advocate who wears a superhero costume; a tour of an inn, in San Luis Obispo, California, in which each room has a unique theme for customers; a real-life Cupid, who will shoot the one you love with his arrows.

Episode Twenty-Two

Original Airdate: February 20, 1980
Featured Segments: Florida State's flying circus; a Los Angeles nightclub featuring mud-wrestling women; a "Bogginhole" competition where jeeps and four-wheel-drive vehicles race in the mud; "Croaker College," in Sacramento, California, where frogs are taught to be weight lifters; a devoutly liberated woman; an interview with Murray Langston, known as the "Unknown Comic," who wears a brown paper bag over his head during his stand-up performance; a man who will backflip anywhere, anytime, for a quarter; Clayton Moore, television's famed Lone Ranger, talks about the controversy that prevented him from wearing his legendary black mask in public; a man who makes rubber bricks to throw at the television when in a fit of anger; a school where people learn to flirt; a Gilmer, Texas, couple who live atop an oil derrick.

Episode Twenty-Three

Original Airdate: February 27, 1980

Featured Segments: A talking refrigerator; Felicia, the toilet-trained cat; a traveling belly-dancing instructor; a psychic who conducts séances for members of Elvis Presley's family; a tiddlywinks championship tournament; an update on Captain Sticky; a Phoenix, Arizona, man who wears a Richard Nixon mask while selling flowers; the Unknown Comic, Murray Langston, is unmasked; Sarah Purcell attends a fashion show for full-figured women; the Golden Age Olympics for senior citizens in Sanford, Florida; fan reactions and dedication to professional wrestling; a commentary on the Susan B. Anthony dollar, by Mark Russell.

Episode Twenty-Four

Original Airdate: March 5, 1980
Featured Segments: Consumer advocate Captain Sticky; a visit to Fiorucci, a fashionable high-end store in New York City; an eight-mile footrace in San Francisco; a Williamsport, Pennsylvania, minister who uses ventriloquism, including a dummy, in his sermons; offbeat versions of skiing; a hotel with an unusual layout; a discount lawyer; a New Orleans disc jockey; a Mark Russell commentary.

Episode Twenty-Five

Original Airdate: March 12, 1980
Featured Segments: Lucky Mike, a 103-year-old gambler; the birdman of Baraboo, Wisconsin; a sandcastle-building contest; a report on the American Medical Association by consumer advocate Herb Denenberg; a beer-drinking contest in Santa Monica, California; a man who skis without skis; a female railroad engineer in Los Angeles; music produced by unusual instruments in Hilton Head, South Carolina; off-duty Chicago police officers who dress up as clowns to entertain hospitalized children; a visit to a summer camp in Georgia; people in Northern California who live and dress in the style of the 1920s; Dennis Holland, a Costa Mesa, California, man who moved his family into a ship he built in his backyard.

Episode Twenty-Six

Original Airdate: March 19, 1980
Featured Segments: A roller-skating elephant; an expert karate demonstration; an unorthodox dietician in Beverly Hills, California; the wild antics of the students at the University of Wisconsin; a woman fired for photocopying her buttocks; homemade-boat races in Oregon; a visit with magician Harry Blackstone Jr.; the city of the future in Arco Santi, Arizona; offbeat ways to ski.

Episode Twenty-Seven

Original Airdate: March 26, 1980
Featured Segments: Byron Allen visits Pepperdine University in Malibu, California, to explore grass skiing; the Suzuki School for Violinists in Pasadena, California; a raft race on the Beaver River in western Canada; a story on three women cycling across the country; a school for baseball umpires; the Polar Bear Club of New York City; a car with two front ends; a man who plays pocket calculator as a musical instrument; a Chicago nightclub with amateur talent; renting a hot tub in Los Angeles; a jump-rope contest; Olympic hopefuls in Oregon.

Episode Twenty-Eight

Original Airdate: May 7, 1980
Featured Segments: A man whose home is made of junk; a man who feeds squirrels as a hobby at Golden Gate Park in San Francisco; a fair for psychics; a best legs contest for men; an eighty-five-year-old self-defense expert; skydiving; a Mark Russell commentary.

Episode Twenty-Nine

Original Airdate: May 14, 1980
Featured Segments: The world's smallest police station; turtle collectors in Los Angeles; a report on the eighty-three-year-old legend that an extraterrestrial being is buried in the small town of Aurora, Texas; the annual tough guy competition in Detroit, Michigan; a cowboy bar in Willits,

Texas; a ten-year-old marathoner in Oakland, California; a bicycle jumping contest; a Mark Russell commentary.

SEASON THREE: 1980–1981, WEDNESDAY, 8 PM

Hosts: Byron Allen, John Barbour, Sarah Purcell, Bill Rafferty, Skip Stephenson
Special Correspondents: Mark Russell

Episode One

Original Airdate: September 17, 1980
Featured Segments: John Barbour attends a Las Vegas, Nevada, reunion of POWs from World War II and the Korean War; part one of a segment featuring Sarah Purcell joining the Los Angeles T-Birds, a female roller derby team; Bill Rafferty interviews a Miami woman who produces a line of custom-made bikinis for women and men; the Fabulous Moolah, a female wrestling champion; a school for baseball umpires; a Florida woman who claims to be the world's fastest oyster shucker; a return visit from Carol Johnston, a one-armed gymnast; a Toledo, Ohio, teenager who runs up walls.

Episode Two

Original Airdate: September 24, 1980
Featured Segments: Sarah Purcell concludes her visit with the T-Birds roller derby team; a man whose hobby is "garbology," which means he sorts through and collects the garbage of celebrities; "Birdman" Abe Johnson of Redland, Oregon, who dedicates his time to feeding birds; punk food at the Mud Club in New York City; the "Scaffold Lady," who cleans and repairs windows on the Empire State Building; the annual "crow off" for roosters at the Rogue River, Oregon; a Frisbee-catching dog; the cast reads a poem by a West Palm Beach, Florida, woman complaining about her problems with a motorbike.

Episode Three

Original Airdate: October 1, 1980
Featured Segments: Monks in Forest Park, Oklahoma, who are also volunteer firefighters; a couple in Bellefontaine, Ohio, who keep alligators, skunks, and wolves in their home; an unusual Beverly Hills health restaurant that also has a gym attached; exercise and health guru Richard Simmons; a snow-skiing dog; hang gliding; a profile of a disabled cowboy from the San Fernando Valley, California.

Episode Four

Original Airdate: October 8, 1980
Featured Segments: Terry Fox, a twenty-two-year-old Canadian man who is running across Canada to raise money for cancer research, despite having lost one of his legs to the disease; a visit to a rodeo in Farmington, New Mexico, where participants are between the ages of six and nine; Bill Rafferty takes a humorous look at the town of Boring, Oregon; a California grape stomp; the "Menopauses," a group of women who won't make concessions to age; an Indiana man fascinated with bubbles as an art form; a middle-aged boxer who wants to turn pro; double-deck bus drivers take their road test.

Episode Five

Original Airdate: October 22, 1980
Featured Segments: Sarah Purcell examines a defensive driving school; Skip Stephenson visits a health spa created to reduce stress for high-powered executives; a feature offering expert opinion on how to avoid hijacking, kidnapping, and robbery; a dude ranch in England; a California man who uses an exercise bicycle to power the family TV; an Ohio man who built his own castle; a man attempts to jump a tank over a car.

Episode Six

Original Airdate: October 29, 1980
Featured Segments: A special Halloween episode: Sarah Purcell attends a Dracula-themed wedding with a monster motif; a visit to a haunted

house in Louisville, Kentucky; a flying lawnmower in Mobile, Alabama; tombstone and cemetery legends from around the country; a visit with Hollywood mask maker Don Post; a story on Rollerena, a New York City man who dresses as a good fairy while roller skating around the city; a karate-practicing chimp; an Elvis Presley séance; an underwater pumpkin-carving contest; a boy who thinks he is the reincarnated form of his own uncle; a haunted house in Santa Barbara, California.

Episode Seven

Original Airdate: November 5, 1980
Featured Segments: In Iowa, a visit with the woman voted by seven thousand truck drivers as the best waitress in America; skiing on melted snow; a coed beauty salon specializing in punk hairstyles; the "Cowboy Chimp," who feeds livestock and drives a tractor on a Mississippi farm; a diminutive artist referred to as the "Midget Michelangelo"; a woman with a collection of 3,300 dolls; a New York woman who dresses birds in costumes and trains them to sing popular songs; a woman's arm-wrestling tournament.

Episode Eight

Original Airdate: November 12, 1980
Featured Segments: An update on Terry Fox, who was running across Canada with a prosthetic leg to raise money for cancer research; unique flying contraptions and experimental aircraft in Oshkosh, Wisconsin; "Confederate Air Force" flying museum in Harlingen, Texas; a sheepdog competition in Phoenix, Arizona; in Ontario, Canada, the eighth annual Ice Floe Race; seventy-one-year-old artist Teresa Fergo, an artist in the medium of junk; Prince Mongo, of Memphis, Tennessee, who claims to be from the planet of Zambodia; the original Chuck E. Cheese's restaurant in San Jose, California.

Episode Nine

Original Airdate: November 19, 1980

Featured Segments: A fifty-year-old Michigan woman living in a tee-pee; a California man who trains household cats to be attack and guard animals; a profile of fourteen-year-old paraplegic actress Suzy Gilstrap; tandem skiing; a school for door-to-door vacuum cleaner salesmen; a Connecticut man who teaches the chauffeurs for rich and prominent people how to elude potential terrorists or abductors; an adoption agency for dolls; a rodeo featuring four-wheel-drive vehicles.

Episode Ten

Original Airdate: November 26, 1980
Featured Segments: A report on a Hawaiian dentist who changed his waiting room into a disco for his patients; an eighty-year-old Minnesota man who has been building his own highway from his town to the city of Duluth, Minnesota; Sarah Purcell learns to fly at Wurtsmith Air Force Base in Michigan; a school for American Indians in Saint Paul, Minnesota; Mark Russell presents a commentary on Washington, DC, after Ronald Reagan's victory in the recent election.

Episode Eleven

Original Airdate: December 3, 1980
Featured Segments: A tour of the gravesites of Hollywood legends; an erotic bakery in New York City; a Los Angeles therapist who encourages his patients to sing their troubles away; a New York artist, Franco Gaskin, who paints inspirational murals on Harlem storefront security gates; a New York City artist who creates paintings that smell like their titles (e.g., ashtray, rush-hour subway, peanut butter sandwich); snowmobile water-skipping races in Siren, Wisconsin; Mark Russell discusses the Vatican's decision to review heresy charges against Galileo.

Episode Twelve

Original Airdate: December 10, 1980
Featured Segments: A look at a hang-gliding squirrel; Sarah Purcell takes a train trip through the Alaska wilderness; a visit to the annual Doo-Dah Parade, a parody of the Tournament of Roses Parade in Pasadena,

California; a gigolo convention in New Jersey; a reunion in Dallas, Texas, of US Air Force Japanese-American pilots who fought in World War II and the people they rescued; the wedding of a ninety-pound sheepdog and a fifteen-pound Lhasa Apso in California; a Philadelphia, Pennsylvania, man who lectures on bathroom plungers; a staring contest championship; a female weight lifter who uses self-hypnosis to build muscle; a visit to a family with nineteen children, fifteen of whom are adopted.

Episode Thirteen

Original Airdate: December 17, 1980
Featured Segments: A visit with an Oklahoma man who lives in a covered wagon and lives off the land; a male exotic dancing contest in Long Beach, California; a tandem skiing exhibition in Durango, Colorado; a look at female body builders; a New York state man who makes music with his false teeth; a woman who dresses her pet turtles and treats them like family members; a national comparison of tap water; a train trip through Alaska.

Episode Fourteen

Original Airdate: January 7, 1981
Featured Segments: A convention of Laurel and Hardy fans; a woman who can read and write backward and forward; handicapped skiers; a Utah man who claims he can control and alter the weather; female "belly-buckers" from California; the Blue Pigs, a rock band from Detroit, Michigan, composed of police officers; a woman who rehabilitates turtles; a meeting of the Sons of the Desert.

Episode Fifteen

Original Airdate: January 14, 1981
Featured Segments: An Aberdeen, Washington, family that paints flagpoles for a living; a Morrow, Ohio, woman who paints everything she owns red, white, and blue; the heavyweight skiing championship at Sugarloaf resort in Maine; people who use crank telephones; men who dress as ballerinas to do comic ballets in New Orleans, Louisiana; a Fullerton,

California, man who teaches boxing to keep local youngsters off the streets; people who wrestle pigs; Salt Lake City, Utah, policemen who engage in drag racing with local teens.

Episode Sixteen

Original Airdate: January 21, 1981
Featured Segments: A visit to a gay rodeo in Reno, Nevada; a sun tanning/tan lines competition in Fresno, California; a profile of a warlock; Paul Knoll, a professional dog walker in New York City; sidecar racing in the Mojave Desert; a New York City cat doctor who makes house calls; a profile of an American Indian from Oregon, who successfully fought the US government over his rights to tribal lands; a whistling contest in Carson City, Nevada; Robert Bowdin, a Los Angeles college student who is a game show expert and fanatic; Fritz Von Berg, a fifty-year-old college football player, who lives out of his car to afford his tuition.

Episode Seventeen

Original Airdate: January 28, 1981
Featured Segments: Pete Moore, from Wetumpka, Alabama, who at sixteen inches tall is the shortest man in America; a baseball game played on mules, in Big Bear, California; a retiree who spends time waving to people going to work; a Cincinnati, Ohio, man who makes music with spoons; a singing poodle in San Francisco; female stevedores in Newark, New Jersey; a transplanted Texan who keeps longhorn steers in his front yard in Quakertown, Pennsylvania; mud-racing vehicles in North Carolina.

Episode Eighteen

Original Airdate: February 4, 1981
Featured Segments: A Durango, Colorado, softball game played in the snow; a hockey game played underwater in Palm Beach, Florida; segments on two belly dancers, one male in Illinois, and one female in California; ballet classes for wheelchair-bound senior citizens in Santa Rosa, California; a woman who keeps a unique array of pets; a visit with

the world's strongest man, John Wooten, of Boston; snowmobile racing in Wisconsin; a Claremont, California, woman who keeps ten alligators as pets.

Episode Nineteen

Original Airdate: February 11, 1981
Featured Segments: Former Dallas Cowboys cheerleader becomes first female professional rodeo clown; Miss Senior Sweetheart Beauty Contest for women over sixty-five; Playboy Bunnies, Los Angeles Rams cheerleaders, and airline stewardesses compete in athletic contests for charity; American Indian artist Peter Toth, who makes wooden sculptures to honor the United States; a dancer named Shabba Doo (aka Adolfo Quinones), who inspires inner-city children to escape poverty and follow their dreams; Bill Cushing from Littleton, New Hampshire, a man who wears skirts in his daily life, rather than pants; a wedding with a donkey for a best man.

Episode Twenty

Original Airdate: February 18, 1981
Featured Segments: A kissing contest in Phoenix, Arizona; a TV station with a novel approach to news; a Wyoming man who travels on motorized roller skates; an update on a woman who refused to sell her Atlantic City, New Jersey, home to make way for a casino; New Hampshire's sixth annual Mud Bowl, a charity football game; a report on Ron Kauk, who climbed one of the highest peaks in Yosemite National Park without ropes.

Episode Twenty-One

Original Airdate: February 25, 1981
Featured Segments: A profile of professional wrestler Lillian Ellison, also known as the Fabulous Moolah, from Columbia, South Carolina; the Arthur Mitchell Dance Troupe, the first classical ballet troupe in Harlem, New York; an artist who creates masterpieces on the streets of Boston; women skiing in bikinis in Dresser, Wisconsin; a look at the Society for

Creative Anachronism, a group dedicated to re-creating the medieval lifestyle; an Oklahoma City, Oklahoma, couple who wallpapered their bedroom with dollar bills; a motocross contest in Los Angeles.

Episode Twenty-Two

Original Airdate: March 4, 1981
Featured Segments: An all-black rodeo in Boley, Oklahoma; a female auctioneer in Garden Grove, California; a male city official in Orange, New Jersey, who dresses in women's clothing; a senior citizen baseball team; a man who raises snails to sell to restaurants; sandcastle building on the Oregon coast; a collection of antique wind-up toys in Lafayette, California; a feature on Arnold the pig, who is treated like a member of his owner's family.

Episode Twenty-Three

Original Airdate: March 18, 1981
Featured Segments: An eleven-year-old stock market investor from Chula Vista, California; a man from Kidderminster, England, who powers small appliances with lemon juice; a police department demolition derby in San Jose, California; Sally Lippman, a seventy-year-old disco queen from New York City; a dancing caterpillar in Clemson, South Carolina; barstool races in Alameda, California; a bagpipe school in Chicago, Illinois.

Episode Twenty-Four

Original Airdate: April 1, 1981
Featured Segments: A "best of" compilation episode with a few new segments; a banjo club in Houston, Texas; female lifeguards; a water-skiing squirrel; a twelve-year-old evangelist; a New Orleans man who plays the ironing board; a pilot who pulls advertisements behind her plane.

Episode Twenty-Five

Original Airdate: May 6, 1981
Featured Segments: Sarah Purcell racing in the Long Beach (California) Grand Prix; the identity of the telephone voice who tells the time; a violinist who performs in the men's room at a Beverly Hills, California, park; a ranger at Yosemite National Park; Madam Lou Bunch Day festival honoring an eighteenth-century madam in Central City, Colorado; female prizefighters.

SEASON FOUR: 1981–1982, WEDNESDAY, 8 PM

Hosts: Byron Allen, John Barbour, Sarah Purcell, Bill Rafferty, Skip Stephenson, Peter Billingsley, Fred Willard
Special Correspondent: Mark Russell

Episode One

Original Airdate: Sept 30, 1981
Featured Segments: Frank Lodato, a New Jersey psychologist who claims he can increase a woman's breast size through hypnosis; John Barbour attends a school for male hula dancers in Hawaii; tractor races in Bakersfield, California; Alice and John Purple, urban ecologists in New York City; a Florida grandmother who races stock cars; a fifteen-year-old writer from Wilmington, Delaware, who writes for *Newsweek*.

Episode Two

Original Airdate: October 7, 1981
Featured Segments: A visit to a tattoo convention in Philadelphia, Pennsylvania; a segment on the plight of teenage runaways in Los Angeles; a profile of a bird psychiatrist in New York City; the All-American Redheads, a female professional basketball team from Caraway, Arkansas, that plays male opponents; "Adopt a Grandparent" program in Prescott, Arizona; a fashion show for dogs in Tonawanda, New York; a Fort Worth, Texas, woman who found a python wrapped around her car's engine; backward roller skating in the hills of San Francisco.

Episode Three

Original Airdate: October 21, 1981
Featured Segments: A visit to Mount Shasta, California; a profile of Hollywood photographer George Hurrell; a group of New Jersey school-children who operate their own cable TV news program; a ninety-two-year-old radio talk show host in Santa Monica, California.

Episode Four

Original Airdate: October 28, 1981
Featured Segments: A Halloween-themed episode: a ghost town in New Mexico; a haunted church in Arizona; an investigation of a reported flying saucer landing at Mount Rainier, Washington; a Santa Monica, California, couple who have transformed their home into a wax museum; a feature on the Amazing Randi, a magician and paranormal skeptic/debunker.

Episode Five

Original Airdate: November 4, 1981
Featured Segments: Ben Gross, an eighty-five-year-old landlord in Venice, California, who has not raised the rent in fifteen years; a one-man band in Butte, Montana; a visit to the town of Derby Line, Vermont, which is split by the US-Canadian border; dogsled racing in the Yukon territory; a twelve-year-old professional cattle auctioneer in Modesto, California; punk rock fashions; chainsaw ice carving; Sarah Purcell rides a mechanical bull.

Episode Six

Original Airdate: November 11, 1981
Featured Segments: A Veterans Day–themed episode: a reunion of the crew of the USS *Lexington* from World War II; a visit to the Tomb of the Unknown Soldier in Arlington National Cemetery; a segment on Navajo Code Talkers who served in World War II; a group of Native American graduates of the US Marine Corps boot camp; a visit to Santa Fe, New Mexico, to profile Bill Maudlin, a noted cartoonist of the World War

II–era cartoon *Willie and Joe*; World War II glider pilots attend a reunion; Dr. David Westphal, a New Mexico man who built a memorial for his son who died in Vietnam, which came to be viewed as a memorial and mourning spot for the families of others killed in Vietnam.

Episode Seven

Original Airdate: November 18, 1981
Featured Segments: Bikini-clad boxers in California; hockey-playing priests, known as the Flying Fathers; Beulah Kershaw, a sixty-five-year-old disco singer from Crossville, Illinois; the Junior Blind of America, an organization which helps young people with visual impairment or disability; Korczak Ziolkowski, a man who is carving a mountain statue in South Dakota, dedicated to Native American hero Chief Crazy Horse.

Episode Eight

Original Airdate: November 25, 1981
Featured Segments: A show dedicated to New York City, "Real People Salutes the Big Apple": a day in the life of Mayor Ed Koch; Sarah Purcell visits a job site with ironworkers finishing a skyscraper; Bill Rafferty plays "bike polo" in Central Park; a Mark Russell commentary on Wall Street and its inhabitants; John Barbour revisits some earlier New York City segments; Skip Stephenson looks at skiing firefighters who raise money for charity while having a good time; Byron Allen introduces several youth-oriented segments; Peter Billingsley profiles Eric Lerner, an accomplished eleven-year-old classical pianist; a new generation of stonemasons who are working to finish the Cathedral of Saint John the Divine.

Episode Nine

Original Airdate: December 2, 1981
Featured Segments: Bill Rafferty interviews Kathy Metcalf, a woman who photographs male nude centerfolds; Sarah Purcell visits Toronto, Canada, to interview "Checkmate Joe," who claims to be the world's fastest chess player; Fred Willard spends time in a disco-themed Laun-

dromat in Azle, Texas; John Barbour travels to Hornet, Missouri, to investigate the source of a mysterious unexplained light, known as the "Spooklight"; a "role reversal" workshop; an Englishman who can whistle in two-part harmony; a look at inner-tube racing in Victoria, British Columbia.

Episode Ten

Original Airdate: December 9, 1981
Featured Segments: A profile of a McKeesport, Pennsylvania, priest who also works as a stand-up comedian; a Chattanooga, Tennessee, man who claims to be the world's best trick shot pool player; a goose that thinks it's a flamingo; a surfing dog; a visit to the palace in Montreal, Quebec, Canada, that was built to house royal family members who were little people; a man who rents decommissioned American battle tanks to the general public; a man who imitates an emergency siren and other common sounds.

Episode Eleven

Original Airdate: December 16, 1981
Featured Segments: A holiday-themed episode: a visit to a toy manufacturers' convention in New York City; skateboarding in the snow (aka snowboarding); a profile of a California man attempting to make the poinsettia tree the world's official holiday tree; a thirty-foot snow mountain at the Lakeland, Florida, Snow Festival; children learn how to ski in Keystone, Colorado; a San Francisco man who decorates his elevator for the holiday season; Skip Stephenson attends a school for Santas.

Episode Twelve

Original Airdate: January 6, 1982
Featured Segments: A "Family Reunion" episode composed largely of clips from previous seasons: one-armed gymnast Carol Johnston; firefighting monks; diet guru Richard Simmons; consumer advocate Captain Sticky; Disco Beulah; Prince Mongo; paraplegic actress Suzy Gilstrap; Sidewalk Sam; female locomotive engineers; Mr. Spoons; the tattooed

granny; the world's fastest oyster shucker; a senior citizen baseball league; a ballet instructor who teaches from a wheelchair; the human echo; disabled park ranger Dennis Almasey; a woman who colors everything in red, white, and blue; a man who walks up walls; the world's fastest beer drinker; America's first female rodeo clown.

Episode Thirteen

Original Airdate: January 13, 1982

Featured Segments: A Pittsburgh, Pennsylvania, hypnotherapist who claims that she has been practicing for one hundred thousand years; a profile of a Dallas woman who has written a book about the two hundred most eligible bachelors in town, and holds a party for women to meet them; a fashion show for frogs in San Diego, California; Joe Smoliij, who bills himself as the world's fastest chess player; a visit to the most isolated woman in America, Dorothy Molter, of Isle of Pine, Minnesota; a Sacramento, California, man who sells advertising on his bald head; a four-hundred-pound man who races go-carts.

Episode Fourteen

Original Airdate: January 20, 1982

Featured Segments: A drive-thru funeral parlor in Jacksonville, Florida; a visit to the fifth annual World Croquet Championship in Vancouver Island, British Columbia, Canada; a photographer for the city of Miami Beach, who spends his days taking pictures of bikini-clad beachgoers; a San Francisco carwash that has a chorus of singing birds; a profile of an eighty-two-year-old bicyclist from Woodbury, New Jersey; a colorful New York City cabdriver; a report on an inspirational dance school for teenage girls in Marblehead, Massachusetts.

Episode Fifteen

Original Airdate: February 3, 1982

Featured Segments: A day in the life of a professional dog walker in New York City; a visit with Robert Asp, a Moorhead, Minnesota, man building a full-scale replica of a Viking ship; a New York City doctor who is also a stand-up comedian; a rodeo for senior citizens in Hyannis, Nebraska; a profile of a teenage fashion model; a Fresno, California, artist acclaimed by critics, but ignored by buyers; Ron Typewriter Mingo, an Oakland, California, teacher who types 1,600 words per minute, with musical accompaniment.

Episode Sixteen

Original Airdate: February 10, 1982
Featured Segments: A Queen Elizabeth look-alike; a look at a Sun Valley, California, couple who teach horseback riding to cerebral palsy patients; profile of ninety-seven-year-old twin sisters in Lemoore, California, both of whom were Ziegfeld Girls in their youth; a beauty pageant for pigeons; a husband and wife team of female/male impersonators; oil wrestling in Southern California; an Alexandria, Virginia, man who used a giant billboard ad to propose to his girlfriend.

Episode Seventeen

Original Airdate: February 17, 1982
Featured Segments: A dog howling contest in Los Angeles' Griffith Park; a Carlson, Minnesota, man who is a devotee of Pyramid Power; a profile of nationally syndicated radio host Dr. Demento; youngsters who race midget cars in Pomona, California.

Episode Eighteen

Original Airdate: February 24, 1982
Featured Segments: A visit to an authentic western dude ranch in the country of Wales; a profile of a Fullerton, California, teacher who counsels gang members to channel their aggression and energy into boxing; two "fruitarians," Tomato and Watermelon Stapleton; a Mont Vernon, New Hampshire, woman who keeps giant lizards as pets; a Los Angeles reunion for black women who served in the WACS during World War II.

Episode Nineteen

Original Airdate: March 3, 1982
Featured Segments: A female sports referee in Philadelphia, Pennsylvania; an eighty-one-year-old Manhattan Beach, California, resident who teaches ballet at $1 a lesson; a junk food critic in Dallas, Texas; the first Miss Bald America contest in New York; a Colorado mountain climber who scales icy peaks; a Los Angeles "dog wash," a car wash for dogs.

Episode Twenty

Original Airdate: March 17, 1982
Featured Segments: A seventy-five-year-old volunteer fireman who drives a 1931 fire truck; the preppy v. anti-preppy controversy on the Princeton University campus; female rock climbers in Vail, Colorado; a blind boxing coach; a comedian who performs with a cutout of a TV around his head and calls himself the "Human TV"; a Florida truck stop where the menus are printed on bikini-clad waitresses.

Episode Twenty-One

Original Airdate: March 31, 1982
Featured Segments: A diminutive Bostonian who is battling civil service height requirements to become a police officer; a kissing contest in Corvallis, Oregon; the National Gay Rodeo in Reno, Nevada; a 103-year-old gambler in Gardena, California; a California guitarist who plays despite not having either arm.

Episode Twenty-Two

Original Airdate: April 28, 1982
Featured Segments: A Russellville, Arkansas, man who is planning to launch his own spaceship; "the Great Antonio," a fifty-six-year-old Montreal, Canada, resident who claims to be the strongest man in the world; a man from Tampa, Florida, who is a champion wheelchair racer; the eighteenth annual bird calling contest at a Piedmont, California, high school; San Francisco's annual Mr. Gay USA contest; the annual re-creation of a ninety-mile pony express ride in Pinetop, Arizona.

Episode Twenty-Three

Original Airdate: May 5, 1982
Featured Segments: A look at a gorilla in an Atlanta, Georgia, zoo, that watches and rates TV programs; a feature on two New York City police officers who started a youth center in the South Bronx; a profile of a cowboy that delivers strip-o-grams; a visit to Lake Champlain, between New York and Vermont, where people claim to have seen a Loch Ness–type monster named Champ; a profile of a Lincolnshire, England, man who is trying to fly like a bird; a Mark Russell commentary on celibacy; a look at a self-proclaimed prince who rules a World War II–era gunnery tower off the coast of England.

SEASON FIVE: 1982–1983, WEDNESDAY, 8 PM

Hosts: Byron Allen, Sarah Purcell, Bill Rafferty, Skip Stephenson, Fred Willard, Peter Billingsley, Kerry Millerick
Special Correspondent: Mark Russell

Episode One

Original Airdate: September 22, 1982
Featured Segments: The ninety-minute season five premiere is the beginning of a trilogy of episodes centered upon a cross-country train trip from Los Angeles to Chicago: the cast, Byron Allen, Sarah Purcell, Skip Stephenson, Fred Willard, Bill Rafferty, and new field reporter Kerry Millerick, are ambushed by desperadoes in Fort Worth, Texas; whistle stops in Phoenix and Tucson, Arizona, and El Paso and San Antonio, Texas; Hub Cap Annie, a woman whose hobby of collecting hubcaps has become a thriving business; Fred Willard tries out for the Oakland A's baseball team; Pamela Wingo, a female steam locomotive engineer; a chat with "Red Neck Granny," a colorful CB radio enthusiast from Pawelekville, Texas; a karate team destroys a house in San Antonio, Texas, with their hands and feet; a tour of the town of Why, Arizona; a segment on an all-female volunteer fire department in Buffalo Gap, Texas (population: 389).

Episode Two

Original Airdate: September 29, 1982

Featured Segments: Part two of the Los Angeles to Chicago train tour: whistle stops in Little Rock, Arkansas, where several thousand fans and a marching band greet the cast; in Dallas, the "Most Perfect Body Contest," both male and female; in Saint Louis, Missouri, a feature on the singing M&M Girls, aged sixty to eighty-seven; a look at the famous Budweiser Clydesdales; a twelve-year-old soccer referee; an Abraham Lincoln look-alike contest in Springfield, Illinois; a breakfast program for disadvantaged children in Little Rock, Arkansas.

Episode Three

Original Airdate: October 6, 1982

Featured Segments: The final segment of the season-opening trilogy features a salute to Chicago, Illinois; Morey Greenblatt, "swimsuit king of Chicago"; a pet motel in Prairie View, Illinois; a day in the life of Mayor Jane Byrne; a visit to the Billy Goat Tavern, made famous in a *Saturday Night Live* skit ("Cheeborger! Cheeborger!"); an ultrapatriotic bar in Fox Lake, Illinois; the Purple Heart Cruise for war veterans; a number of earlier Chicago stores are revisited; "Human Drummer" Joe Wright, who plays his body as his instrument; Disco Beulah; Sally's Stage, featuring daily talent shows; a bagpipe teacher; a cat who predicts the weather; Chicago police officers who become clowns and entertain at children's hospitals; Steve Hart and his Bungee Bird Circus visit sick children; a visit to Wrigley Field.

Episode Four

Original Airdate: October 27, 1982

Featured Segments: The Peabody Hotel in Memphis, Tennessee, where four ducks are treated like royalty, including being given a daily parade; a cardboard-box race in Minot, North Dakota; a Pennsylvania sheriff and his family who live in the county jail; two construction teams in California competing to see who can build a house more quickly; an eighty-eight-year-old nun who runs a home for abandoned animals.

Episode Five

Original Airdate: November 3, 1982
Featured Segments: A four-year-old body builder; a Los Angeles supper club that features female impersonators; a look at the work of search-and-rescue dogs at Lake Tahoe, Nevada; a look at WOOF; a massive hat collection in Eldora, Iowa; people who wear pontoons on their feet; National Pig Day celebration in Lubbock, Texas.

Episode Six

Original Airdate: November 10, 1982
Featured Segments: A Veterans Day special: the Dallas Cowboys cheerleaders visit servicemen on the DMZ in South Korea during the Christmas season; a reunion for WACs who served in World War II; George Baker, creator of *Sad Sack* cartoons popularized in World War II; Douglas Albert Munro, the first US Coast Guard member to receive the Congressional Medal of Honor, for his service in World War II; Boss Markham, a Dayton, Ohio, man, who impersonates General George S. Patton; a visit to the USS *Laffey* in Charleston, South Carolina, where it is being restored by men and the widows of men who served on the ship in multiple wars; the "River Rats," American fighter pilots from the Vietnam War, at their annual reunion; a feature on MIAs from the Vietnam War and the efforts of their families to have them returned.

Episode Seven

Original Airdate: November 17, 1982
Featured Segments: The "Ultimate Valley Girl Contest" in Sherman Oaks, California, with judges Moon Unit Zappa and Bert Parks; a seventy-five-year-old newlywed who is also an extreme jogger; a trick shot golfer performs; a feature on the marriage of a *Real People* favorite, consumer superhero Captain Sticky.

Episode Eight

Original Airdate: November 24, 1982

Featured Segments: Sterling Beemis, a man who lives in a lighthouse near Chicago; a San Francisco barbershop for babies; a seventy-year-old Wisconsin man and his pet worm; a male wet T-shirt contest; nutrition class at Syracuse University; a Denver man who skips rope without a rope; one of the oldest Kelly Girls (temporary office workers) in the country.

Episode Nine

Original Airdate: December 1, 1982
Featured Segments: Tricycle racing in New Iberia, Louisiana; playing golf in the snow in Prince George, British Columbia; Jacques d'Amboise, a former ballet star who teaches modern dance to children; a mother of two who is also a centerfold model; an eighty-five-year-old fraternity house mother; a man who claims to be the fastest bartender in the west.

Episode Ten

Original Airdate: December 8, 1982
Featured Segments: A report on the fans of the *Rocky Horror Picture Show* at a theater in Portland, Oregon; Lenny Skutnick, the hero of an Air Florida crash in Washington, DC; a Rochester, New York, collector of telephones; a look at garage sales; animal trainer Ray Berwick; a man who plays Mozart on wine goblets; an acrobatic troupe, the Flippo Morris Tumblers, from Chattanooga, Tennessee, composed largely of disadvantaged youth.

Episode Eleven

Original Airdate: December 15, 1982
Featured Segments: A holiday-themed show: an eighty-two-year-old woman from Maryland, known as "Mrs. Santa" because of her work repairing toys for needy youth; the Volunteers of America in New York City, who bring Christmas gifts to the disadvantaged; a family that adopted a polar bear; a West Orange, New Jersey, radio station that only operates during Chanukah; a truck driver who makes his rounds dressed as Santa.

Episode Twelve

Original Airdate: January 12, 1983
Featured Segments: A segment on a drug raid by Los Angeles narcotics detectives; a convention of cheerleaders and mascots from 150 American colleges; the training of the US women's alpine ski team; a traveling pianist in Eugene, Oregon, who plays concerts from the back of a van; a South Dakota journalist who travels by horse and mule; a publication for pig framers; a centerfold photo shoot for *Playboar* magazine, a satirical publication; a California couple who have a passion for the color purple in every aspect of their lives.

Episode Thirteen

Original Airdate: January 19, 1983
Featured Segments: The All-American Male beauty pageant in Washington, Indiana; a look at hibernating bears in Minnesota; a sports memorabilia collector who has his own ten-room museum in Pittsburgh, Pennsylvania; the finals of the National Mechanical Bull Championships in Las Vegas, Nevada; blind athlete Janet Rowley; an examination of the growing national fad of aerobic exercise.

Episode Fourteen

Original Airdate: January 26, 1983
Featured Segments: Report on the Loch Ness Monster in Scotland, who inspired the "Nessie Hunters"; a "love witch" in New York City; a horse auction in Scottsdale, Arizona; a dog that runs errands for its owners and others; a pig that acts like a watchdog, in Jackson, Mississippi; modern-day Gypsies; a home that has been transformed into a western fantasy land; the national Wheelchair Games in Long Beach, California.

Episode Fifteen

Original Airdate: February 9, 1983
Featured Segments: Tassos Chronopoulos, a Chicago man who erected a controversial memorial to the eight servicemen who died trying to rescue the American hostages in Iran; a costumed ski competition in Vail,

Colorado; a ski club for senior citizens over seventy in upstate New York; a couple celebrating their seventy-fifth anniversary; a hang-gliding dog in Buffalo, Colorado.

Episode Sixteen

Original Airdate: February 16, 1983
Featured Segments: A scuba-diving dog; a San Francisco artist who creates portraits made of jelly beans; Maggie Kuhn, founder of the Gray Panthers, an advocacy organization for senior citizens; a pair of preteen disco dancers in Chicago; a Mississippi university that offers football players a class in fashion modeling.

Episode Seventeen

Original Airdate: February 23, 1983
Featured Segments: The fifth annual Stuntman's Rodeo in Phoenix, Arizona; a florist who delivers dead flowers; a man who made his car look like a hippopotamus; the "Best Chest in the West Competition"; a profile of a man who trains tigers; the Las Floristas Ball in Beverly Hills, California, where celebrities sport elaborate headdresses made of flowers.

Episode Eighteen

Original Airdate: March 2, 1983
Featured Segments: A feature on an allegedly talking cow; the American Avalanche Institute in Jackson Hole, Wyoming; bicycle moto-cross racing in Southern California; a ninety-five-year-old woman about to be inducted into the Chili Hall of Fame; a former Skid Row dweller who now helps the poor and the homeless on the streets; the Golden Rollers skating club from San Francisco; a Mark Russell commentary on warnings and product labels.

Episode Nineteen

Original Airdate: March 9, 1983

Featured Segments: Women who wrestle in Jell-O; a children's circus in Peru, Indiana; a pair of senior citizens who operate a portable disco business; a man and his pet chicken; a man who ties cherry stems into knots with his tongue; dune buggy racing on a mountain of gravel.

Episode Twenty

Original Airdate: March 16, 1983
Featured Segments: An all-female rodeo in Canada; Pat and the "Chili Bordello"; a man who helped his daughter overcome mental and physical obstacles to become an outstanding student; a ten-year-old private detective; a "hug club" in Southern California; the one-hundredth birthday party for a volunteer fireman on Long Island, New York; male cheerleaders for a women's basketball team.

Episode Twenty-One

Original Airdate: March 23, 1983
Featured Segments: A women's tackle football team where the husbands are the cheerleaders; the Miss L.A. Best Body Contest, in Los Angeles; a classical violinist who fiddles for his cows; a pilot who specializes in spreading the ashes of the deceased from his airplane; an eighty-year-old man from Wilson, Wyoming, who is known as Dancin' George; a program that teaches skating to disabled children; a California surfer who surfs against the waves.

Episode Twenty-Two

Original Airdate: April 6, 1983
Featured Segments: Report on a "hearing ear dog," a dog that helps its deaf owner; a grand national Kung Fu champion; a marathoner who runs despite needing a pacemaker; the sport of grape catching; Bill Rafferty visits Scarsdale, New York; Peter Mosen, who offers his services as an "extraterrestrial" at parties, meetings, and weddings; the Chub Club in Saint Louis, Missouri; underwater shopping cart races.

Episode Twenty-Three

Original Airdate: April 27, 1983
Featured Segments: A zucchini festival in Harrisville, New Hampshire; Fred Willard talks to an actor who makes a living dressed as King Kong; Sarah Purcell profiles the highest-ranking female cadet officer in the history of West Point; Skip Stephenson looks at the unique lifestyle and some unusual residents of Key West, Florida; the Grand National Wild Turkey Calling Contest in Orlando, Florida; Bill Rafferty visits with an eighty-five-year-old radio news reporter in Kingston, Oklahoma, who does her reporting from a public phone booth; Mark Russell reports on a man who expressed his support of the people of Poland and the Solidarity movement with a protest sign near the Bering Straits.

Episode Twenty-Four

Original Airdate: May 4, 1983
Featured Segments: Wisconsin pool players who use their noses instead of cue sticks; a Canadian college professor who claims he can make nutritious food out of garbage; the first winner of the Real People Film Award; people flying in a wind chamber; a report on missing children, including a child fingerprinting program, and advice for teaching children how to recognize danger.

SEASON SIX: 1983–1984, WEDNESDAY, 8 PM

Hosts: Byron Allen, Sarah Purcell, Bill Rafferty, Skip Stephenson, Peter Billingsley, David Ruprecht
Special Correspondent: Mark Russell

Episode One

Original Airdate: September 14, 1983
Featured Segments: The season six ninety-minute premiere is the beginning of a trilogy of episodes centered upon a cross-country train trip from Chicago to Washington, DC: a futuristic car that can talk back to the driver; the Silver Belles, a team of precision ice skaters; a sixty-nine-

year-old female racquetball champion; a look at the various sports teams from Michigan; Jerry "Mr. Softball" Burton, who can throw a softball over 100 MPH; a commentary by Mark Russell on the lure of Niagara Falls, including stories of those who went over the falls in a barrel; a visit with a cook who tosses pancakes to his customers.

Episode Two

Original Airdate: September 21, 1983
Featured Segments: The second part of the train trip from Chicago to Washington, DC: a tour of upstate New York; a reenactment of the Boston Tea Party in Boston Harbor; a dancer who believes that stress and anxiety can be tap-danced away; a theology student who works part-time as a stripper; an eighty-eight-year-old woman dedicated to protecting beavers; a punk rock club run by Evelyn "Granny" Knoll.

Episode Three

Original Airdate: September 28, 1983
Featured Segments: Part three of the Chicago to Washington, DC, train trip: the Philadelphia Bell Ringers, a group that has been ringing the bell at Independence Hall on special occasions for thirty years; Raymond Cormier, from Temple University, gives a lesson on the value of learning foreign languages; a bikini-clad hot dog vendor; a feature on New York City disc jockey Don Imus; a feature on investigative reporters and some of the stories they cover.

Episode Four

Original Airdate: October 12, 1983
Featured Segments: Skip Stephenson is shipped in a life-sized envelope via courier express to Mill Valley, California; a Juilliard student who took the music of Mozart to the natives of New Guinea; a story on a Monterey, California, program where homeless pets are taken to visit convalescent homes to cheer up the residents; Byron Allen takes on the winner of a Las Vegas, Nevada, arm wrestling contest; a demolition derby on ice; a Santa

Barbara man who crusades against safety laws that allegedly do more harm than good.

Episode Five

Original Airdate: October 19, 1983
Featured Segments: Families of Vietnam POWs/MIAs meet with the UN ambassador from Vietnam to plead for cooperation in the recovery of their loved ones; male strippers from Chippendales nightclub put Sarah Purcell through an aerobics routine; a female skydiving team from Perris Valley, California; a woman who teaches models to act like mannequins; the Polar Bear Club in Salt Lake City, Utah; an elderly Minneapolis, Minnesota, man gives his pigs obedience training.

Episode Six

Original Airdate: October 26, 1983
Featured Segments: A Halloween special: a man who wears a red gorilla suit and lives in a spaceship; a sci-fi ball held in San Diego (the original Comic-Con); a warlock from Florida who sculpts alien creatures; a Los Angeles TV horror hostess, Elvira (Cassandra Peterson), who introduces campy B movies late at night; a psychic who claims to have antennae in the back of his head; strange happenings in Scotland.

Episode Seven

Original Airdate: November 2, 1983
Featured Segments: An episode based in Hawaii: world champion sand sculptor Joe Maize; a female outrigger canoe team; Sarah Purcell gets married to Dr. Robert A. McClintock; Skip Stephenson gets a hula lesson; Sarah gets a lesson from pro surfer Buttons Kaluhiokalani; a traditional luau; the art of making leis; comedian Andy Bumatai; the fifth annual Underwater Pogo Stick Championships; a 1,100-pound pig.

Episode Eight

Original Airdate: November 9, 1983

Featured Segments: A Veterans Day special, "A Salute to American Veterans": a piece on Army Sergeant Roy Benavidez, a Vietnam veteran and a Congressional Medal of Honor recipient, who is fighting for full benefits for himself and other veterans; a profile of the WASPs (Women Airforce Service Pilots) of World War II, who flew domestic military missions; Bill Rafferty goes through US Marine Corps boot camp; a reunion of World War II paratroopers who landed in the Normandy invasion; a look at the most famous pinup girls of previous wars; a look at the history of the USS *North Carolina* in Wilmington, North Carolina; home cooking and daily life for the crew of aircraft carrier USS *John F. Kennedy*.

Episode Nine

Original Airdate: November 16, 1983
Featured Segments: A new road trip arc, going down the Ohio and Mississippi Rivers on the *Mississippi Queen* steamboat; stops include Cincinnati, Ohio; Saint Louis, Missouri; Louisville, Kentucky; Evansville, Indiana; Paducah, Kentucky; and Cairo, Illinois, where the cast is greeted by 12,000 people; segments include a visit to Mark Twain's hometown, Hannibal, Missouri; a tour of Elvis Presley's mansion, Graceland, and the recollections of his former high-school classmates; a motorcyclist whose sheepdog rides with him everywhere; a salute to the "Eagle Lady," a woman who worked for twenty years to protect the American bald eagle; a feature on a paralyzed man who kayaked down the Mississippi from Minnesota to Louisiana; the cast performing a spoof of *Gone with the Wind*.

Episode Ten

Original Airdate: November 30, 1983
Featured Segments: "A Salute to Women": a hearing-impaired woman from Port Washington, New York, who taught a deaf dog to understand sign language; a female auto racer from Pulaski, Virginia; a wife and mother who is the shift boss of a mining crew in Leadville, Colorado; a 108-year-old bowler; Sarah Purcell goes skydiving with a female skydiving team in Perris Valley, California; Skip Stephenson visits a class for flirts.

Episode Eleven

Original Airdate: December 14, 1983

Featured Segments: A holiday special: a Santa who talks to hearing-impaired children via sign language; a twelve-year-old boy from Saint Louis who saved a young girl's life; a helicopter pilot honored by President Ronald Reagan for outstanding contributions to aviation; a man who spreads holiday cheer from an elevator; a bowling pig; an unusual Christmas parade in Steamboat Springs, Colorado; a visit to Santa's Village in Cherokee, North Carolina.

Episode Twelve

Original Airdate: January 4, 1984

Featured Segments: A profile of former Olympic star Wilma Rudolph; a look at the "fortune bagel" craze in Chicago; three-wheeled go-cart racing in Oregon; a calendar featuring Los Angeles firefighters.

Episode Thirteen

Original Airdate: January 11, 1984

Featured Segments: "A Salute to Olympians Past and Present": filmmaker Bud Greenspan; boxing gold medal winner George Foreman; decathlete Rafer Johnson; Japanese gymnast Shun Fujimoto, who competed despite a broken leg at the 1976 Olympics; a piece on Jesse Owens, recalling his life and accomplishments at the 1936 Berlin Olympics, including winning four gold medals; 1972 eight-hundred-meter gold medal winner Dave Wottle; the origins of the "Truce of God" march in 1956, which became the closing athlete procession in every subsequent Olympic games; Olympic diver Pat McCormick and her daughter Kelly, who hopes to compete in the 1984 Los Angeles Olympics.

Episode Fourteen

Original Airdate: January 18, 1984

Featured Segments: A female skating coach in the National Hockey League, who used to teach ballet; a man who risks his life to save baby seals and whales; a wet nightie contest in Fort Lauderdale, Florida; a twelve-year-old soccer coach; a pet pig named Spot, being raised by a dog; a Burbank, California, man who covers his van in ornaments.

Episode Fifteen

Original Airdate: January 25, 1984

Featured Segments: An eighteen-year-old mountain climber who has no feet; a California woman who makes art out of dryer lint; a Boston disc jockey who operates an on-air singles forum; Peter Billingsley skis on coal; a woman who adopted an elephant.

Episode Sixteen

Original Airdate: February 1, 1984

Featured Segments: A reunion of Bataan Death March survivors in Montgomery, Alabama; Sarah Purcell attempts water-ski ballet at Cypress Gardens, Florida; Byron Allen talks to a husband and wife who are both members of the California Highway Patrol; a fashion show for dogs; a horse that plays soccer; Mark Russell looks at Latin entertainer Iris Chacón, who became a celebrity in an antifreeze commercial.

Episode Seventeen

Original Airdate: February 8, 1984

Featured Segments: A Valentine's Day special episode from Hawaii: sand sculpture champion Joe Maize; a man who entertains tourists with his individual calls for each of his many exotic birds; a woman who operates a company specializing in Hawaiian travel for the handicapped and elderly; Sarah Purcell learns how to windsurf; a Tahitian fire dancer; a state legislator with a thousand-pound pig named Suey.

Episode Eighteen

Original Airdate: February 15, 1984

Featured Segments: An interview with Tom Selleck, who is attending an Olympic fundraiser; a disabled man from Pocatello, Idaho, who takes disabled people on river rafting trips; Sherry Blair, an eleven-year-old world champion rodeo barrel racer from Oklahoma; Sergio Aragones, often called the world's fastest cartoonist; a Saint Paul, Minnesota, woman who raises baby gorillas in her home.

Episode Nineteen

Original Airdate: February 22, 1984
Featured Segments: Photographer Peter B. Kaplan, who "hangs out" on the ledges of New York City's tallest buildings; a triple amputee disabled-tennis coach; a seventy-year-old expert boat-in-a-bottle builder in Toronto, Canada; canoe skiing in Maine; the official skunk catcher of North Syracuse, New York; Dustin Schuler, a "pop artist" who nailed a Cessna airplane to the side of the American Hotel in Los Angeles.

Episode Twenty

Original Airdate: February 29, 1984
Featured Segments: The Make-A-Wish Foundation, which grants wishes to terminally ill children; a reunion of the 42nd Infantry Rainbow Division, once commanded by General Douglas MacArthur; mountain climber John Bacher, who uses no equipment to scale peaks; a seventy-five-year-old stripper who lives in a nursing home.

Episode Twenty-One

Original Airdate: March 7, 1984
Featured Segments: A bull-riding champion from the Los Angeles Watts neighborhood, who teaches Byron Allen to ride; seventy-six-year-old marathoner Johnny Kelly, who recently won his fifty-second race; an investigation of the death of Wild West legend Jesse James; Sarah Purcell examines the collection of food that supermarkets and restaurants throw away to feed the needy; a sardine-packing contest in Rockland, Maine; a woman who performs opera for her cows to increase their milk production.

Episode Twenty-Two

Original Airdate: March 21, 1984
Featured Segments: The plight of Ameri-Asian children who were born out of the war in Vietnam and a minister, Alfred Keane, who helps find homes for them; a sixty-year-old skateboard champion; a segment explaining how flight simulators work to train pilots for emergencies; a man who rescued a woman from a burning building; a record-breaking game of musical chairs; a mosquito festival in Clute, Texas; a homemade bikini contest; a Los Angeles couple who grow grass on the roof of their home.

Episode Twenty-Three

Original Airdate: May 9, 1984
Featured Segments: Byron Allen reports on Mother Waddles, a senior who helps the needy and disadvantaged; a visit to an underground home that is a repurposed US government missile silo; Sarah Purcell travels to Phoenix, Arizona, to fly on an ultralight, an experimental aircraft; Skip Stephenson profiles a Minnesota woman who has run a café single-handedly for fifty-two years, acting as the cook, waitress, cashier, dishwasher, and entertainer; a tollbooth attendant who yodels while he works.

APPENDIX B

Reality-Themed Shows 1976–1992

The following list features reality-themed shows that were broadcast nationally, with the year the series premiered.

1976

PM Magazine (Syndicated)

1978

Crazy and Wonderful (Home Box Office)
Lifeline (NBC)
What's Up America? (Showtime)

1979

Guinness Games (Syndicated)
Real People (NBC)

1980

The Amazing World (Syndicated)
Fantasies Fulfilled (Syndicated)
Games People Play (NBC)
Hour Magazine (Syndicated)
Look at Us (Syndicated)
The New You Asked for It (Syndicated)
No Holds Barred (CBS)
Non-fiction TV (PBS)
Speak Up America (NBC)
That's Incredible (ABC)
That's My Line (CBS)
Those Amazing Animals (ABC)
What's Happening America? (Syndicated)
The World of People (Syndicated)

1981

The People's Court (Syndicated)
Real Kids (NBC)
Real Live People (Syndicated)

1982

Counterattack: Crime in America (ABC)
Couples (Syndicated)
Custody Court (Syndicated)
Family Court (Syndicated)
Getting Personal (Syndicated)
Inside America (CBS)
Police Court (Syndicated)
Ripley's Believe It or Not (ABC)
Shoot, Don't Shoot (ABC)
Singles Only (Syndicated)
So You Think You've Got Troubles (Syndicated)
That Awful Quiz Show (Syndicated)
Wedding Day (NBC)

1983

America's Heroes: The Athlete Chronicles (NBC)
Lie Detector (Syndicated)
Love Connection (Syndicated)
Miller's Court (Syndicated)
Survive (Syndicated)
This Is Your Life (Syndicated)

1984

Anything for Money (Syndicated)
Bill Burrud's Quest (Syndicated)

Every Second Counts (Syndicated)
Lifestyles of the Rich and Famous (Syndicated)
On Stage America (Syndicated)
People Are Funny (NBC)
People Do the Craziest Things (ABC)

1985

All about Us (Syndicated)
America (Syndicated)
American Almanac (NBC)
Divorce Court (Syndicated)
It's a Great Life (Syndicated)
Life's Most Embarrassing Moments (ABC)
What's Hot? What's Not? (Syndicated)

1986

The Barbour Report (ABC)
A Current Affair (Syndicated)
Superior Court (Syndicated)

1987

Strictly Confidential (Syndicated)

1988

America's Most Wanted (FOX)
Funny People (Syndicated)
Group One Medical (Syndicated)
High Risk (CBS)
Incredible Sunday (ABC)
Love Court with Pearl Bailey (Syndicated)

On Trial (Syndicated)
Private People, Private Lives (Syndicated)
Unsolved Mysteries (NBC)

1989

America's Funniest Home Videos (ABC)
Cops (FOX)
From the Heart (Syndicated)
Hard Copy (Syndicated)
Inside Edition (Syndicated)
Inside Report (Syndicated)
Rescue 911 (CBS)
Totally Hidden Video (FOX)

1990

American Chronicles (FOX)
Memories Then and Now (Syndicated)
Missing: Reward (Syndicated)
On Scene: Emergency Response (Syndicated)
Real Life with Jane Pauley (NBC)
Reunion (Syndicated)
Top Cops (CBS)

1991

Amazing Love Stories (Syndicated)
America's Funniest People (ABC)
American Detective (ABC)
Candid Camera (Syndicated)
Emergency Call (Syndicated)
Exposé (NBC)
Love Stories (Syndicated)
Now It Can Be Told (Syndicated)

Real People Reunion (NBC)
Studs (Syndicated)
Stunt Masters (Syndicated)
Trial Watch (NBC)
Verdict (CBS)
Yearbook (FOX)

1992

I Witness Video (NBC)
The Real World (MTV)
What Happened (NBC)

APPENDIX C

Map of *Real People* Filming Locations, 1979–1984

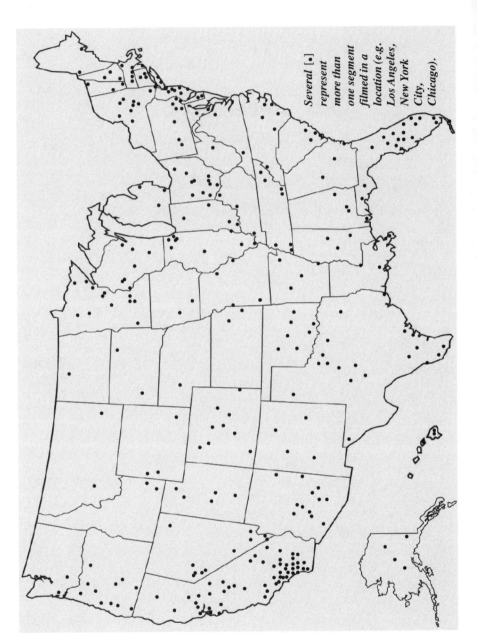

Several [•] represent more than one segment filmed in a location (e.g. Los Angeles, New York City, Chicago).

NOTES

PREFACE

1. Tom Shales, "TV Goes Bananas for Real People," *Washington Post*, 17 August 1980, L1.

2. The two apparent exceptions to these examples are westerns and variety shows, both of which were programming stalwarts for several decades from the 1950s into the 1970s, but have essentially disappeared from either network or cable television in the first two decades of the twenty-first century.

3. Alex McNeil, *Total Television* (New York: Penguin Books, 1996), passim.

4. The Rosetta Stone, discovered in 1799, became an archeological and linguistic tool used to decipher and translate Egyptian hieroglyphs.

5. Susan Murray and Laurie Ouellette, eds., *Reality TV: Remaking Television Culture* (New York: New York University Press, 2004); Misha Kavka, *Reality TV* (Edinburgh: Edinburgh University Press, 2012); Kristie Bunton and Wendy Wyatt, *The Ethics of Reality TV* (London: Continuum Publishing, 2012); Leigh H. Edwards, *The Triumph of Reality TV* (Santa Barbara, CA: Praeger Publishing, 2013).

6. Richard Crew, "*PM Magazine*: A Missing Link in the Evolution of Reality Television," *Film and History* 37.2 (2007), 23.

7. Michael McKenna, *The ABC Movie of the Week: Big Movies for the Small Screen* (Lanham, MD: Scarecrow Press, 2013), passim.

8. Anna McCarthy, "Stanley Milgrim, Allen Funt, and Me: Postwar Social Science and the 'First Wave' of Reality TV," *Reality TV: Remaking Television Culture*, ed. Susan Murray and Laurie Ouellette (New York: New York University Press, 2004), 21–25.

9. Jeffrey Ruoff, *"An American Family": A Televised Life* (Minneapolis, MN: University of Minnesota Press, 2001), passim. *An American Family*, *Candid Camera*, and a variety of other earlier reality-themed programs are discussed in greater depth in the introduction.

10. Rob Tannenbaum, *I Want My MTV: The Uncensored Story of the Music Video Revolution* (New York: Penguin Publishing, 2012), 505–509. It is illustrative of the lack of clarity on the origins of the reality genre that the four examples cited in this preface come from four different decades: *Candid Camera* (1960s), *An American Family* (1970s), *Real People* (1980s), and *The Real World* (1990s).

11. Ken Auletta, *Three Blind Mice: How the TV Networks Lost Their Way* (New York: Random House, 1991), chapter 4; Gary Edgerton, *Columbia History of American Television* (New York: Columbia University Press, 2009), 487–489.

12. Further enhancing the appeal of reality programming were separate actors' and writers' strikes, which shut down most, though not all, television productions for extended periods in the 1980s. With no actors or writers, reality programs were not impacted by the strikes, and were therefore deemed immune to future labor strife.

INTRODUCTION

1. Eric Burns, *Invasion of the Mind Snatchers: Television's Conquest of America in the Fifties* (Philadelphia: Temple University Press, 2010), 6–8.

2. Harry Castlemon and Walter Podrazik, *Watching TV: Six Decades of American Television* (Syracuse, NY: Syracuse University Press, 2010), 19.

3. Mary Ann Watson, *Defining Visions: Television and the American Experience in the 20th Century* (New York: Wiley-Blackwell, 2009), 8.

4. Jeff Kisseloff, *The Box: An Oral History of Television, 1920–1961* (New York: Penguin Books, 1995), 110, 121, 129. *What's It Worth?* bears a strong resemblance to the contemporary Public Broadcasting stalwart *Antiques Roadshow* (1997–).

5. Burns, *Invasion of the Mind Snatchers*, 54–56.

6. Alexander Kendrick, *Prime Time: The Life of Edward R. Murrow* (Boston: Little, Brown, 1969), 52–53.

7. Edwin R. Bayley, *Joseph McCarthy and the Press* (Madison, WI: University of Wisconsin Press, 1981), 201–202.

8. James Reston, "Unintended Consequences of Senator McCarthy," *New York Times*, 30 May 1954, E6; Gladwin Hills, "McCarthy Charges Plot to Halt Him," *New York Times*, 22 April 1954, 1; Bayley, *Joseph McCarthy and the Press*, 204.

9. John Crosby, "Crime Attracts 1,000,000 TV Fans," *Boston Globe*, 4 March 1951, A7; "Bar Group Cautions Kefauver on TV Use," *New York Times*, 27 February 1951, 28.

10. James Hagerty, "Costello's Power in Politics, Crime Shown at Hearing," *New York Times*, 13 March 1951, 1; Jack Gould, "Video Captures Drama of Inquiry," *New York Times*, 13 March 1951, 27.

11. "The U.S. Gets a Close Look at Crime," *Life*, 26 March 1951, 33; Gould, "Video Captures Drama of Inquiry," 27; Thomas Doherty, *Cold War, Cool Medium: Television, McCarthyism and American Culture* (New York: Columbia University Press, 2003), 112–113; Burns, *Invasion of the Mind Snatchers*, 147. The remarkable ratings success of the Kefauver hearings had a lingering effect on the television industry as well. Daytime programming in many cities had been sparse before 1951; however, the record viewership convinced the networks that an audience existed in the daytime, resulting in more regular and commercially lucrative morning and afternoon programs. There was also a noticeable increase in the number of crime/police programs on the network's prime-time schedule over the next few years.

12. "Senator Kefauver Cited for TV Inquiry," *New York Times*, 20 February 1952, 37.

13. Jack Gould, "Bishop Fulton J. Sheen Preaches Absorbing Sermons in *Life Is Worth Living* Series," *New York Times*, 22 February 1952, 27; "132 Stations to Carry Bishop Sheen Next Fall," *Boston Globe*, 26 July 1953, C58; "Microphone Missionary," *Time*, 14 March 1952, 74–76; Burns, *Invasion of the Mind Snatchers*, 279–284; Doherty, *Cold War, Cool Medium*, 153–157.

14. Marsha F. Cassidy, *What Women Watched: Daytime Television in the 1950s* (Austin: University of Texas Press, 2005), 89–90; Henry La Cossit, "They Say He's a Funny Man," *Saturday Evening Post*, 17 May 1952, 7–9.

15. David Halberstam, *The Fifties* (New York: Villard Books, 1993), 567–568.

16. Cassidy, *What Women Watched*, 104–112; Burns, *Invasion of the Mind Snatchers*, 241–243; Castlemon and Podrazik, *Watching TV*, 59–60; Joseph Dinneen, "She May Strike It Rich for the Sake of Her Son," *Boston Globe*, 2 June 1952, 1.

17. Jack Gould, "A Look at *Strike It Rich* as Video Entertainment: Human Emotions and Commercial Appeal," *New York Times*, 9 November 1951, 34; "Family of 11 Fails to 'Strike It Rich,'" *New York Times*, 9 March 1954, 29; "Ex-convict Strikes It Rich on TV, but Fame Proves a Give-Away to Police," *New York Times*, 27 January 1954, 19; "Strike It Rich Bill Slated in Congress," *New York Times*, 15 February 1954, 23.

18. Burns, *Invasion of the Mind Snatchers*, 118–120; Howard Blake, "The Worst Program in TV History," in *TV Book: The Ultimate Television Book*, ed.

Judy Fireman (New York: Workman Publishing, 1977), 96–100; "Troubles and Bubbles," *Time*, 15 April 1957, 78; Cassidy, *What Women Watched*, 187–191.

19. Cassidy, *What Women Watched*, 192–193.

20. Halberstam, *The Fifties*, 644–648; Alex McNeil, *Total Television* (New York: Penguin Books, 1996), 762; Burns, *Invasion of the Mind Snatchers*, 75; James L. Baughman, *Same Time, Same Station: Creating American Television 1948–1961* (Baltimore: Johns Hopkins University Press, 2007), 146.

21. Halberstam, *The Fifties*, 650–659, 563; "The People Getters," *Time*, 25 August 1958, 67; "The Wizard of Quiz," *Time*, 11 February 1957, 46–48.

22. Karal Ann Marling, *As Seen on TV: The Visual Culture of Everyday Life in the 1950s* (Cambridge, MA: Harvard University Press, 1994), 183.

23. "Scandal of the Quizzes," *Time*, 1 September 1958, 40–41; "Quiz Scandal," *Time*, 8 September 1958, 45–48; "Meeting of the Minds," *Time*, 15 September 1958, 49.

24. Cassidy, *What Women Watched*, 194–196.

25. "Secret Longings," *Time*, 15 April 1951, 58.

26. John Crosby, "Are Real People Too Real For TV?" *St. Petersburg Times*, 19 January 1959, C7.

27. McNeil, *Total Television*, 140; the traditional *Candid Camera* would reappear both on network and in syndicated television in 1974–1978 and 1991–1992.

28. Anna McCarthy, "Stanley Milgrim, Allen Funt, and Me," in *Reality TV: Remaking Television Culture*, ed. Susan Murray and Laurie Ouellette (New York: New York University Press, 2004), 26–28; John P. Shanely, "Candid Words from Allen Funt," *New York Times*, 5 November 1961, X19.

29. Fred Nadis, "Citizen Funt: Surveillance as Cold War Entertainment," *Film and History* 37.2 (Fall 2007), 15–21; McCarthy, "Stanley Milgrim, Allen Funt, and Me," 21–25.

30. Mary Roiphe, "Things Are Keen but Could Be Keener," *New York Times*, 18 February 1973, 292; John J. O'Conner, "TV: *An American Family* Is a Provocative Series," *New York Times*, 23 January 1973, 79.

31. Jeffrey Ruoff, *"An American Family": A Televised Life* (Minneapolis, MN: University of Minnesota Press, 2001), 95–110; Roiphe, "Things Are Keen but Could Be Keener," 48; Bruce McCabe, *"An American Family* Fights Back," *Boston Globe*, 22 February 1973, 39.

32. "Ultimate Soap Opera," *Time*, 22 January 1973, 150–151; "Sample of One?" *Time*, 26 February 1973, 123–125; John J. O'Conner, "Mr. and Mrs. Loud Meet the Bradys," *New York Times*, 4 March 1973, 137; Stephanie Harrington, "An American Family Lives Its Life on TV," *New York Times*, 7 January 1973, 141. It may have no bearing on Mead's opinion, but it is worth noting that Craig

Gilbert had produced a TV series entitled *Margaret Mead's New Guinea Journal*.

33. "Ultimate Soap Opera," *Time*, 22 January 1973, 150.

34. Richard Crew, "*PM Magazine*: A Missing Link in the Evolution of Reality Television," *Film and History* 37.2 (2007), 23–25; John J. O'Conner, "*PM Magazine*, Focus on Features," *New York Times*, 9 July 1980, C19.

35. Crew, "*PM Magazine*," 23.

36. McNeil, *Total Television*, 228, 334.

1. THE GOLDEN GUT STRIKES AGAIN

1. Sally Bedell, *Up the Tube: Prime-Time in the Silverman Years* (New York: Viking Press, 1981), 107–122; Harry Castlemon and Walter Podrazik, *Watching TV: Six Decades of American Television* (Syracuse, NY: Syracuse University Press, 2010), 274–275.

2. "The Man with the Golden Gut," *Time*, 5 September 1977, 46–49; Les Brown, "Silverman Is Likely to Surprise NBC Affiliates," *New York Times*, 19 June 1978, C19.

3. "The Man with the Golden Gut," 49; Castlemon and Podrazik, *Watching TV*, 275; Alex McNeil, *Total Television* (New York: Penguin Press, 1997), 1154; Bedell, *Up the Tube*, 222.

4. Richard Reeves, "The Dangers of Television in the Silverman Era," *Esquire*, 25 April 1978, 32–34, also quoted in Bedell, *Up the Tube*, 222, 230.

5. Brown, "Silverman Is Likely to Surprise NBC Affiliates"; William A. Henry III, "Conscious of a TV Boss," *Boston Globe*, 26 June 1978, 43; Tom Shales, "At NBC Fred Silverman Is Putting in a Bid for Respectability," *Washington Post*, 21 June 1978, B1; "The Man with the Golden Gut," 47.

6. "Silverman Puts Stamp on First Changes," *Broadcasting Magazine*, 19 June 1978, 34; Rudy Maxa, "NBC Bets on Reality," *Washington Post*, 13 August 1978, 4; William Henry, "Nudity and Blood—Limited TV Realism," *Boston Globe*, 6 September 1978, 1; episodes of *Lifeline* can be viewed at the UCLA Film and Television Archives on the Westwood campus.

7. Tom Shales, "*Lifeline*: Moving Medical Drama beyond the Hospital Hope Operas," *Washington Post*, 7 September 1978, D1; "In Brief," *Broadcasting Magazine*, 27 November 1978, 27; Jay Sharbutt, "*Lifeline* Is Compelling Medical Show," Associated Press, 7 September 1978, AM cycle; "Display Ad 158," *New York Times*, 14 November 1978, C26.

8. Tom Shales, "NBC Closed Circus: After a Clean Sweep, and 'Update' of Nine New Shows," *Washington Post*, 13 December 1978, D1.

9. Jerry Buck, Associated Press, 9 May 1979, PM cycle; George Schlatter, interview by Rob Owen, Syracuse University symposium on the career of Fred Silverman, "From Test Patterns to Pixels: Envisioning the Future of Television," session 3, 8 April 2009, www.silverman.syr.edu, retrieved 11 May 2011. Schlatter had attempted a somewhat similar show entitled *Whacky World* in 1973.

10. Jerry Buck, "Viewers Say TV Shows Look Alike," *Eugene Register Guard*, 14 April 1979, 5; "6 New Series in NBC Spring Cleaning," *New York Times*, 9 March 1979, C29.

11. McNeil, *Total Television*, 1155; "Humor Gets Spotlight on Real People," *Schenectady Gazette*, 14 April 1979, 31; "Just Plain Folks," *Broadcasting Magazine*, 5 March 1979, 130; William Beamon, "*Real People* Humor Is for Real," *Evening-Independent* (St. Petersburg, FL) 19 April 1979, B1.

12. Promotional ad, *Boston Globe*, 25 April 1979, 41.

13. John J. O'Conner, "There May Be Turkeys amid the Peacocks," *New York Times*, 3 June 1979, D29; "Crazy Folks on *Real People*," *Robesonian* (Lumberton, NC), 29 July 1979, TV 8 (article borrowed heavily from NBC promotional materials). Episodes of *Real People* were found in various archives, and some episodes were purchased online from unofficial sources. The most useful archives for *Real People* episodes are the Paley Center for Media (both New York and Los Angeles) and the UCLA Film and Television Archive.

14. O'Conner, "There May Be Turkeys amid the Peacocks"; "Television Reviews," *Variety*, 25 April 1979, 59; Tom Shales, "The Realities of Real People," *Washington* Post, 18 April 1979, B1; Kay Gardella, "Live Shows Make a Comeback," *Boston Globe*, 28 May 1979, 53.

15. Eric Pace, "NBC, CBS Release Schedules for Fall," *New York Times*, 2 May 1979, C17; Les Brown, "Silverman Maps Road Back for NBC," *New York Times*, 16 May 1979, C28.

16. "Mail Pours In," *Robesonian* (Lumberton, NC), 11 January 1980, TV 5 (article borrowed heavily from NBC promotional materials).

17. Shales, "The Realities of Real People," B1; Tony Schwartz, "Blurring the Line between Entertainment and News," *New York Times*, 7 September 1980, D1; Schlatter, interview by Rob Owen, www.silverman.syr.edu.

18. H. F. Waters, "TV Sends in the Freaks," *Newsweek*, 28 April 1980, 79–80.

19. Vernon Scott, "*Real People* Co-host Says TV Going down Tube," *Milwaukee Sentinel*, 9 November 1979, part 3, 2; George Maksian, "How to Cheat the Black Box," *Boston Globe,* 19 November 1979, 37.

20. Gary Deeb, "*Real People* Has Lunacy Warmth," *Deseret News*, 8 February 1980, C1.

21. Deeb, "*Real People* Has Lunacy Warmth."

22. "Weekly Ratings," Associated Press, 10 October 1979, AM cycle; "TV Ratings," *New York Times*, 28 November 1979, C28; Les Brown, "ABC Ties with CBS for Lead in TV Ratings," *New York Times*, 6 February 1980, 73; "1979–80 Regular Season Series Ratings," *Daily Variety*, 4 June 1980, 48.

23. Frank Swertlow, "The Un-real People," *Boston Globe*, 25 February 1980, 19; Arthur Unger, "TV's Real People Trend, Is It News Gone Astray?" *Christian Science Monitor*, 3 July 1980, 22.

24. Peter Boyer, Associated Press, 27 February 1980, PM cycle; Waters, "TV Sends in the Freaks," 79; "Catholic Church Calls 15 Shows Unfit for Children," Associated Press, 15 November 1979, PM cycle.

25. Gary Deeb, "*Real People*, Zany, Warm and Downright Courageous," *Chicago Tribune*, 12 March 1980, 45; Deeb, "*Real People* Has Lunacy Warmth."

26. William A. Henry III, "*Real People*: Reality Comedy," *Boston Globe*, 27 November 1979, 29; "The 70s' Most Important TV Series," *Chicago Tribune*, 9 December 1979, G61.

27. "Real People or Highly Rated Freak Show," *Washington Post*, 27 April 1980, TV 6.

28. Jack Loftus, "NBC's Prime-Time Profits: The $$ from the Shows," *Variety*, 30 April 1980, 15; "Starting Over in 1980," *Broadcasting*, 30 June 1980, 32–33.

29. "ABC TV Planning Magazine Show to Fight Others," *Palm Beach Post*, 14 February 1980, B6; Bill Carter, "Incredibly People Watch *That's Incredible*," *Baltimore Sun*, 6 April 1980, TV 2.

30. "Display Ad 98," *New York Times*, 3 March 1980, C18; "ABC TV Planning Magazine Show to Fight Others."

31. Jerry Buck, "*That's Incredible* Wasn't Incredible," Associated Press, 10 March 1980, AM cycle; Carter, "Incredibly People Watch *That's Incredible*"; Tom Shales, "TV Goes Bananas for Real People," *Washington Post*, 17 August 1980, L1.

32. Kay Gardella, "Real Life Trend Luring Back Viewers," *Boston Globe*, 30 March 1980, 1; Harry Waters, Lucy Howard, and Cynthia Wilson, "TV's Local Magazines," *Newsweek*, 31 December 1979, 50–51; Howard Rosenberg, "Fluffy *PM* Gets LA Outlet," *Los Angeles Times*, 14 April 1980, G1.

33. John J. O'Conner, "TV: *PM Magazine* Focus on Features," *New York Times*, 9 July 1980, C19; Howard Rosenberg, "Fluffy *PM* Gets LA Outlet"; Carter, "Incredibly People Watch *That's Incredible*"; Gardella, "Real Life Trend Luring Back Viewers."

34. Gary Edgerton and Jeffrey P. Jones, *The Essential HBO Reader* (Frankfurt, KY: University of Kentucky Press, 2013), 154; Shales, "TV Goes Bananas for Real People"; John J. O'Conner, "Diary of an Occasional Cable TV Watcher," *New York Times*, 2 March 1980, D35–D36; Tom Jory, "Chuck Braverman:

No Modesty Intended, No Modesty Needed," Associated Press, 1 May 1980, PM cycle.

35. "Access on Cable TV Reaches Grass Roots," *New York Times*, 12 February 1980, C22.

36. O'Conner, "Diary of an Occasional Cable TV Watcher"; Peter Boyer, "Networks, Networks, Everywhere," Associated Press, 29 May 1980, AM cycle.

2. BRANDING A GENRE: NONFICTION, ACTUALITY, REALITY!

1. Robert Lindsay, "Movie and TV Actors Strike," *New York Times*, 22 July 1980, C7; Anna Quindlen, "Actors Star in Show of Strike Support," *New York Times*, 28 August 1980, C1; Roger Ebert, "Actors Want Profit," *Boston Globe*, 7 August 1980, 33; Jay Arnold, "Actors Ratify New Contract," *Boston Globe*, 24 October 1980, 63.

2. Much of the discussion of the format and content of *Real People* is culled from viewing episodes of the show. Episodes of *Real People* were found in various archives, and some episodes were purchased online from unofficial sources. The most useful archives for *Real People* episodes are the Paley Center for Media (both New York and Los Angeles) and the UCLA Film and Television Archive. For more specific references to content, episode dates will be used.

3. Source of quotes in order: *Politics*, audience member, 9 September 1980, the cast, 1 October 1980, audience member, 3 December 1980; *Women's Liberation/ERA*, letter, 17 September 1980; *Sarah Purcell*, 1 October 1980; *Cold War*, audience member, 17 September 1980; *Mariel Boatlift*, cast, 3 December 1980; *Mark Twain*, 17 September 1980.

4. Quote from the 17 September 1980 episode.

5. See the episode guide, appendix A, for more specific information on broadcast dates.

6. Episode originally aired 21 January 1981; James T. Patterson, *Restless Giant: The United States from Watergate to Gore v. Bush* (New York: Oxford University Press, 2005), 172.

7. The episode originally aired on 17 September 1980.

8. Margo Miller, "Pedal Vision, a Father's Remedy for TV Addiction," *Boston Globe*, 12 November 1980, 65.

9. Alex McNeil, *Total Television* (New York: Penguin Books, 1996), 1155; Jack Hicks, "This Is a Big Slice of American Life," *TV Guide*, 15 August 1980, 18–24.

10. *Saturday Night Live* transcript, season 5, episode 19, http://snltranscripts.jt.org/79/79sreal.phtml, retrieved 5 July 2014.

11. "Sally Bedell, *Up the Tube: Prime-Time in the Silverman Years* (New York: Viking Press, 1981).

12. *Real People* Fosters *Speak Up America*," Associated Press, 10 August 1980, PM cycle.

13. John J. O'Conner, "TV's New Populism Is an Old Style Hustle," *New York Times*, 4 May 1980, D37.

14. Bob Michals, "America Tells All for TV," *Palm Beach Post*, 30 July 1980, B4; Jerry Krupnick, "*Speak Up* Tuning On," *Boston Globe*, 1 August 1980, 27; Tom Shales, "Keep Quiet America," *Washington Post*, 1 August 1980, C10; Tom Shales, "TV Goes Bananas for Real People," *Washington Post*, 17 August 1980, L1; Barbara Holsopple, "So Jimmy Carter's Got a Brother? Tough (Bleep)," *Pittsburgh Press*, 17 August 1980, TV 8–10; Peter J. Boyer, Associated Press, 22 August 1980, AM cycle; Tony Schwartz, "Show on Who Shot JR Sets a Viewing Record," *New York Times*, 26 November 1980, C18.

15. "Jenner Hosts Sunday Games," *Dispatch* (Lexington, NC), 25 April 1980, 11 (taken directly from NBC promotional materials); Win Fanning, "The Average Man's Competitive Spirit Will be Showcased," *Pittsburgh Post-Gazette*, 22 April 1980, 29.

16. Bill Carter, "Real People or Trashsports? Another NBC Big Event," *Baltimore Sun*, 10 July 1980, B8.

17. Blaik Kirby, "TV Presents Nerdling for the Masses," *Toronto Globe and Mail*, 22 August 1980, 33.

18. "NBC with Shogun Gets Its Best Rating," *New York Times*, 24 September 1980, C25; "NBC Again Tops Ratings," *New York Times*, 1 October 1980, C26.

19. Peter J. Boyer, "They Were Fun Despite the Efforts of the People," Associated Press, 30 August 1980, PM cycle.

20. Tony Schwartz, "NBC Tops Ratings," *New York Times*, 10 October 1980, C26; Steven Reddicliffe, "Bad TV as Usual," *Boston Globe*, 22 December 1980, 36; Tony Schwartz, "ABC-TV Will Replace 8 Shows in 6 1/2 Prime-Time Hours," *New York Times*, 30 April 1981, C30; McNeil, *Total Television*, 986.

21. "Amusing Situations Viewed," *Robesonian* (Lumberton, NC), 17 August 1980, 3 (taken directly from ABC promotional materials).

22. Cynthia Wilson, "Is It Incredible or Inexcusable?" *Newsweek*, 25 August 1980, 75; David Gritten, "That's Incredible—or Is It Reprehensible? TV Mayhem Stirs Protest over a Top-Rated Show," *People*, 14 October 1980, 93–99; Peter J. Boyer, Associated Press, 13 October 1980, PM cycle.

23. Vernon Scott, United Press International, 3 February 1981; Mike Drew, "The Shock of Reality," *Milwaukee Journal*, 3 February 1981, Accent 6; Blaik Kirby, "*That's My Line* Contrived TV," *Toronto Globe and Mail*, 11 August 1980, 39; McNeil, *Total Television*, 828.

24. "Visit Kenny Rogers' America," *Robesonian* (Lumberton, NC), 16 November 1980, 39 (taken directly from CBS promotional materials).

25. John J. O'Conner, "*Hanging On* Visits New York Boatmen," *New York Times*, 11 September 1980, C19.

26. John J. O'Conner, "On TV, Illness Is an Epidemic," *New York Times*, 19 October 1980, 35.

27. Albin Krebs, "A Writer, though Gracious, Gets the Name Wrong Two," *New York Times*, 11 October 1980, 26; Kuralt transitioned to the anchor chair of the *Sunday Morning* program, on which he would ultimately revive the "On the Road" segment.

28. Kenneth R. Clark, United Press International, 15 April 1981, PM cycle; Howard Rosenberg, "Number of Real Shows—Unreal," *Sarasota Herald Tribune*, 23 April 1981, 12C; John J. O'Conner, "Real Life Stories in Soaps Time," *New York Times*, 13 April 1981, C22.

29. Tony Schwartz, "New Talk Series, with Non-professionals Discussing Life," *New York Times*, 27 September 1980, 48.

30. John J. O'Conner, "Breaking Away Begins Tomorrow," *New York Times*, 28 November 1980, C26; Tom Shales, "Can *Roadshow* Save Saturday Night?" *Washington Post*, 29 November 1980, B1.

31. John J. O'Conner, "Crackpot Comedy Series and a Film Made in Israel," *New York Times*, 10 October 1980, C23.

32. Peter Boyer, Associated Press, 25 September 1980, PM cycle; Herb Michelson, "*World of People* Grinding Out Events," *Variety*, 9 July 1980, 68.

33. "Airtime Buys Airtime," *Broadcasting Magazine*, 4 February 1980, 50; advertisement, *Broadcasting Magazine*, 16 March 1981; advertisement, *Broadcasting Magazine*, 11 August 1980, 54.

34. Terry Ann Knopf, "It's Just a Poor Man's *Donahue*," *Boston Globe*, 25 January 1981, J2; C. Gerald Fraser, "NBC Expands *Hour Magazine* to 3 Major Cities," *New York Times*, 29 December 1980, C20.

35. "TV Plus: Weekly Listings," *Schenectady Gazette*, 7 March 1981, 2–11.

36. Dale Pollock, "Belt Tightening a New Look for TV?" *Los Angeles Times*, 15 July 1980, G1.

37. Holsopple, "So Jimmy Carter's Got a Brother?"; Peter J. Boyer, Associated Press, 22 August 1980, PM cycle.

38. Thomas Rizzo, "QUBE: The TV Revolution Is Still in the Making," Associated Press, 27 October 1980, PM cycle; Les Brown, "TV Lets Homes Boo, Buy, Vote," *New York Times*, 13 April 1978, C22; Jean Bethke Elshtain, "Democracy and the QUBE Tube," *Nation*, 7–12 August 1982, 108–109; Dale Leach, "Failure of QUBE Not Seen as End of Two Way Television," Associated Press, 19 January 1984, PM cycle. QUBE was also used by ABC for test screenings of future programming, to elicit viewer opinions on proposed series.

39. Tony Schwartz, "NBC Continues to Lag in 3rd Place," *New York Times*, 1 April 1980, C28; Lee Winfrey, "Silverman's Rating Low," *Boston Globe*, 28 March 1981, 23; Tony Schwartz, "Silverman Quits at NBC: Tinker to Succeed Him," *New York Times*, 1 July 1981, C23.

3. WHACKOS, FREAKS, ECCENTRICS . . . GOD BLESS AMERICA

1. Aljean Harmetz, "Hollywood Writers to Vote Tomorrow on Strike," *New York Times*, 9 April 1981, C19; Aljean Harmetz, "Tentative Accord Reached in Strike of Screen Writers," *New York Times*, 12 July 1981, 20.

2. Jerry Buck, "Fred Willard, *Real People*, Back on NBC," Associated Press, 23 September 1981, AM cycle; Ruth Thompson, *Real People* Holds Reunion," *TV Data Service*, 20 November 1981 (found in *Kingman Daily Miner*, same date, 6); Billingsley's age limited the amount of hours he could legally work, so he would be used sparingly in the field and in the studio.

3. Tony Schwartz, "George Schlatter Finds the Fun in TV," *New York Times*, 6 May 1982, C28.

4. James T. Patterson, *Restless Giant: The United States from Watergate to Bush v. Gore* (New York: Oxford University Press, 2005), 158–159. Much of the discussion of the format and content of *Real People* is culled from viewing episodes of the show. Episodes of *Real People* were found in various archives, and some episodes were purchased online from unofficial sources. The most useful archives for *Real People* episodes are the Paley Center for Media (both New York and Los Angeles) and the UCLA Film and Television Archive. For more specific references to content, episode dates will be used.

5. The parting-shot quotes are from the 21 January 1981 episode.

6. Rita Kempley, "TV's Real People Zooms in on Goosebump City," *Washington Post*, 16 August 1981, G1.

7. Jack Hicks, "This Is a Big Slice of American Life," *TV Guide*, 2 August 1980, 18–19.

8. Episode originally aired 25 November 1981; Tom Shales, "New York's Riper Reflections on *Real People*," *Washington Post*, 25 November 1981, C1.

9. The Navajo Code Talkers would eventually get their presidential citation in August 1982, an event that would be featured on *Real People* during the 1982–1983 season.

10. Tom Shales, "The Vet: The Real Thing on *Real People*," *Washington Post*, 11 November 1981, E1; Kempley, "TV's *Real People* Zooms in on Goosebump City." The entire Veterans Day episode is available for viewing at the Paley Center for Media (both New York and Los Angeles).

11. "Season Tally: CBS-TV Chalks Up Three in a Row," *Broadcasting Magazine*, 26 April 1982, 64; Alex McNeil, *Total Television* (New York: Penguin Press, 1997), 342, 1156.

12. Tom Shales, "One Shiny Apple: New York's Ripe Reflections on *Real People*," *Washington Post*, 25 November 1981, C1; "Broadcast Journalism's Report Card," *Broadcasting Magazine*, 16 August 1982, 61; Marvin Barrett, ed., *Alfred I. DuPont/Columbia University Survey*, vol. 8, parts 1979–1981 (New York: Everest House, 1981), 146–147.

13. John J. O'Conner, "An Exploration of the Fanciful," *New York Times*, 21 June 1981, D25; Harry F. Waters with George Hackett, "Reality Strikes Again," *Newsweek*, 29 June 1981, 73; Mike Drew, "Man, Wife and Showbiz," *Milwaukee Journal*, 9 June 1981, Accent 7.

14. John J. O'Conner, "Kentucky Derby and Shooting Test," *New York Times*, 30 April 1982, C30; Rocky Pomerance and Ray Johnson, "Hotlines Are the Latest Weapons in Fight against Crime," *Miami News*, 6 July 1982, 15A; Fred Rosenberg, "ABC Shows to Mix Reality and Crime," Associated Press, 30 April 1982, AM cycle; Win Fanning, "ABC Staging Counterattack," *Pittsburgh Post-Gazette*, 30 April 1982, 27; "Ratings Roundup," *Broadcasting Magazine*, 17 May 1982, 42.

15. Fred Rothenberg, "*Inside America* on ABC Sunday Night," Associated Press, 3 April 1982, AM cycle; Jaime Gold, "New Bits 'n' Pieces Program the *People* Magazine of TV," *Washington Post News Service*, 3 April 1982; "Season Tally CBS-TV Chalks Up Three in a Row," *Broadcasting Magazine*.

16. John J. O'Conner, "*Up to the Minute* Too Slick," *New York Times*, 4 October 1981, 31.

17. Jerry Buck, Associated Press, 31 March 1982, AM cycle; "Display Ad 21," *New York Times*, 24 October 1981, 5; advertisement, *Broadcasting Magazine*, 8 June 1981, 71; advertisement, *Broadcasting Magazine*, 17 August 1981, 52.

18. Telepictures promotional ad, *Broadcasting Magazine*, 1 June 1981, 12–13; Julie Salamon, "The People's Court Makes Routine Cases a Hit on Television," *Wall Street Journal*, 6 November 1981, 1; Waters and Hackett, "Reality Strikes Again"; John J. O'Conner, "*People's Court*, Reality in the Morning," *New York Times*, 8 September 1981, C22; Walter Shapiro, "Have I Got a Show for You," *Washington Post*, 6 June 1982, 6.

19. "That Agile NATPE Marketplace," *Broadcasting Magazine*, 23 March 1981, 37; Amy Huttunen, "Tarzan Lives," *Palm Beach Post*, 27 May 1982, B1; "Programming Eyes on Fringe, Late Night," *Broadcasting Magazine*, 8 March 1982, 57; McNeil, *Total Television*, 599.

20. Jerry Buck, "Emotions Run Gamut on *Couples*," Associated Press, 2 June 1982, PM cycle; John J. O'Conner, "An Exhibitionism Epidemic," *New York*

Times, 20 June 1982, H31; Harry F. Waters and David T. Friendly, "Season of the Locust," *Newsweek*, 23 August 1982, 60; John J. O'Conner, "Sister, Sister Film and Couples Series," *New York Times*, 7 June 1982, C20.

21. Shapiro, "Have I Got a Show for You"; Waters and Friendly, "Season of the Locust," *Newsweek*; promotional ad, *Broadcasting Magazine*, 15 March 1982, 113.

22. Waters and Friendly, "Season of the Locust"; Sharon Lee Doubler, "Funt's Camera Slated for HBO Quite Candidly," *Hollywood Reporter*, 12 November 1981, 47.

23. Arthur Unger, "The People of Middletown Decades Later: Is This a True Picture?" *Christian Science Monitor*, 23 March 1982, 66; John J. O'Connor, "Middletown in Video Verité," *New York Times*, 24 March 1982, C23; Tony Schwartz, "Final PBS *Middletown* Segment Is Withdrawn," *New York Times*, 31 March 1982, C29.

24. James Mann, "Network's Heyday in Television Coming to a Close?" *U.S. News and World Report*, 5 April 1982, 62; "*TV Guide* Says Networks Share of Audience Shrinking," Associated Press, 16 March 1981, AM cycle.

25. Jill Williams, "The Drive to Clean Up Television," *Saturday Evening Post*, November 1981, 74–77; Harry F. Waters with George Hackett, "The New Right's TV Hit List," *Newsweek*, 15 June 1981, 101; William Henry III, "Another Kind of Ratings War," *Time*, 6 July 1981, 19–23; Walter Goodman, "TV Boycotts," *New York Times*, 6 April 1981, A19; Roger Gillott, "Chairman Discounts Religious Boycotts Effect," Associated Press, 5 June 1982, AM cycle; Bernice Kanner, "How the Coalition Is Changing TV," *New York*, 28 September 1981, 25–27.

4. SLIDING DOWN THE TV FOOD CHAIN: SYNDICATED REALITY

1. Lee Margulies, "Without Barbour, Will *Real People* Unreal?" *Los Angeles Times*, 18 March 1982, J1; Alan J. Gansberg, "*Real People* Star Firing Bitterest Episode," *Copley News Service*, 25 April 1982.

2. Tom Jicha, "People' Essayist Will Be 'Real' Irish Miamian," *Miami News*, 30 June 1982, 6C; "Kerry Millerick Joins *Real People*," Associated Press, 23 July 1982, AM cycle.

3. Episodes of *Real People* were found in various archives, and some episodes were purchased online from unofficial sources. The most useful archives for *Real People* episodes are the Paley Center for Media (both New York and Los Angeles) and the UCLA Film and Television Archive. For more specific references to content, episode dates will be used.

4. "Whistle-Stop Train Trek Carries *Real People* Crew from L.A. to Windy City," *Variety*, 18 August 1982, 52; Tom Shales, "Night of the Real and Ridiculous," *Washington Post*, 22 September 1982, B1; Rogers Worthington, "*Real People* Meets the Real People," *Chicago Tribune*, 9 August 1982, B1.

5. Tony Schwartz, "Mixed Ratings for NBC," *New York Times*, 14 October 1982, C29; "New Season Off to a Semi-start," *Broadcasting Magazine*, 4 October 1982, 50; "Whistle-Stop Train Trek Carries Real People Crew from L.A. to Windy City."

6. "Valley Girls Try to Make It as 'Real People,'" *St. Petersburg Times*, 28 September 1982, 16A; "Valley Girls," Associated Press, 27 September 1982, PM cycle.

7. Barbara Holsopple, "The Legacy of Adam Walsh," *Pittsburgh Press*, 9 October 1983, TV 3. The made-for-TV movie, entitled *Adam*, aired in October 1983, drawing 19 million viewers and finishing as the seventh-rated show for the week. John Walsh would transition from his crusade for child protection into the host of one of television's longest-running reality-themed crime shows, *America's Most Wanted*.

8. "Iran Dead Get Monument," Associated Press, 7 July 1980, AM cycle.

9. "Missing Veterans," United Press International, 9 November 1982; "Sarah Purcell Is for Real," Associated Press, 10 November 1982, AM cycle.

10. Alex McNeil, *Total Television* (New York: Penguin Press, 1997), 1156; "Charting the Competition," *Broadcasting Magazine*, 16 May 1983, 32; John Carmody, "Now Here's the News," *Washington Post*, 31 May 1983, C6.

11. "NATPE Bids FCC Ban *Real People* from Access Time," *Variety*, 29 September 1982, 35; "A Question of Content of *Real People*," *Broadcasting Magazine*, 13 September 1982, 94; "In Brief," *Broadcasting Magazine*, 18 October 1982, 88.

12. William Beamon, "*Magic or Miracle* Pits Psychic vs. Scientific," *Evening Independent* (St. Petersburg, FL), 8 February 1983, 15B; John Carmody, "Now Here's the News," *Washington Post*, 16 February 1983, B11; John J. O'Conner, "Keeping On, a Drama of Life in a Mill Town," *New York Times*, 8 February 1983, C14.

13. Mike Drew, "Good Specials Give Us the Facts of TV Life," *Milwaukee Journal*, 6 May 1983, Accent 11; John Carmody, "Short but Sweet," *Washington Post*, 4 May 1983, B16.

14. David Handler, "*Ripley's* Tells Some Gruesome Tales," *Rome New Tribune* (GA), 25 February 1983, TV 6; Jerry Buck, "*Ripley's* Loses to *60 Minutes*," Associated Press, 7 December 1982, AM cycle; McNeil, *Total Television*, 698.

15. Promotional ad, *TV Guide* (NY metro edition), 10 January 1983, A65; Tommy Stevenson, "Portrait of State Limited, Positive," *Tuscaloosa News* (AL), 5 September 1987, 5.

16. Tony Schwartz, "Cable TV Presses Hunt for Shows to Fill Airtime," *New York Times*, 2 June 1981, C15.

17. Arthur Unger, "Cable Documentary Tests the Boundaries of TV and Real Life," *Christian Science Monitor*, 9 August 1983, 57–58; John Corry, "The Louds 10 Years Later," *New York Times*, 11 August 1983, C21.

18. Bernice Kamerer, "*That Awful Quiz Show* and Other Coming Attractions," *New York Times Magazine*, 5 April 1982, 11–13; "Programming Eyes Are on Fringe, Late Night," *Broadcasting*, 8 March 1982, 61; Walter Shapiro, "Have I Got a Show for You," *Washington Post Magazine*, 6 June 1982, 6.

19. Charles Leerhsen with Ron LaBrecque, "Lies, Lies—and F. Lee Bailey," *Newsweek*, 4 February 1983, 81; promotional ad, *Broadcasting Magazine*, 18 October 1982, 64; "The Fugate Graphs," *New York Times*, 20 February 1983, D9; George Maksian, "*Lie Detector* May Not Pass the Test," *Boston Globe*, 4 May 1983, TV 1; Tom Shales, "*Lie Detector*: It's Really Awful, Honest," *Washington Post*, 22 January 1983, B1; "News in Brief," *Broadcasting Magazine*, 12 September 1983, 89.

20. Kamerer, "*That Awful Quiz Show* and Other Coming Attractions," 12; "Little Hosts Shine on *That Quiz Show*," Associated Press, 8 December 1982, AM cycle; promotional ad, *Broadcasting Magazine*, 8 March 1982, 60.

21. Kamerer, "*That Awful Quiz Show* and Other Coming Attractions," 12; Ella Taylor, "Your Show of Woes," *Boston Phoenix*, 15 March 1983, section 3, 3; "Television Syndication at a Glance," *Variety*, 16 March 1983, 80; McNeil, *Total Television*, 769.

22. Ellen Farley, "Fantasy' Show Underscores Hard Times," *Los Angeles Times*, 10 May 1983, C6; Bob Thomas, "Another Lemon Makes His Way in Hollywood," *Philadelphia Inquirer*, 6 February 1983, I3.

23. Marilyn Matelski, "Jerry Springer and the Wages of Fin-Syn: The Rise of Deregulation and the Decline of TV Talk," *Journal of Popular Culture* 33:4 (Spring 2000), 66–67; Taylor, "Your Show of Woes," 3; promotional ad, *Broadcasting Magazine*, 10 May 1982, 76; James Wolcott, "Shrink to the Stars," *New York*, 13 December 1982, 88–89.

24. Promotional ad, *Broadcasting Magazine*, 8 March 1982, 61; Shapiro, "Have I Got a Show for You," 6; Matelski, "Jerry Springer and the Wages of Fin-Syn," 70.

25. Harry F. Waters and David T. Friendly, "Season of the Locust," *Newsweek*, 23 August 1982, 60; promotional ad (*Singles Only*), *Broadcasting Magazine*, 8 March 1982, 74; promotional ad (*Queen for a Day*), *Broadcasting Magazine*, 8 March 1982, 63.

26. Ken Auletta, *Three Blind Mice: How the TV Networks Lost their Way* (New York: Random House, 1991), 72–75; Haynes Johnson, *Sleepwalking*

through History: America in the Reagan Years (New York: W.W. Norton 1991), 141–142.

27. "Television," *New York Times*, 31 January 1983, C25.

5. EBB TIDE

1. Richard King, "David Ruprecht Is Now Spreading 'Real' Word," *Free Lance Star* (Fredericksburg, VA), 7 January 1984, TV 23.

2. "Specials and New Shows Give ABC Ratings Win," *Broadcasting Magazine*, 26 September 1983, 44; "ABC Takes First; *Hardcastle* Upsets *60 Minutes*," *Broadcasting Magazine*, 3 October 1983, 38; "Premiere Week Goes to CBS," *Broadcasting Magazine*, 10 October 1983, 78. Episodes of *Real People* were found in various archives, and some episodes were purchased online from unofficial sources. The most useful archives for *Real People* episodes are the Paley Center for Media (both New York and Los Angeles) and the UCLA Film and Television Archive. For more specific references to content, episode dates will be used.

3. R. D. Heldenfels, "*Real People* Passes through Area," *Schenectady Gazette*, 25 May 1983, 41–42.

4. "Mass Celebration or Mass Confusion for *Real People*," Associated Press, 17 August 1983, AM cycle.

5. "American Hawaii, *Real People*'s Sarah Purcell to Wed aboard SS *Constitution*," *Business Wire*, 28 September 1983, 58; "Jerry Buck, ABC Wins Opening Salvo of November Television Sweeps," Associated Press, 8 November 1983, AM cycle. To fans, observers, and scholars of the history of television, it is evident that *Real People* was cycling through a list of narrative clichés, which indicates the decline of ratings and a desperate attempt to stay relevant or at the very least remain on the air. Though typically applied to scripted fare, including some classic or well-known series, *Real People* fell in line with this trend. These standard tropes included cast changes, a new location or vacation setting (e.g., Hawaii, train and boat trips), the addition of a new child character (e.g., Peter Billingsley), and a wedding.

6. "It's CBS Six Days a Week," *Broadcasting Magazine*, 12 December 1983, 90.

7. Steve Aschburner, "Olympic 'Real People' Real Nice," *Milwaukee Journal*, 5 January 1984, part 3, 3.

8. "Vietnam Hero Spurns White House Aid," United Press International, 31 May 1985, AM cycle.

9. Alex McNeil, *Total Television* (New York: Penguin Press, 1997), 1088.

10. Fred Rothenberg, "NBC's *V* Series Key to Success Next Season," Associated Press, 10 May 1984, AM cycle; John Carmody, "Now Here's the News," *Washington Post*, 11 May 1984, B10; "Wendy's Star Twists Cranky Query for NBC," *Hartford Courant*, 3 July 1983, C8. NBC's and *Real People*'s main prime-time reality competitor, *That's Incredible*, was also canceled in 1984.

11. "Television Reviews," *Variety*, 16 March 1984, 47; Gail Schuster, "Sawyer Won't Leave CBS Show," *Philadelphia Inquirer*, 28 March 1984, E11; Barbara Holsopple, "New Flip Wilson Show Uses *Candid Camera* Format," *Pittsburgh Press*, 23 March 1984, D10; Tom Jory, "*People Are Funny* Is Back," Associated Press, 7 April 1984, AM cycle.

12. John Corry, "On Gossip, Glitz and Other Real Stuff," *New York Times*, 21 August 1983, H25; Tom Shales, "NBC's 'Personal' Insult," *Washington Post*, 1 August 1983, C1.

13. Arthur Unger, "Television Celebrates the Spirit of America," *Christian Science Monitor*, 29 June 1984, 23; Jack Thomas, "*Summer Sunday* to Be Innovative," *Boston Globe*, 13 June 1984, 1; Gail Schuster, "Nell Carter's on the Set with a $15,000 Raise," *Philadelphia Inquirer*, 1 August 1984, G11.

14. William E. Geist, "Charles Kuralt Continues to Wonder What's around the Bend: Charles Kuralt," *New York Times*, 26 June 1983, H25; Fred Rothenberg, "Off Season Flops—Reruns Outdraw 6 of 8 New Shows," 19 September 1983, *Philadelphia Inquirer*, E8.

15. Martha Bayles, "News for a Summer Night," *Wall Street Journal*, 16 July 1984, 16; Howard Rosenberg, "It Rains on CBS' *Parade*," *Los Angeles Times*, 27 April 1984, G1; Tom Shales, "Oasis in the Wasteland: *The American Parade*: TV's Last Great Hope," *Washington Post*, 29 March 1984, D1.

16. Though reality programs thrived in the first decade of the twenty-first century, there was virtually no syndication of the most popular shows in the genre. The shows typically saturated their home networks, particularly on cable television, but reality series were rarely sold into syndication the way network sitcoms and dramas were.

17. McNeil, *Total Television*, 457; Lee Margulies, "Three Daytime Programs Debut," *Los Angeles Times*, 21 September 1983, D1.

18. Charles Whitbeck, "*This Is Your Life* Comes Back Strong," United Press International, 30 December 1983; Val Adams, "Television Is Dusting Off Oldie, *This Is Your Life*," *Toledo Bee*, 14 January 1983, 8.

19. McNeil, *Total Television*, 551; promotional ad, *Broadcasting Magazine*, 17 January 1983, 86.

20. "New Rumblings," *Broadcast Magazine*, 24 October 1983, 62; "Series in Syndication," *Broadcasting Magazine*, 2 May 1983, 56; promotional ad, *Broadcasting Magazine*, 17 January 1983, 68.

21. Carol Burton Terry, "Off Camera," *Newsday*, 6 March 1983, G66; "TV Shorts," *Newsday*, 8 September 1983, B48; McNeil, *Total Television*, 785.

22. Arthur Unger, "Cable Documentary Tests the Boundaries of TV and Real Life," *Christian Science Monitor*, 9 August 1983, 18.

23. Joe Mandese, "Network Erosion Accelerates to More Than 4 Percent," *Adweek*, 16 July 1984, 24.

24. In 1997, *Real People* was briefly revived on a short-lived cable network called CBS Eye on People. The network featured people-oriented shows, notably reruns of CBS network's *60 Minutes*, *48 Hours*, and *Real People*.

EPILOGUE

1. Ken Auletta, *Three Blind Mice: How the TV Networks Lost Their Way* (New York: Random House, 1991), 5–6, 526; Leonard Goldenson with Marvin J. Wolf, *Beating the Odds: The Untold Story behind the Rise of ABC* (New York: Charles Scribner's Sons, 1991), 462–467; Daniel Kimmel, *The Fourth Network: How FOX Broke the Rules and Reinvented Television* (Chicago: Ivan R. Dee, 2004), 147–149.

2. Rob Tannenbaum, *I Want My MTV: The Uncensored Story of the Music Video Revolution* (New York: Penguin Group, 2011), 193; Bill Keveney, "MTV's *Real World* Launched a Revolution," *USA Today*, 9 October 2007, 27.

3. Alex McNeil, *Total Television* (New York: Penguin Books, 1996), 43–44, 861; Tom Shales, "Homespun Flashes of Fear," *Washington Post*, 15 August 1992, D1.

4. Promotional ad (*Divorce Court*), *Broadcasting Magazine*, 30 December 1985, 72; promotional ad (*On Trial*), *Broadcasting Magazine*, 14 December 1987, 140; Matt Roush, "NBC's Day Duo Sleazy and Breezy," *USA Today*, 29 January 1991, 3D; McNeil, *Total Television*, 884.

5. Bill Carter, "Police Dramas on TV Were Always Popular, Now Are They Real?" *New York Times*, 17 October 1990, C13; Kevin Goldman, "CBS and FOX Adopt Risky TV Strategies in Fight to Capture Prime-Time's Crown," *Wall Street Journal*, 30 May 1990, B3; McNeil, *Total Television*, 859, 879.

6. Promotional ad (*Strictly Confidential*), *Broadcasting Magazine*, 25 February 1987, 64; John Koch, "*Studs* Shows Just How Low TV Can Go," *Boston Globe*, 9 August 1991, 43; Marilyn Matelski, "Jerry Springer and the Wages of Fin-Syn: The Rise of Deregulation and the Decline of TV Talk," *Journal of Popular Culture* 33:4 (Spring 2000), 68–69.

7. Howard Rosenberg, "*Inside Edition* Puts a Chill on TV's Hard News Coverage," *Los Angeles Times*, 11 January 1989, 1; Noel Halston, "Tabloid TV—It's a New Low," *Minneapolis Star Tribune*, 17 July 1988, 1F; "Can TV

Tell Us What Is Real?" *Christian Science Monitor*, 10 October 1991, 27; Bill Carter, "Now It Can Be Told: Tabloid TV Is Booming," *New York Times*, 23 December 1991, D10.

8. Promotional ad (*On Scene: Emergency Response*), *Broadcasting Magazine*, 9 July 1990, 63; "New in Syndication," *Broadcasting Magazine*, 21 January 1991, 29; Bruce McCabe, "An Overwhelming Drive for Reality on Screen," *Boston Globe*, 30 October 1988, B1.

9. Eric Mink, "Quantum Link Gets a Second Chance," *St. Louis Post-Dispatch*, 6 March 1991, 7E; McNeil, *Total Television*, 928.

10. Sally Bedell Smith, "*Inday* New Step in TV Syndication," *New York Times*, 5 September 1985, C21; Howard Rosenberg, "No Heat and No Meat on *Inday* Menu," *Los Angeles Times*, 9 October 1985, 1.

11. Michael Tanaka, "*High Risk* Boasts a Dose of Reality," *New York Times News Service*, 9 October 1988; Monica Collins, "The Mysterious Lure of Reality Shows," *USA Today*, 4 October 1988, 3D; Steve Weinstein, "The Lynch/Frost View of America Series," *Los Angeles Times*, 29 July 1990, 40; Steve Daly, "New TV Season Covered in Mold," *Chicago Tribune*, 14 October 1988, 1.

12. Howard Rosenberg, "*America*: Welcome to Bozovision," *Los Angeles Times*, 25 September 1985, 1; Peter J. Boyer, "CBS Cancellation Jeopardizes *America*," *New York Times*, 18 December 1985, C26; Jerry Buck, "Barbour Gets 10 Nights to Capture Audience," Associated Press, 6 March 1986, AM cycle.

13. Jerry Buck, "George Schlatter's *Funny People* Has Its Roots in *Real People*," Associated Press, 26 July 1988, PM cycle; Eleanor Blau, "TV Notes," *New York Times*, 18 July 1988, C16.

14. Mike Drew, "*Real People* Returns with Its Own Kind of Reality," *Milwaukee Journal*, 10 October 1991, D1; "List of Week's TV Ratings," Associated Press, 8 October 1991, AM cycle; Rick DuBrow, "*Real People* Changed the Face of TV in Its Five Years on NBC," *Los Angeles Times*, 1 October 1991, 64; Rick Sherwood, "TV Reviews: *Real People Reunion*," *Hollywood Reporter*, 1 October 1991, 47.

BIBLIOGRAPHY

Archive of American Television, "Archive Interview Part 4, Fred Silverman," http://www.emmytvlegends.org/interviews/shows/real-people (10 January 2014).
———. "Archive Interview Part 4, George Schlatter," http://www.emmytvlegends.org/interviews/people/george-schlatter (15 January 2014).
———. "Archive Interview Part 2, Fred Willard," http://www.emmytvlegends.org/interviews/people/fred-willard (20 January 2014).
Associated Press, 7 September 1978–8 October 1991.
Auletta, Ken. *Three Blind Mice: How the TV Networks Lost Their Way*. New York: Random House, 1991.
Baltimore Sun, 10 July 1980–7 August 1984.
Barnouw, Erik. *Tube of Plenty: The Evolution of American Television*. New York: Oxford University Press, 1990.
Barrett, Marvin, ed. *Alfred I. DuPont/Columbia University Survey*. Vol. 8, parts 1979–1981. New York: Everest House, 1981.
Baughman, James L. *Same Time, Same Station: Creating American Television 1948–1961*. Baltimore: Johns Hopkins University Press, 2007.
Bayley, Edwin R. *Joseph McCarthy and the Press*. Madison, WI: University of Wisconsin Press, 1981.
Bedell, Sally. *Up the Tube: Prime-Time in the Silverman Years*. New York: Viking Press, 1981.
Blake, Howard. "The Worst Program in TV History." In *TV Book: The Ultimate Television Book*. Edited by Judy Fireman. New York: Workman Publishing, 1977.
Boston Globe, 11 November 1978–30 October 1988.
Broadcasting Magazine, 19 June 1978–21 January 1991.
Bunton, Kristie, and Wendy Wyatt. *The Ethics of Reality TV*. London: Continuum Publishing, 2012.
Burns, Eric. *Invasion of the Mind Snatchers: Television's Conquest of America in the Fifties*. Philadelphia: Temple University Press, 2010.
Cassidy, Marsha F. *What Women Watched: Daytime Television in the 1950s*. Austin: University of Texas Press, 2005.
Castlemon, Harry, and Walter Podrazik. *Watching TV: Six Decades of American Television*. Syracuse, NY: Syracuse University Press, 2010.
Chicago Tribune, 9 December 1979–14 October 1991.
Christian Science Monitor, 3 July 1980–10 October 1991.
Crew, Richard. "*PM Magazine*: A Missing Link in the Evolution of Reality Television." *Film and History* 37.2 (2007).

Devine, Jeremy M. *Vietnam at 24 Frames a Second*. Austin: University of Texas Press, 1995.

Doherty, Thomas. *Cold War, Cool Medium: Television, McCarthyism and American Culture*. New York: Columbia University Press, 2003.

Edgerton, Gary. *Columbia History of American Television*. New York: Columbia University Press, 2009.

Edgerton, Gary, and Jeffrey P. Jones. *The Essential HBO Reader*. Frankfurt, KY: University of Kentucky Press, 2013.

Edwards, Leigh H. *The Triumph of Reality TV*. Santa Barbara, CA: Praeger Publishing, 2013.

Esquire, 25 April 1978, 32–34.

Gitlin, Todd. *Inside Prime Time*. New York: Pantheon Books, 1983.

Goldenson, Leonard H., and Marvin J. Wolf. *Beating the Odds: The Untold Story behind the Rise of ABC*. New York: Charles Scribner's Sons, 1991.

Halberstam, David. *The Fifties*. New York: Villard Books, 1993.

Hallin, Daniel C. *The "Uncensored War": The Media and Vietnam*. New York: Oxford University Press, 1986.

Hollywood Reporter, 12 November 1981–1 October 1991.

Johnson, Haynes. *Sleepwalking through History: America in the Reagan Years*. New York: W.W. Norton, 1991.

Kavka, Misha. *Reality TV*. Edinburgh: Edinburgh University Press, 2012.

Kendrick, Alexander. *Prime Time: The Life of Edward R. Murrow*. Boston: Little, Brown, 1969.

Kimmel, Daniel. *The Fourth Network: How FOX Broke the Rules and Reinvented Television*. Chicago: Ivan R. Dee, 2004.

Kisseloff, Jeff. *The Box: An Oral History of Television, 1920–1961*. New York: Penguin Books, 1995.

Los Angeles Times, 14 April 1979–1 October 1991.

Marling, Karal Ann. *As Seen on TV: The Visual Culture of Everyday Life in the 1950s*. Cambridge, MA: Harvard University Press, 1994.

Matelski, Marilyn. "Jerry Springer and the Wages of Fin-Syn: The Rise of Deregulation and the Decline of TV Talk." *Journal of Popular Culture* 33:4 (Spring 2000).

May, Elaine Tyler. *Homeward Bound: American Families in the Cold War*. Basic Books, 1988.

McCarthy, Anna. "Stanley Milgrim, Allen Funt, and Me: Postwar Social Science and the 'First Wave' of Reality TV." In *Reality TV: Remaking Television Culture*. Edited by Susan Murray and Laurie Ouellette. New York: New York University Press, 2004.

McKenna, Michael. *The ABC Movie of the Week: Big Movies for the Small Screen*. Lanham, MD: Scarecrow Press, 2013.

McNeil, Alex. *Total Television*. New York: Penguin Books, 1996.

Miami News, 30 June 1982–7 September 1984.

Milwaukee Journal, 6 May 1979–1 October 1991.

Murray, Susan, and Laurie Ouellette, eds. *Reality TV: Remaking Television Culture*. New York: New York University Press, 2004.

Nadis, Fred. "Citizen Funt: Surveillance as Cold War Entertainment." *Film and History* 37.2 (Fall 2007).

Newsweek, 28 April 1980–10 November 1983.

New York Times, 27 February 1951–23 December 1951.

Patterson, James T. *Restless Giant: The United States from Watergate to Gore v. Bush*. New York: Oxford University Press, 2005.

Pittsburgh Press, 17 August 1980–9 October 1983.

Ruoff, Jeffrey. *"An American Family": A Televised Life*. Minneapolis, MN: University of Minnesota Press, 2001.

Sackett, Susan. *Prime-Time Hits: Television's Most Popular Network Programs*. New York: Billboard Books, 1993.

Schenectady Gazette, 14 April 1979–11 November 1983.

Schulman, Bruce J. *The Seventies: The Great Shift in American Culture, Society and Politics*. New York: Free Press, 2001.

Tannenbaum, Rob. *I Want My MTV: The Uncensored Story of the Music Video Revolution.* New York: Penguin Publishing, 2012.

Time, 15 April 1951–7 November 1982.

Toronto Globe and Mail, 11 August 1980–1 October 1991.

TV Guide, 2 August 1980–4 July 1984.

United Press International, 3 February 1981–5 May 1984.

Variety, 25 April 1979–8 October 1991.

Wall Street Journal, 6 November 1981–30 May 1990.

Washington Post, 7 November 1978–15 August 1992.

Watson, Mary Ann. *Defining Visions: Television and the American Experience in the 20th Century.* New York: Wiley-Blackwell, 2009.

INDEX

A Current Affair, 141, 145
All about Us, 142
All-American Pie, 51–52
Allen, Byron, 12, 34, 92, 117, 123
America, 143
American Broadcasting Company (ABC), x, 44, 50, 79, 104, 127, 137
American Chronicles, 138, 143
American Family Revisited—The Louds Ten Years Later, 108–109
The American Parade, 130
America's Funniest Home Videos, 139
America's Funniest People, 139
America's Heroes: The Athlete Chronicles, 106–107
America's Most Wanted, 79, 133, 134, 138, 140
An American Family, xii, xl–xliii; and origins reality TV, xliii; critical response to, xli–xliii
Art Linkletter's House Party, xxix

Barbour, John, 6, 34, 91–92, 143
The Barbour Report, 143–144
Barris, Chuck, xlv
Billingsley, Peter, 64, 92, 117
Breslin, Jimmy, 7

cable television, 30; early development of, xiii; and expansion of programming, 30–31, 88, 134–135

Candid Camera, xi, xxxviii–xl, 128; format of, xxxviii–xxxix; Playboy channel version, 86
Code 3, 139
Columbia Broadcasting Company (CBS), xiii, 44, 53, 80, 129–130, 137
Cops, 79, 134, 138
Counterattack: Crime in America, 79
Couples, 84–85
Court TV, 139
Crazy and Wonderful, 30
A Current Affair, 134
Custody Court, 109

daytime talk shows, 56
Divorce Court (1957), xxxvii
Divorce Court (1986), 139
Divorce Hearing, xxxvii
Dotto, xxxv

Emergency Call, 142
Emmy Awards, xxviii, xxix, 126
Everything Goes, 86

Falwell, Jerry, 88–89
Family Court, 109–110
Fantasies Fulfilled, 58
Fantasy, 112–113
Finders Seekers, 132
Fox Network (FOX), 134, 138
Funt, Allen, xxxviii–xl

Games People Play, 48–50; critical response to, 49
game shows, xxx–xxxvi; and "misery shows," xxx–xxxiii; and quiz show scandal, xxxiii–xxxvi
Getting Personal, 114
Glamour Girl, xxxii–xxxiii
The Gong Show, xlv, 133
The Greatest American Hero, 76
Group One Medical, 142

Hard Copy, 141
High Risk, 142–143
Home Box Office (HBO), xliv, 30, 31, 108
Hour Magazine, 59, 131

I Witness Video, 139
Incredible Sunday, 143
Inside America, 79–80
Inside Edition, 141
It Could Be You, xxxvi–xxxvii
It's a Great Life, 142

Kefauver, Estes, xxv–xxvi, xxviii; and organized crime committee hearings, xxv–xxvii; and reception of televised hearings, xxvii–xxviii
Kenny Rogers' America, 54–55

Lie Detector, 110–111
Life with Linkletter, xxix
Lifeline, 4–5, 142
Lifestyles of the Rich and Famous, 142
Linkletter, Art, xxix, 128. *See also Life with Linkletter*; *Art Linkletter's House Party*; *People Are Funny (1954)*
The Lives We Live, 56–57
Look at Us, 80–81
Love Connection, 115, 131, 134, 140

Magic or Miracle, 106
Marx, Groucho, xxix–xxx
McCarthy, Joseph, xxiii–xxiv; and anti-communism efforts, xxiv–xxv; and reception of televised hearings, xxv
Middletown, 87–88
Millerick, Kerry, 92, 117
Miller's Court, 132–133
More Real People, 105, 131

National Broadcasting Company (NBC), viii, 44, 62, 77, 90, 91, 105, 127, 137, 144
network television: and challenges to major network supremacy, xiii–xiv; corporate takeover of, 137–138; and the decline of viewership, 31, 88; and the softening of network news, xiv–xv, 92–93, 145; and the threat of viewer boycott, 88–90. *See also* American Broadcasting Company (ABC); Columbia Broadcasting Company (CBS); Fox Broadcasting (FOX) National Broadcasting Company (NBC)
The New You Asked, 76, 84
Nice People, 108
No Holds Barred, 57

On Scene: Emergency Response, 141–142
On the Road, xiv, 55–56, 129–130
On Trial, 139
On Your Account, xxxiii

People Are Funny (1954), xxix
People Are Funny (1984), 128
The People's Court, 81–82, 109, 131, 135
The People Versus, 133
Personal and Confidential, 128–129
The Phil Donahue Show, 113
PM Magazine, x, xliii–xlv, 29, 75, 131; expansion of, 29, 59; format of, xliv, 29, 59–60; and origins of reality TV, xliv, 29
Police Court, 110
Portrait of America, 107–108
Purcell, Sarah, 6, 34, 92, 117, 143; wedding of, 119–120

QUBE, 61–62
Queen for a Day, xxxii–xxxiii, 115

The Radio Corporation of America (RCA), xxi–xxii
Rafferty, Bill, 6, 92, 117, 123
Real Kids, 50
Real Life Stories, 56
Real People, viii, 91, 108, 117, 130, 134, 135, 142, 143, 144; alternative lifestyles

featured on, 18, 37–38, 124–125; animals featured on, 14–15, 38, 96, 124–125; and audience/viewer participation, 13–14, 34–37, 65–66; and advocacy for Vietnam MIAs, 103–104, 124; and advocacy for veterans, xvi, 22–23, 41–42, 72–75, 101–105, 122–124; cancellation of, 127; critical response to, 7, 10–11, 18, 23–25, 37, 42–44, 68, 75, 76–77, 126; and cultural/social fads of the era, xv–xvi, 70, 97–98; cultural legacy of, xviii, 135, 145; format of, xvi; and "infotainment," xiv–xv, 14, 98–99, 104, 125–126, 141; inspirational stories featured on, 19, 40–41, 70, 99–100, 121; and racial diversity, 12–13; and the origins of reality TV, xv–xvi; populist themes featured on, 20–21, 42, 66–67, 68, 118; and patriotic themes, xvi, 10, 19, 22–23, 41, 72, 100–101, 122–124; ratings for, xiv, 10, 23, 42, 75–76, 91, 120, 127; and the Real People Express, 93–95, 117–119; sexual themes featured on, 17–18, 39, 70, 94, 98; unique occupations featured on, 15, 38, 68, 70–72, 94–95, 96, 118–119, 120, 124–125; uniquely talented people featured on, 14–15, 68, 94–95, 118–119, 120, 121, 124–125; unusual events/competitions featured on, 17, 38, 68, 69–70, 94–95, 96–97, 118–119, 120, 124–125; and women's issues, 13, 120–121, 122–123

Real People Reunion Special, 144

Real Sex, 87

The Real World, xii–xiii, xliii, 138–139

reality television: contemporary programming, ix, xiii, xv, 77, 114, 133; and daytime talk shows, 140; early origins of, xi–xiii; economic advantages of, xiii–xiv, 25–26, 134–135, 137–138; expansion of, vii–viii, 55, 115–116, 134, 138–144; studies of, ix

Rescue 911, 79, 133, 134, 140

Ripley's Believe It or Not, 107, 130

Roadshow, 57

Ruprecht, David, 117

Russell, Mark, 6

Schlatter, George, 6, 91–92, 106, 119, 145; and the creation of *Real People*, 6–9; and the creation of *Speak Up America*, 44–45; and his criticism of other reality shows, 29; and his defense of *Real People*, 25, 37, 119, 145; and *Laugh-In*, 11–12

Sheen, Bishop Fulton, xxviii; *Life Is Worth Living*, xxviii–xxix; wide spread popularity of, xxviii–xxix

Shoot, Don't Shoot, 79

Silverman, Fred, 1–2, 44; and the creation of *Real People*, 6; criticism of, 2, 3–4; early career of, 1–3; and hiring by NBC, 2–4; and resignation from NBC, 62; and scheduling of *Lifeline*, 4–5

Singles Magazine, 86

Singles Only, 114–115

The $64,000 Question, xxxiii

60 Minutes, 79, 80, 130

So You Think You've Got Troubles, 112

Speak Up America, viii, 44–47; controversy surrounding, 45–47

Star Search, 133

Stempel, Herb, xxxiv–xxxv

Stephenson, Skip, 6, 34, 92, 117, 124

Strictly Confidential, 140

Strike It Rich, xxx–xxxii; controversy surrounding, xxxi–xxxii

Studs, 140

Summer Sunday U.S.A., 129

Superior Court, 139

Tartikoff, Brandon, 127, 128

television: deregulation of, 115; early experiments in, xxi–xxiii; labor unrest in, 33–34, 63–64; origins of various genres, viii, x; rising production costs in, 60–61; syndication of, xv, 57–60

That Awful Quiz Show, 111–112

That's Incredible!, viii, 26, 52–53, 80, 107, 128, 130, 134, 135, 143; critical response to, 28–29, 52–53; controversy surrounding, 52–53; format of, 26–28; ratings for, 28

That's My Line, 53–54

This Is Your Life, 132

Those Amazing Animals, 50–51

Tom Cottle: Up Close, 113–114

Top Cops, 140
Totally Hidden Video, 138, 139
Trial Watch, 139
TV's Bloopers and Practical Jokes, 127
Twenty-One, xxxiii–xxxvi; and quiz show
   scandal, xxxv–xxxvi

Unsolved Mysteries, 79, 133, 134, 140
Up to the Minute, 80
U.S. Chronicle, 55

Van Doren, Charles, xxxiv–xxxv
Verdict, 139
The Verdict Is Yours, xxxvii

Wanted by the FBI, 133
Wedding Day, 77
What's Hot? What's Not?, 143
What's It Worth?, xxii–xxiii
What's Up America?, xliv, 30
Wildmon, Donald, 88–90
Willard, Fred, 6, 64, 92, 117, 143
The World of People, 57–58
World's Fair (1939), xxi–xxii
WTBS, 31, 107–108

Yearbook, 138, 142
You Asked for It, xxxvii
You Bet Your Life , xxix–xxx

ABOUT THE AUTHOR

Michael McKenna teaches and writes about history. His primary research interests are in urban history, with a focus on New York City, and American popular culture, particularly television programming.

This is the author's second book. His previous study, *The ABC Movie of the Week: Big Movies for the Small Screen* (2013), explored the early history of made-for-TV films and the seminal impact of the *Movie of the Week* series.